A People of Two Kingdoms

The Political Acculturation of the Kansas Mennonites

JAMES C. JUHNKE

Faith and Life Press
Newton, Kansas

Mennonite Historical Series

International Standard Book Number 0-87303-662-X

Library of Congress Catalog Card Number: 74-84697

Printed in the United States of America
Copyright © 1975 by Faith and Life Press
724 Main Street, Newton, Kansas 67114

Foreword

WHEN PROFESSOR JUHNKE ASKED ME TO PROVIDE A WORD OF INTRO-
duction for his book, I felt honored; I was also gratified to learn that
this excellent contribution to the history of the Mennonites in America
will become more generally accessible than it has been. It often happens, unfortunately, that substantial works of scholarship remain
unread outside of the seminar rooms of the universities under whose
aegis they are created; examples include Cornelius C. Janzen's social
study of the Kansas Mennonite communities and Raymond Miller's
history of Kansas Populism, both done at Chicago in the late 1920s,
and both of which helped me greatly when I wrote my own dissertation on Kansas Populism and immigrant groups. It is delightful to
know that Professor Juhnke's work will now be within reach of the
readership it deserves.

One of the virtues of this book is essential to good immigration
histories: it is free of filiopietism. Many of the studies of immigrant
groups which were produced in the earlier decades of this century
(and sometimes since) were unable to avoid a patronizing or even
nativist approach if the author was an outsider, or the curse of
glorification and defensiveness if the author was writing about his own
ethnic group. One of my concerns several years ago when a graduate
student named Juhnke began to discuss with me his idea of writing a
doctoral dissertation on the acculturation of the Mennonites was the
possibility of filiopietism, since his own roots as a Mennonite were so
profound and so conscious. The concern was needless. The author,
I discovered, is not only a good Mennonite but a good historian. As a
consequence, this book will not only provide aid and comfort (and at
times perhaps a little discomfort) to Mennonite readers seeking seriously to understand their own past in America, but also will inform all

v

students of the processes of immigration and immigrant acculturation in the United States.

The story told here is not simply a description of the political behavior of an immigrant group, though that is part of it. It is also a record and analysis of intercultural contact which in some important ways was unique. When Swedes came to Kansas from Sweden, or Germans from Germany, they were leaving a society exclusively or dominantly their own, and they entered a society in which they became one of about two dozen distinct ethnic-religious minorities operating within a majority culture which differed from theirs in language, legal tradition, religion, and political structure and practice. For the German-Russian Mennonites, however, minority status was itself traditional, as a result both of a century's experience as an ethnic-religious enclave in Russia, and of the experience of politically nonparticipating Anabaptist life for over two hundred and fifty years before the movement to Catherine the Great's Russia in the late eighteenth century. With such a long history as an out-group, and given the fact that such out-group status was strongly reinforced by the theology of the "two kingdoms" and the ideals of political nonparticipation and nonresistance (*Wehrlosigkeit*), the Mennonites might have been expected to remain an out-group peculiarly resistant to the acculturation and assimilation to America which overtook the Swedes, the Germans, and other ethnic-religious groups.

In certain respects the Mennonites did indeed remain partially or largely unassimilated, as this book shows. In other respects, however, they fit in to the Kansas of the late nineteenth and early twentieth centuries to a degree, and with a rapidity, that seems surprising in view of their previous history. Professor Juhnke delineates the hows and whys of their political acculturation as well as their resistance to it, and his touch is sure. In a unique and complex way, he describes how the Mennonites came to terms with Kansan and American society more completely in the first fifty years after the immigration of the 1870s than they had done over much longer periods in Russia and central Europe. America's magnetic ability to assimilate ethnic-religious minorities has obviously not been frictionless, as the history of racial as well as immigrant groups clearly testifies, but it has been powerful in comparison to other countries; witness the great differences in assimilation patterns and treatment of minorities today between the United States and the Soviet Union. Juhnke points out, for example, that the Mennonites had become a predominantly English-speaking group within sixty years after their arrival in America, while after a much longer time in Russia they still spoke German. Even *Wehrlosigkeit* underwent some erosion by the 1920s.

Perhaps things would have been different if the Mennonites had been linguistically French rather than German, or if the United States had gone to war with someone other than Germany in 1917. But these are counterfactuals. As it happened, political acculturation did go on, slowly and incompletely, between the mid-seventies and World War I, and then traumatically during that war. The Mennonites then shared with other ethnic Germans what the historian John Hawgood called "the tragedy of German-America," the shocking and undreamt-of conflict between the old fatherland and the new; in addition, Mennonites underwent the crisis of conscience generated by the imposition of military conscription without adequate provision for conscientious objection. As Juhnke shows, World War I was a climacteric in the history of Kansas Mennonite acculturation. After that episode they tended to be more solidly Republican and more actively a part of the fundamentalist movement than they had been before, apparently in an effort to try even harder than before to be "good Americans," at least by the standards of central Kansas at that time. In these ways too, the magnetism of the culture that surrounded them proved to be irresistible.

Political historians will be interested in this book, especially the growing number concerned with the social and cultural bases of political behavior. They will notice among other things the unusual degree of Mennonite support for third-party movements, including the Populists (where Juhnke corrects my published assertion that the Mennonites seldom voted Populist), Theodore Roosevelt in 1912, La Follette in 1924, and Dr. Brinkley in 1930 and 1932. But I will not anticipate any more of the story. Professor Juhnke states his own case admirably, and I encourage the reader to proceed with it.

WALTER T. K. NUGENT

Bloomington, Indiana
July 4, 1974

vii

Many changes have occurred in the century since 1874 when most of the Mennonites of the Kansas prairies left South Russia to settle in this country. The changes have involved the Mennonites as they have lived in Kansas. Some changes are quite obvious to even the most uninitiated observer; other changes are much more difficult to observe and even more difficult to evaluate. Such is the slow and subtle process of adapting to the political process of a new land.

James C. Juhnke has attempted to study this ethnic and religiously oriented people in the light of their "political acculturation." He has succeeded and has brought new insights and understanding of the saga of the Mennonites, "a people of two kingdoms."

With pleasure we present this volume as the tenth in the Mennonite Historical Series. It takes its place as another "stone of remembrance" placed for those who ask, "What mean these stones?" To the previous volumes this study adds understanding, insight, and reflection in the story of the Mennonites who settled in Kansas and participated in its glory, its errors, and its hopes. At all times this people has been concerned about the kingdom in this world as well as the kingdom of our Lord and of His Christ.

LORIS A. HABEGGER, GENERAL EDITOR

General Conference Mennonite Church
Commission on Education
Newton, Kansas
November 1974

Preface

Like many other books written by Mennonites about Mennonites or books by Americans about Americans, this volume represents a quest for a usable past. The readers deserve a word about the author's standpoint and values. I am a Mennonite in America, a pacifist and a citizen. When I became a peace candidate for Congress in the Kansas fourth congressional district in 1970, a Mennonite Sunday school class became my base for discussions on how to work out Anabaptist-Mennonite principles in the contemporary political world. A sense of dialogue between the church and the political world is part of the heritage I share with many of the politically active Mennonites who appear in this book.

This book is also an effort in objective scholarship. I have attempted to reconstruct a piece of the past as it actually happened. No information has been intentionally disregarded—no skeletons hidden—simply because they might not serve the needs of my own self-definition or the cause of those liberal Mennonite Christian values I espouse. I accept full responsibility for errors of small detail or major interpretation which appear in the book. At some points I revise the work of previous historians. I hope my work may be revised in turn.

Many people helped in the development of this book. Walter T. K. Nugent planted some important ideas initially and then stood ready with enthusiasm and practical suggestions as the work proceeded toward a Ph.D. dissertation. Indiana University offered a year of fellowship money to finance research and writing. Much of the research was done in the Mennonite Library and Archives at Bethel College, North Newton, Kansas, where Cornelius Krahn, director, and John F. Schmidt, archivist, provided essential assistance in making resources available and in suggesting avenues for investigation. Loris Habegger and Muriel Stackley of Faith and Life Press helped editorially to polish the text at numerous points. A grant from Schowalter Foundation helped finance publication.

While the book was in process, the Bethel College student and faculty community, through their lively debate and protest against the war in Vietnam, provided an atmosphere conducive to reflection on the meaning of Mennonite political acculturation. My greatest debt is to this community and the tradition it bears.

James C. Juhnke
July 1974

Contents

LIST OF TABLES

The line drawings preceding each chapter were done by the Mennonite artist John P. Klassen in a Russian Mennonite village in the post-World War I years. The drawings typify cultural styles of pre-industrial Mennonites whether on the Russian steppes or the Kansas prairies. They are reproduced here by courtesy of *Mennonite Life*. (See "Sketches from a Chortitza Boyhood," *Mennonite Life,* December 1973, pp. 104-113.)

Photos, newspaper illustrations, and masthead are reproduced by courtesy of Mennonite Library and Archives, North Newton, Kansas 67117.

ABBREVIATIONS

BC   Bethel College
GC   General Conference (Mennonite)
KMB   Krimmer Mennonite Brethren
MB   Mennonite Brethren
MCC   Mennonite Central Committee
ML   *Mennonite Life*
MLA   Mennonite Library and Archives, Bethel College, North
        Newton, Kansas
MQR   *Mennonite Quarterly Review*
OM   Mennonite Church, often referred to as (Old) Mennonite

"God led the Mennonites to America"
(C. H. WEDEL, 1901).

CHAPTER 1

Mennonite Political Acculturation: Introduction

THE MENNONITES WHO CAME TO KANSAS IN THE 1870s SETTLED AT the crossing of the trails. A few miles southwest of the spot where the Chisholm cattle trail crossed the Santa Fe Trail, Mennonite ploughs bit the sod and turned the dew under. The prairie grasses, which had waved at passing wagon trains and cattle herds, now yielded to the productive tyranny of Russian Turkey Red winter wheat.

A hundred years later the descendants of the Kansas Mennonites saw their land crossed by other trails. In the early 1970s Interstate Highway I-35 from Wichita to Salina split Mennonite territory in half with a gash as wide as a farmstead through some of the richest grain fields on earth. Some Mennonites of the diaspora returned by Trans-World Airlines to Wichita Municipal Airport on their way to the 1974 Mennonite centennial celebrations. It had been a century of change.

The Mennonite 1974 centennial plans and celebrations reflected how far these people had become Americanized. The Mennonites recognized that they had found a permanent home in America. They were proud of their unique contribution to America, especially the wheat which in 1974 was priced over five dollars per bushel. They were aware that their celebrations were part of a more general ethnic revival which was a typically American phenomenon.

However, the dominant theme of the Mennonite 1974 centennial was not how Mennonites had a share in America's greatness. The Mennonites focused on honoring their parents for their faithfulness in recovering and preserving the faith of their Anabaptist forebears.

The central questions were these: Have we been disciples of Christ? Have we been obedient to the New Testament? How can we renew the Anabaptist vision?[1]

The Kansas Mennonites bore the stamp of both their Anabaptist history and of the American social and political environment. They had been remarkably persistent in adhering to doctrines and traditions which marked them as a peculiar people from generation to generation. In addition, they had also taken on characteristically American traits. Many Mennonite sons and daughters had merged with American society and lost all traces of Mennonite identity. Others had tenaciously clung to their historical roots. In no case could the Kansas Mennonites be separated from the American drama. They had become what they were because of their interaction with America.

The changing Mennonite attitude toward American political institutions and values is a particularly interesting case of Americanization. The immigration of the Mennonites was a political act. It had to do with power. It had to do with the ability of these people to keep control over their own lives, their language, their education, their practice of nonresistance, and in fact their entire way of life. The Mennonites wanted autonomy. The freedom they sought was not the freedom of each individual to choose his own values and do his own thing. They sought freedom as the power to maintain their distinctive and severely disciplined communities.

In America the Mennonites met a challenge to their autonomy and power of self-control which was as severe as the more obvious threats of Russianization from which they fled. In Kansas they were faced with American county commissioners, American tax assessors, American school boards, and eventually American draft board officials. Mennonites responded variously in their interaction with American political institutions and values. At the end of a century of living in America, the invariable tendency was for Mennonites to think and to behave more and more like Americans.

The political Americanization, or acculturation, of the Kansas Mennonites was a multifaceted and complex process. Political behavior, of course, involves more than voting or paying taxes. It involves the Mennonite understanding of American political authority and relating to it. The Mennonites were behaving politically when they applied for citizenship, when they refused to take office on religious grounds, when they claimed exemption from military service, and when they discussed the rights and responsibilities of Christians in a free and democratic country.

To think clearly about Mennonite political acculturation, it is necessary to define the American norm. What are the typically American political values and behavior patterns which Mennonites gradually adopt? This question is not easily answered. No single American community can be said to constitute a wholly typical norm. Each community has its peculiar mix of population, economic resources, social relationships, and moral creeds. To whom shall we compare the Mennonites?

In the quest for an American norm by which to measure Mennonite political acculturation, it is helpful to keep in mind a number of levels of community thought and action which can serve as a comparative basis. On the broadest level there is the American* national community which occasionally achieves a high degree of unity in policy and sentiment. For the First World War, for example, it is possible to speak of a national "wartime spirit" which includes a consensus upon the special responsibilities of American citizens, including Mennonites, in response to the war crisis. There is a statewide political community whose special characteristics are suggested by such events as the adoption of Prohibition in 1880, the flourishing of Populism, and the near election of John R. Brinkley to the governorship in 1930. To compare the behavior of Kansas Mennonites with their contemporaries, it is possible to select a specific county of substantial nonimmigrant population and of similar size and geographical location. For this study, Chase County in east central Kansas serves as such a unit.[2] Mennonites can also be compared to other Protestant immigrants who came to the same area at about the same time: the Swedish community centered around Lindsborg in northern McPherson County provides another control for several comparisons in the course of the study.

There will be no systematic attempt to compare the Mennonites with these four different communities at every turn in the history of Mennonite political acculturation. For analysis of voting statistics, the norm most often used will be the state of Kansas, although the state norm deviates so slightly from the voting records of the Chase County

*I use "America" as a term equivalent to "the United States." "North America" will include both the United States and Canada. The Canadian Government was strongly interested in the Mennonite immigration and offered to meet Mennonite demands for full autonomy. Many Mennonites went from Russia to Canada in the 1870s.

nonimmigrant norm that either standard might have been used. The national norm is most relevant here as it provides an ideology of nationalism to which immigrant communities are expected to conform. The Swedish community is particularly interesting here because it is so unexpectedly different from the Mennonite community in relationship to the state norm. The "American norm," then, which must be the standard for judging Mennonite political acculturation is in this study a composite construct rather than a single community. Comparisons are made on various levels as seems most useful and illuminating.

Mennonite political acculturation in Kansas is a complex, uneven, and unfinished process. Three primary indexes of that process may help to introduce several leading problems of interpretation. These indexes are: (1) The percentage of Mennonite voters as compared to the American norm, (2) Mennonite votes by political party as compared to the American norm, (3) Mennonite political officeholding. The following introductory statistical survey will clarify some of the possibilities and problems of the concept of acculturation in understanding the political behavior of Kansas Mennonites.

Mennonite nonvoting. The traditional Anabaptist-Mennonite position, shaped by a persistent theological distinction between church and state and by a history of governmental persecution, is one of noninvolvement in political affairs. In view of this apolitical heritage, one would expect that in the early years after immigration a substantially smaller percentage of Mennonite voters would go to the polls than in a non-Mennonite, nonimmigrant county. One would further expect the percentage of Mennonite voters to increase as the community became acclimated to American democracy. The process of political acculturation could be measured by the gradual increase in the number of Mennonite voters until it approached the American norm.

Four predominantly Mennonite townships in Marion, McPherson, and Harvey counties were selected and the number of voters as a percentage of the total population from 1880 to 1948 were tabulated. The results were compared with equivalent statistics from Chase County and charted on a bar graph. (See Appendixes A and B, pages 160 and 161.) The graph confirmed prior expectations that Mennonite townships had a smaller percentage of voters than non-Mennonite areas in the early years. In the area which included present-day Menno Township in Marion County, only 2 percent of the population voted in the 1880 general elections and only 1.1 percent in 1882, compared with 23.8 percent and 25.6 percent in the same elections in Chase County.

A rough pattern was established by 1886 or 1888 with the percentage of voters in predominantly Mennonite townships being somewhat over one-half that in Chase County. Contrary to expectations, *this pattern continued for election after election beyond the Second World War.* The percentage of Mennonite voters in state or national elections never approximated the norm. In only one election since 1878 did the percentage of voters in a selected Mennonite township exceed the percentage of Chase County. The divergence between the Mennonite and non-Mennonite voter percentages for the 1930s was as great as that of forty or fifty years earlier.

If acculturation means the adoption of behavior patterns of the American society, and if the statistics used here constitute a valid basis for comparative analysis, one cannot look upon Mennonite political acculturation as a completed process by the mid-twentieth century. For some reason, Mennonites persisted in staying away from the polls. This fact is particularly interesting because the processes of acculturation had been proceeding apace during this period. The isolation of the Mennonite community had begun breaking down since the time Mennonites arrived as they gradually adopted American patterns of education, language, and technology. One might expect their habits of voting also to conform to the American norm by the Second World War.

The persistence of Mennonite nonconformity to the American norm in voter turnout in spite of the adoption of other American patterns of behavior demands explanation.

Mennonite party vote. The Mennonite vote by political party can also be calculated and viewed over a period of time as a measure of acculturation. Although many Mennonites failed to exercise their voting privileges, there were also some who voted in elections from the outset.

One might expect to find a measure of acculturation in the party vote if, for example, the Mennonites voted solidly for one particular party in the early years but later began to scatter their votes in proportions similar to the norm. The elections in which the shift or shifts took place could be identified, and this could possibly be correlated with other aspects of the general acculturation process.

It is instructive in this regard to compare Mennonite voting patterns with those of the Swedish community in northern McPherson County. (See Appendix C, page 162.) The Swedes were Republicans from the beginning. In 1880 in five selected townships they voted 80.7 percent for Garfield; in 1884, 86.1 percent for Blaine; in 1888, 73.7 percent for Harrison; and a peak of 89.9 percent in 1904 for Roosevelt. In each of these elections the Swedish Republican vote was over twenty percentage points higher than the average in the state of Kansas.[3] But the size of the majorities for Republican party candidates in relation to the state norm decreased until the 1930s when it approximated the pattern in Kansas. This approach of the Swedish vote to the state norm may be taken as a measure of political acculturation. The Swedish community presumably was subjected to forces from the outside American world which resulted in a political behavior pattern which was not significantly different from a non-Swede, nonimmigrant area.

The vote in Mennonite townships, meanwhile, was surprisingly different from the Swede vote. The "Mennonite vote" was more evenly divided between the major parties from the beginning. The Mennonite variation from the Kansas average was considerably less than the strongly Republican Swedish variation. It could neither be said that the Mennonite voting patterns by party moved in the direction of a norm nor could the votes be understood as a measure of acculturation from 1880 to the mid-1930s. (Appendix D, page 163.)

Interestingly enough, a distinctive Mennonite pattern did emerge around 1940, shortly after the Swedish distinctiveness disappeared. With the 1940 presidential election, the Mennonites began to return a Republican majority which was fairly consistently about 15 percent higher than the state average. The Mennonites had become more distinctively Republican by the mid-twentieth century, whereas the Swedes had lost their former Republican distinctiveness.[4]

What does it mean for the concept of acculturation that Mennonite voting patterns did not deviate significantly from the Kansas average until the late 1930s, and that the deviation thereafter was significant? If one adheres to the definition of acculturation as the acceptance of culture traits and behavior of the surrounding society, the voting statistics must be taken as negative evidence. If one had only these figures by which to draw conclusions, it would appear that a high degree of acculturation had been achieved from the earliest years in America but that something happened about 1940 to reverse that pattern.

Mennonite officeholding. A third measure of Mennonite political behavior worth surveying, in advance of the historical narrative that follows, is the number of Mennonites who have run for or held political office. Here again may be a possible measure of acculturation. An increasing number of Mennonites running for political office would indicate that the distinctive Mennonite resistance to political involvement was being overcome and that the cultural characteristics of the American society were being adopted.

Again the facts of the case fail to conform neatly to a model of acculturation. Mennonites first gained county offices in the late 1880s and elected their own state representative in the 1890s. To date, the Kansas Mennonites have never had a person elected to national political office. The number of Mennonites seeking and gaining office on the county and state level is fairly constant throughout the entire period, with mild increases in the early teens and early thirties. There is no point at which one could say that the Mennonites definitely turned their energies toward or against the prospects of political officeholding. No broader trends are visible to indicate a pattern of acculturation for the Mennonite community as a whole.

There is much more to Kansas Mennonite political acculturation than a skeleton of unexpected statistics on how Mennonites voted and ran for political office. Political acculturation involves Americanization, and Americanization involves the changing expectations, achievements, and self-conceptions of the community as it adjusted to a new way of life on the American frontier and beyond. The statistics take their meaning from the broader story.

The facts already cited make it abundantly clear, however, that Mennonite political acculturation will not easily be squeezed into some preconceived mold. Our initial survey of statistics regarding Mennonite voter turnout, voting by party, and office-seeking gives scant encouragement to the view that Mennonite political behavior fits a simple model of acculturation or can be smoothly correlated with social or economic acculturation. A historical narrative of Anabaptist-Mennonite experience can shed some light on the complexities of their changing political attitudes and behavior in America.

"America is the land of freedom" (ABRA-
HAM J. MOSER, 1876).

CHAPTER **2**

The Two Kingdoms and the Coming to Kansas

ORIGINS

THE MENNONITE ATTITUDE TOWARD POLITICAL AUTHORITY HAS BEEN decisive in the life of the group from its beginnings in the Anabaptist left wing of the sixteenth-century Protestant Reformation. Mennonites trace their origins to a small group of youthful, impatient reformers gathered around the leadership of Ulrich Zwingli in Zurich, Switzerland, in the 1520s. When Zwingli curbed his ambitious church reforms in the face of opposition from the Zurich City Council, his followers protested that truth was independent of political authority. "You have no authority to place the decision in the hands of My Lords [the Council]," exclaimed one incipient Anabaptist, "for the decision is already made; the Spirit of God decides."[1] Their conviction that the church dare not take final orders from the government led the rebels to break with Zwingli, to begin a separate church fellowship, and to engage in an unchurchly, unauthorized, new baptism. They became rebaptizers, Anabaptists, outlaws.

Banned in Zurich, the Anabaptist movement spread with alarming speed into the Swiss Confederation, Austria, Bavaria, Wuerttemberg, the Palatinate, and the Netherlands. The symbol of rebaptism, standing for a voluntary church separated from state control, frightened all established church and state authorities. There was good reason for fear. Even though most of the Anabaptists eschewed violence and wanted simply to restore the early church of the New Testament, their program had socially-disruptive implications which were unacceptable for the sixteenth-century mind.[2]

The charge of social disruption, leveled by both Protestant Reformers and Catholic churchmen, contained an element of self-fulfilling prophecy. Vicious persecution by church and state eliminated many of the most competent peaceful Anabaptist leaders and led some of the more zealous adherents into an apocalyptic rejection of the present world and an attempt to usher in Christ's kingdom by the sword. The violent revolutionary Anabaptist kingdom at Muenster turned into a disastrous fiasco which opponents of Anabaptism could use to condemn indiscriminately all Anabaptists without respect to their particular ideas or actions.[3]

The mainstream Anabaptists rejected revolutionary violence and emphasized, rather, the suffering way of the cross as the call of the Christian. An orthodox Anabaptist-Mennonite view of the state emerged gradually out of the experience of persecution and their reading of the Bible in terms of what was happening to them. The Schleitheim Confession, the result of a meeting of Anabaptists in 1527, gave an identity to the movement and provided a standard for the main group of left-wing dissenters. The consolidating and organizing work of Menno Simons after 1536 in the Netherlands helped salvage the movement in the region. The once dangerous sect eventually made its peace with the world through withdrawal into separate, quiet, and relatively isolated communities.

At the heart of the Anabaptist view of the state—as it grew out of the left wing of the sixteenth-century Reformation and eventually made its way to Kansas in the nineteenth century—was the doctrine of the two worlds.[4] Both the state and the state churches belonged to the evil kingdom; the new community of regenerated believers was part of the kingdom of Christ. The state, although it was ordained of God to maintain order in an evil world and therefore deserved obedience, had no authority over Christ's kingdom or the church. The kingdom of Christ in itself had no need for the state, and Christians who chose to accept the discipline of Christ in the new kingdom must renounce the sword, the taking of oaths, and the holding of political office. The Anabaptists knew from bitter experience that the kingdom of this world was hostile to true Christianity; their doctrine regarding the state reflected their experience of two alien kingdoms whose proper relationship was decisive and thorough separation.[5]

The history of the Mennonites, from the origins in the 1520s through four and one-half centuries, can be told as the story of an uneasy and ill-defined truce between their church and the state. The turning points in that history, often marked by persecution and migration, resulted from the shattering of the truce. After the first several generations, during which persecution taught the Mennonites the values of accommodation, it was the state rather than the Mennonites who disturbed the basis of peace. But throughout their history the Mennonites have maintained a claim to be taking orders from a higher authority than the government on certain decisive matters. The symbol of Mennonite dissent, in an age of intensifying nationalism and militarism, became their rejection of military service in their doctrine of *Wehrlosigkeit* (defenselessness) or nonresistance. Upon this explosive issue the Mennonites continued to re-echo the affirmation of their founders: "You have no authority to place the decisions in the hands of government; the Spirit of God decides such matters."

Mennonite doctrinal opposition to participation in politics tended to break down as the Mennonites won full privileges of citizenship in European countries around 1800[6] Mennonite voting and office-holding followed soon after toleration, though remnants of the doctrine of the two kingdoms survived to remind the believers of more difficult days. The Mennonites who established colonies in South Russia after 1788 were a special case because they were granted not only toleration but virtually complete autonomy over their religious and political affairs. The Czarist policy for settling and developing the rich farmlands in the Ukraine, initiated by Catherine II, involved the promise that the invited German colonists could govern themselves. Mennonite self-government at times approached theocracy, although church and civic offices were kept separate. Mennonites elected village mayors from their own membership and took responsibilities in village assemblies and in special committees for working out the financial budget, the distribution of the tax burden, and whatever local problems the community faced.

The experience in Russia introduced the Mennonites to the arts and frustrations of local politics. It was no smooth course. Some problems were too large to be solved by the Mennonite community alone; on occasion the state, held to be necessary to maintain order in an evil world, was called upon to maintain order among the Mennonites. Concentration of Mennonite land ownership and the creation of a disenfranchised landless class resulted in community dissension which was solved only after the requested intervention of the Russian Government. When a group of dissatisfied Mennonites formed a separate church in 1860 in an attempt to restore spiritual vitality to the community, the established church leaders requested the imperial government to revoke the special privileges of the schismatics and deport them to Siberia. The government disregarded the request. During the Crimean War the Mennonites exhibited their appreciation for their privileged exemption from military service by providing food and medical supplies for the armies and by caring for five thousand soldiers wounded at the front.

In 1866 the Russian Government embarked upon the reform and nationalization program which resulted in the emigration of some eighteen thousand Mennonites. Three developments threatened the ethnic and religious identity of the Mennonite communities: the prospects for Russian language teaching in the schools, minority status of some Mennonite communities in new Russian administrative districts, and revocation of exemption from military service. The Mennonites undertook a vigorous lobbying program to oppose the changes, a program which was not helped by their obvious unfamiliarity with the Russian language and customs. Faced with the prospect of mass emigration, the Russian Government offered a compromise which included exemption from direct military service but required the Mennonites to perform alternative forestry service in lieu of military service. The Mennonites who came to Kansas were among those who were unwilling to compromise.[7]

IMMIGRATION AND GOVERNMENT

A puzzling disparity between intention and act marked the coming of the Mennonites from Russia to Kansas. On the one hand, the Mennonites left Russia in search of cultural autonomy. They desired a separated and self-contained community in which they could perpetuate their distinctive religious and ethnic tradition without the encroachments of the world. They demanded complete exemption from military service as the symbol of their special status in the political world. The fact, however, is that Mennonites settled the American frontier without legal guarantees of isolation and autonomy. They immigrated without insurance that they could establish their own local government or that their settlement areas would be legally reserved for Mennonite land ownership. They received no guarantee of exemption from national military conscription. On the face of it, America did not provide what the Mennonites were looking for.[8]

Why did the Mennonite immigrants to Kansas accept conditions of settlement which contradicted their stated intentions for leaving Russia? The answer to this question is as clouded and uncertain as are all fragmentary historical reconstructions. But the answer is of overwhelming importance to the broader issue of the accommodation of the Mennonite immigrant community to the American environment. Immigration itself was an accommodation. The first giant step in the Americanization of the Mennonites is found in the character of their immigration. It is found especially in the remarkable flexibility of the supposedly doctrinaire and rigid Mennonites in accepting conditions of settlement which guaranteed no immunity from the declared evils which occasioned their flight from Russia, Prussia, and elsewhere in Europe.

The first enthusiastic advocate of Mennonite emigration from Russia to America was Cornelius Jansen, a Prussian consul in Berdiansk. Early convinced that the new Russian imperial policy of nationalization and the removal of special Mennonite privileges might make emigration necessary, Jansen opened a correspondence with Mennonite leaders in America in 1870 to inquire about settlement possibilities. He published a series of letters from American Mennonites for distribution in Russia in 1872 and introduced them with a brief preface explaining the meaning of American freedom.[9]

The structure of Jansen's argument reveals the ambivalence of Russian Mennonites' attitudes toward the ideal of freedom. Jansen found it necessary to apologize for freedom and defend it as a positive virtue in the American context:

Although America is a land of freedom, this certainly does not mean freedom from the law but rather freedom within the law; and in regard to religion it does not mean "irreligiosity" but rather "protection for religion"....[10]

Jansen admitted that America's freedom may have provided a haven for lawbreakers, but he argued that America was *also* a place of refuge for those who are persecuted for their faith. The introduction of general military service in Prussia and Russia, Jansen felt, was sufficient inducement to look to America for a new home.

The American Mennonite leaders whose letters Jansen printed in his brochure saw no ambiguity at all in American freedom. John F. Funk, Mennonite leader of Indiana and editor of the *Herald of Truth*, wrote in a letter of April 8, 1870, that in America one enjoys "complete freedom of conscience." There is "nothing to fear" in America so far as government and military service is concerned. "We have a good government that protects us well," Funk wrote to Russia, "and in this regard we live as peacefully and happily as possible."[11] Funk did mention that Mennonites who did not want to fight in the Civil War had to hire substitutes or pay a $300 commutation fee, but this was no apparent infringement upon the American Mennonite non-resistant conscience.

John M. Oberholzer of Pennsylvania, in a letter dated September 9, 1871, expressed the same point of view after reviewing the question of military service in America: ". . . No country in the world could give a better guarantee for lasting freedom of conscience."[12] Already in reading these letters the Russian Mennonites began to lose their reservations about freedom as a great ideal. Whereas the traditional Mennonite community had placed greatest value upon the disciplined church which followed the way of Christ (and had questioned the ideal of freedom as perhaps related to lawbreaking), it eventually began to make room for the nationalistic ideal of American freedom alongside their traditional concept of freedom as autonomy.[13]

Bernhard Warkentin was another Mennonite whose shift of loyalties from Russia to America was as rapid as his geographical transplanta-tion. Warkentin was one of a group of four adventurous young men who toured America in 1872 and sent reports of their experiences back to their homes in Russia. So impressed was Warkentin with the opportunities in America that he decided not to return to Russia after hearing of the death of his fiancée. His letters to his friend David Goerz tell of growing enthusiasm for a Mennonite migration, and of his exhaustion in responding to requests for information from Russia plus the demands by railroad men and real estate agents that he accompany them to look over prospective settlement areas.[14] In the promise for state laws exempting religious objectors from military service, Warkentin saw a possible answer to Mennonite fears regarding their doctrine of nonresistance.[15] Caught up in enthusiasm for Amer-ica, Warkentin delightedly responded when Goerz's replies began to echo his own sentiments: "[I] must grant you the commendation," wrote Warkentin to his youthful friend, "that you will become a real American patriot."[16] Warkentin spoke more truly than he knew, for David Goerz not only eventually joined him in settling in Harvey County, Kansas, but became a great leader in promoting immigration and in establishing Mennonite institutions of education, publication, and welfare which became potent agents in the Americanization of the Mennonite community.[17]

When Mennonite restlessness and uneasiness in Russia reached a peak in 1873, various congregations chose official representatives to spy out the land and make advance arrangements for settlement if it seemed advisable. The delegates went in four separate groups, each with instructions from the churches. Delegates Leonhard Sudermann of Berdiansk and Jacob Buller of Alexanderwohl, both of whom eventually settled in Kansas, had instructions to seek the following concessions from the governments with which they dealt:

1. Legal assurance of complete religious freedom; specifically, full exemption from military service.
2. Sufficient land of good quality at low prices and easy terms.
3. Closed settlements with the German language and local self-determination.
4. Financial assistance for the journey.[18]

The first three demands were considered essential; the fourth was desirable. Of the first three, one scholar has suggested, the "most important" was military exemption and the second most important was the closed settlement.[19] The question remains, then: Why did so many Mennonites come to Kansas where their two foremost requests were not guaranteed? Could it be that free land outweighed all other considerations, in spite of Mennonite insistence that they came for religious reasons?

To say that the Mennonites talked like religious men but acted like economic men would be to substitute a simple slogan for a more complex reality. The instructions of the congregations made clear that the Mennonites expected the economic and religious concessions to come from *governments*. They had originally come to Russia upon government invitation, and now another imperial edict was prompting their emigration. It was quite natural for them to expect that if they were to go to America, the way would have to be paved for them by political arrangements. Indeed, they already had assurances from the Canadian Government that all their demands would be met if they would settle in Canada. But the experiences of the Mennonite official delegation in touring the prospective settlement areas demonstrate that it was not the American Government but rather the American railroad that played the decisive role in settling the Mennonites on the frontier. Railroad salesmanship, together with the positive description of America by American Mennonites, were key factors which modified and softened Mennonite ideas regarding the essential preconditions of their settlement in America.

Railroad representatives, aware by 1873 of the potential of the immigration of Mennonite farmers, were on hand to greet the Mennonite official delegations at their port of debarkation. Railroad agents financed the exploratory tours of the delegates, introduced the Mennonites to state officials, and assured the Mennonites that they had nothing to fear for freedom of conscience and availability of land. Symbolic of the railroads' role as the mediator of America to the Mennonites was the visit of several of the delegates to Independence Hall in Philadelphia where they were favored with an explanation of the United States Constitution by the president of a railroad company.[20]

The salesmanship of the railroads and the reassurances of the American Mennonites were so effective that only three of the twelve delegates thought it necessary to approach the national government in Washington for specific guarantees of religious freedom and exemption from military service before returning to their home congregations in Russia. The railroads, with the Mennonites securely under their wing, provided the entrée. Jay Cooke, trustee of the Northern Pacific Railroad, gave the Mennonites a persuasive illustration of the political potency of railroad power by writing out a letter of introduction which produced an interview with President Ulysses S. Grant to plead the cause of special concessions for immigrating Mennonites. The delegates seemed more impressed with Grant's inauspicious manner and dress than by the fact that he was unwilling to extend extraordinary rights and privileges to them as an immigrating group. One delegate wrote in his diary:

He was a plain man and very friendly. He informed us that the constitution has a concession that it will not override a man's conscience and religious freedom is guaranteed. We appreciated this information, expressed our gratitude and bid him adieu. He then offered us his hand and gave us a very warm friendly goodbye.[21]

President Grant could not offer the Mennonites any promises of land for closed settlements or legal guarantees of exemption in case of a national conscription law; nor were such concessions forthcoming.[22] The absence of the full delegation at the audience with Grant, and the apparent lack of acute disappointment that no specific promises for concessions were received, indicate that a good number of the Mennonite delegates were already indoctrinated to the point of advising immigration regardless of government action. Had not the railroads made clear that they would serve as the Mennonite benefactors? Did not the dangers of national military conscription evaporate in the face of American constitutional guarantees of religious freedom? Was not abundant land awaiting settlement?

Mennonite political naiveté and confusion regarding the principle of federalism in United States Government contributed to a blurring of the issue of exemption from military service. The Mennonites were told that state laws would be passed to exempt them from militia service; they were *not* told that national conscription legislation superseded state enactments in case of national emergency. C. B. Schmidt, settlement agent for the Santa Fe Railroad who toured Mennonite areas in South Russia "preaching the gospel of emigration to Kansas from village to village," assured the Mennonites that Kansas had a constitutional provision exempting religious objectors from militia duty.[23] For the Mennonites already predisposed to settle in Kansas, the knowledge of this provision could be grasped as sufficient legal protection for the doctrine of nonresistance. Not until national military conscription in the First World War did the Mennonites finally learn that the state exemption law had been cleverly presented by the railroads primarily to attract their settlement rather than to provide genuine religious freedom.

The "Mennonite question" actually did reach the floor of the Senate in 1874 in the form of a bill to set aside special lands for a Mennonite settlement.[24] The bill was the result of lobbying by American Mennonite leaders and by Cornelius Jansen, who was by now in the United States. But the railroads, who wanted to sell their own lands to the Mennonites, did not support the measure and it was never brought to a vote. The Senate debate revealed American political attitudes toward immigrating communities, but it was insignificant in terms of effects on the actual migration. The failure of the bill simply confirmed the primacy of the railroads in establishing the Mennonites in America and the fact that the Mennonites had made their decision to move or stay irrespective of the action of Congress.[25]

DEBATE AND INVOLVEMENT

The emigration of Russian Mennonites to Kansas in the 1870s was a community undertaking. The decision to move was preceded by extensive community debate over the advisability of pulling up stakes, the chances that the Russian Government would relax its nationalization policies, and the prospects for a better social and political situation in America. Although most Mennonite colonists elected to stay in Russia and the departure of the minority was often a severe wrench to established community relationships, the significant fact was that most Mennonites moved in groups rather than as isolated individuals or families. They could expect the sympathy and support of the broader Mennonite community both in Russia and in America for their venture. The shocks of loneliness, unfamiliarity, and isolation— the lot of so many immigrants to America—were for the Mennonites cushioned by an undergirding community.

The immigrant newspaper was the communities' primary publishing instrument for the assistance of Mennonite adjustment to their new environment. In Kansas the most important Mennonite immigrant newspaper was *Zur Heimath,* edited by David Goerz who was himself an immigrant from Russia in 1872. Goerz was secretary of the Mennonite Board of Guardians, the American Mennonite committee for aiding the immigrants. *Zur Heimath,* published initially as a monthly in Summerfield, Illinois, was at first subsidized by the Santa Fe Railroad and distributed free to Mennonite immigrants.[26] When Goerz moved to Halstead, Kansas, in late 1875, he founded the Western Publishing Company and continued *Zur Heimath* on a bimonthly basis with regular subscriptions. The editor of the *Marion County Record,* greatly impressed by the rapid influx of Mennonite settlers in the area, reported enviously and inaccurately that the new Mennonite newspaper had 3,700 subscribers before starting.[27] In fact the *Zur Heimath* subscription list remained in only three figures until over four years later when Goerz announced that the goal of a thousand subscribers had been finally achieved.[28] The paper was more significant as a frontier socializing institution than suggested by the size of its circulation. In those earliest years when the immigrants were preoccupied with establishing dwellings and planting crops, *Zur Heimath* was their most important published resource for discussion of their experience, for information about the homeland, for instructions and ideas regarding citizenship and education in America, and for building the sense of community which provided continuity with Russia and a step toward new identity shaped by and adapted to the American environment.

The political environment into which the Russian Mennonites moved was confusing and complex in that it offered less autonomy within a more democratic political system than the Mennonites had known in Russia and Europe. Mennonites had less political autonomy in America because they were not organized in colonies governed by political officials of their own choosing. Rather, they were settled in previously constituted political units of state and county in which they were a minority and in which political affairs were conducted in unfamiliar language and procedure.

Their new environment confronted them with a series of decisions relating to the political world. Should they take out citizenship papers? Should they vote in elections? Should they establish their own township and school board political structure in conformity to the American pattern?

The education problem served as the sounding board for other issues. An American Mennonite, one "D. S. H.," expressed his educational concerns for the immigrating Mennonites in *Zur Heimath*. He began with some elementary political instruction. The American political chain of command from state to county to township and school district, he said, makes American education a government enterprise. The government schools, dominated by the spirit of the world rather than the Spirit of Christ, use textbooks filled with fables rather than Scripture and hire teachers who provide pupils with living examples of cursing, lying, deception, and drinking. A more fundamental concern was at stake, however:

I hear that they [the immigrants from Russia], in part, are deciding to become citizens in order to obtain the right to vote and to be able to take part in the worldly things of government. . . . I know only two citizenships, an earthly and a heavenly, and although I am a native citizen of the United States I do not find that this citizenship does me any good. . . . The Savior says: You cannot serve God and Mammon.[29]

The Anabaptist two-kingdom dualism, conceived by those facing martyrdom at the hands of a brutal state, was here held adequate for guiding man's relationship to the American liberal democratic government. But not everyone agreed. Abraham J. Moser of Bethel, Missouri, likewise a native-born American Mennonite, undertook to instruct the immigrants in American history from a different point of view. "America is the land of freedom," he began his article.

From the very beginning, he wrote, America has been a land of refuge for oppressed peoples. When the "despotic yoke" of England became unbearable, the people rose to throw it off and establish a new republic in which a free people would rule themselves. American education, wrote Moser, is the means of preserving the freedom and promoting the well-being of this great people. In this task the schools are doing an excellent job. Moser avoided a direct assault on the absolutist doctrine of two worlds and two citizenships. But he clearly believed that the appearance of the great American republic invalidated the dualistic basis for Mennonite withdrawal from the world: "I do not believe that God called this great republic into existence so that His people could withdraw in idle calm without bothering themselves about the welfare of the people in general." Moser could quote Scripture too. The Mennonites, he wrote, should be "the salt of the earth." They should use whatever means are available, including the political, for promoting "Christianity, civilization, culture, and progress." The condition which made participation in such work possible was American freedom. Moser's word to the Mennonites was infused with national pride.[30]

D. S. H. replied to Moser, and to another writer who saw American politics as worthy of involvement,[31] with an even more radical dualistic division of the world. There are only two kinds of people, he wrote, believers and unbelievers. Believers are called by God to reject the world: ". . . I have chosen you out of the world; therefore the world hateth you."[32] The Christian is a fugitive whose very vocation excludes politics. Furthermore, D. S. H. argued, political participation contradicts the doctrine of nonresistance. To vote for the government which wields the sword is to express approval of and responsibility for the use of the sword. If we vote, we are logically "obligated to do military service."[33]

The argument over schools, citizenship, and political participation took on new participants and added intensity in subsequent issues of *Zur Heimath*. Editor Goerz vainly appealed for more love and less contentiousness.[34] The recent immigrants, whose arrival occasioned the debate, contributed only a portion of the articles. At stake was the vitally important issue of the attitude and behavior of Kansas immigrant Mennonites to political authority.

On a continuum representing the various positions between the opposing poles of separation from and involvement in politics, D. S. H. would appear at the far right—the position of total separation including refusal to accept citizenship. This extreme position became the whipping boy for everyone who favored at least some involvement in politics, but especially for writers on the other end of the continuum who saw no danger in political involvement. One D. R. Hirschler, for example, chopped away at the core of Mennonite nonresistance with his argument from nature that because man is endowed with the power and inclinations of self-defense and destructiveness, he therefore ought to exercise this power.[35]

Ph. Schmutz took the middle position that it was sin to vote in elections where it was merely a question of which party will win, "as is most often the case in this country," but that when one had a political choice between a believer and an unbeliever, then voting became not only permissible but a Christian obligation. Since Schmutz had never voted, he apparently felt that United States' elections were meaningless in terms of significant choices of candidates. Where the Mennonites were the majority and had responsibility for civil government, as was true in Russia, Schmutz was quite willing to accede in their political involvement, at least so far as they did not go against the Word of God.[36]

Wilhelm Ewert, elder of the Bruderthal congregation near Hillsboro and immigrant from Prussia in 1874,[37] took a positive view of the state which would place him somewhat left of center on the Mennonite continuum. Ewert collapsed the structure of D. S. H.'s church-world dualism by challenging the notion that the American Government was equivalent to the biblical word "world." World in the biblical sense, said Ewert, meant "that hostile creature (feindliche Wesen) which stands in the service of the prince of darkness against God, His kingdom, and to the persecution of His children." The American Constitution simply does not fit such a conception, said Ewert. America promotes the Christian element and has long been the refuge for religious exiles.[38]

Ewert identified with a laudable national tradition. In America the Mennonites could be proud of their religious history of steadfastness in the face of persecution as well as of their adopted country's history of toleration and freedom for people such as they. When America became a positive symbol, however, the possibility was virtually eliminated of sustaining the traditional church-world dualism which defined the relationship of the Mennonite to the state. American democracy was death to old-world dualisms.

A schematic representation of the viewpoints of Mennonite writers in Zur Heimath on church-state relations in these years belies the fragmentary nature of the arguments. The articles were not treatises in systematic theology but were designed to confront the immediate problems of immigrant Mennonites in working out a new relationship to the political order. The writers, mostly of limited education, used whatever arguments were at hand. Editor David Goerz printed an extended learned article by a Quaker, but most contributors wrote spontaneously about specific problems such as the public schools or the voting question rather than laying out the theological basis for a comprehensive view of humanity and human institutions.[39]   They quoted the Bible to good advantage on all sides of the question and called upon the authority of Menno Simons to justify both a positive and a negative view of the state.[40]   Most of the writers avoided what they considered to be the extremes of complete withdrawal or separation and complete involvement in government.   The majority believed the advantages of American public schools outweighed the disadvantages; they believed that at least some participation in government was permissible.

More often than not, the theological arguments advanced in support of or warning against political involvement reflected the biases of the particular Mennonite group to which the writer belonged.   For although the Kansas Mennonites constituted a religious community, they were also divided into separate competing groups which were extremely self-conscious of their distinctiveness in cultural background, religious doctrine, and conference affiliation.   The lack of an overall ecclesiastical organization allowed each group to establish its own polity and to make its own separate decisions on such issues as church discipline, education, and relationship to the outside world.   A brief outline of the origins and differences between the main groups is essential for an adequate understanding of their political acculturation.

THE SPLINTERED COMMUNITY

No less than five main groups made up the bulk of Kansas Mennonites.   On a liberal-conservative continuum, the churches ranged from left to right as follows: The General Conference Mennonite Church (GC), Mennonite Brethren (MB), (Old) Mennonite (OM)*, Krimmer Mennonite Brethren (KMB), and Church of God in Christ, Mennonite (Holdeman).   The most numerous groups in Kansas tended to be the most liberal.   All of these groups were subject to the processes of acculturation, but individual members who were dissatisfied with the pace of their own church occasionally moved along the continuum by joining a congregation to the left which was more open to social change.

The largest body was the General Conference Mennonite Church,

---

*The official designation for this body is "Mennonite Church."

organized in 1860 in Iowa by a number of progressive leaders who undertook a separate movement aimed at church renewal through evangelism, education, and unity. As the most ecumenical of the Mennonite conferences, the General Conference attracted to its membership most of the Mennonite immigrants from Europe, including the Russian Mennonites to Kansas in the 1870s. After joining the General Conference individually over a period of years, the Kansas GC churches were formally organized in 1892 as the Western District of the General Conference. Kansas eventually became a cultural and administrative center of the conference with the national headquarters in Newton and with Bethel College near Newton as a leading institution of higher education.[41]

The second largest branch, the Mennonite Brethren Church, began as an evangelical reform movement, influenced by the Pietist movement, among the Russian Mennonites in 1860. The formation of the MB church, with its emphasis upon personal conversion, baptism by immersion, and aggressive mission work among nonreforming churches, brought new life and new dissension which lasted well into the twentieth century. Hillsboro became the American mecca for the Mennonite Brethren. Tabor College, founded in 1906, grew into their cultural and intellectual center. Theologically the Mennonite Brethren were strongly influenced by the subjectivism of Pietism and the biblical literalism of the fundamentalist movement. Both in Russia and the United States the MBs have felt kinship with the Baptist church.[42]

The third conference is the (Old) Mennonites who trace their background in a direct line to the original Anabaptist movement of the sixteenth century. Although this was the largest body of Mennonites in America and although the first Mennonite settlers in Kansas were from eastern OM churches, they were a minority in Kansas. The Kansas (Old) Mennonites tended to take cues from their eastern conference leadership rather than from other Kansas groups. They emphasized nonconformity and separation from the world more than did their GC and MB neighbors. Hesston College, founded in 1909 by the OM Kansas-Nebraska regional conference, became the third Mennonite college in Kansas within a radius of twenty miles.

The foundation of colleges by the three conferences at Newton, Hillsboro, and Hesston was a measure of intellectual and cultural vitality as well as of ecclesiastical division. A handful of smaller Mennonite groups in Kansas either were too small or too conservative to undertake enterprises in higher education. The Krimmer Mennonite Brethren group, for example, coming from the Russian Crimea, established only four congregations in central Kansas. The KMBs were very conservative and put up strong resistance to Americanizing changes of social customs and institutions. The KMBs eventually joined the Mennonite Brethren Church in 1960, but their strictness long kept them apart from other Mennonites.[43]

The work of a dynamic Mennonite evangelist, John Holdeman of Ohio, created another distinctive Mennonite group in Kansas in the early years after immigration. Holdeman stressed nonconformity to the world, including the requirement of the beard for male members, opposition to secondary or higher education, withdrawal from all forms of political participation, and strict use of the ban in church discipline. The Holdeman church, officially the "Church of God in Christ, Mennonite," has been more successful than any of the others in resisting Americanization and in maintaining sectarian distinctiveness.[44]

In addition to the five Mennonite groups mentioned above, Kansas also had representatives from the Old Order Amish, the Conservative Amish, the Evangelical Mennonite Brethren, and the Evangelical Mennonite Church, all of which could trace their history back to the Anabaptist movement. But these groups were either too small, too far from the geographical center of Kansas Mennonitism, or theologically and culturally so far out of the Mennonite mainstream that they will not be considered in this study.

A pattern of stability in conference affiliations was not set for several decades after immigration. At times it appeared that inter-Mennonite cooperation in the face of the challenges of immigration and initial settlement would break down some of the established barriers between Mennonite groups. But it was also evident from the outset that continuing Mennonite animosities and suspicions were present on the frontier and would prevent either the homogenization of the various Mennonite branches or their full cooperation in establishing common educational and social institutions.[45]

Within the conference groupings existed ethnic differences due to the national origin and migration history of the various congregations. The most fundamental difference was rooted in origin from the northern and southern wings of the Anabaptist movement. Those whose ancestors were from the Netherlands spoke a Low German dialect; those from the south spoke a Swiss or South German dialect. Migrations of Mennonite groups from country to country led to the adoption of distinctive customs and the modification of dialects. The resulting differentiation accounts for the fact that Kansas Mennonites were often blessed with a sense of identity which included, in order of increasing specificity, the Christian faith, the German national culture, the Mennonite sectarian heritage, and social differences derived from migration to specific regions. Within the General Conference Kansas churches alone there were at least eight distinguishable types which would be characterized by special social traits. In one listing, these included South Germans, Prussians via South Russia, Prussians via Polish Russia, Prussians via Volhynia, Swiss via Russia, Prussians, Galicians, and Swiss.[46]

The diversity and divisions in the Anabaptist-Mennonite movement, from its sixteenth-century European origins to its twentieth-century American development, have been the frustration of scholars who attempt to generalize about the movement as a whole.[47] One need not deny those basic inter-Mennonite differences which result in varying rates of acculturation, however, to recognize that all Mennonites were subject to Americanizing influences which, in many cases, were more significant than petty Mennonite disagreements. Nor is it necessary to forget the remarkable degree to which some congregations succeeded in remaining socially isolated from other Mennonites, in order to concentrate attention upon ways in which a common Mennonite identity issued in common responses to forces of social and political change.

All the Mennonites who came to Kansas in the 1870s, including the (Old) Mennonite homesteaders of 1870 and 1871, mixed religious and economic motives in the decision to migrate. The Santa Fe Railroad Company smoothed the way with cheap land, free transportation, and sweet talk about American freedom so that the Russian Mennonites were enticed to settle in Kansas even without guarantees of the preconditions of a closed settlement and exemption from national military service. The entire community gradually came to accept a positive image of the American Constitution, Government, and national tradition—an image which took the harshness out of Anabaptist church-state dualism and blurred Mennonite clarity about the evils of the outside world.

All the Kansas Mennonites were likewise subject to the invasion of American influences which closed in on the frontier. Paradoxically, the very railroads which carried the Mennonites to presumed isolation served, in turn, as channels for changes from the outside. The railroads brought new farm equipment, building materials, more non-Mennonite settlers, and agents to promote bond issues for the building of even more railroads. In time the Mennonites themselves would welcome improvements in transportation and communication—the bicycle, improved roads, American newspapers and periodicals, telephones, rural mail service, radios, and television. The Mennonites were up against the same dilemma as all traditional societies faced with the impact of a modernizing, industrializing world. The Kansas Mennonites, on the whole, opted for modernization. But all the while they clung tenaciously to their Mennonite identity and remained firm in the illusion that their common response to a changing world was less important than those immediate problems which distinguished one Mennonite congregation from its neighbor across the Dry Turkey Creek.

How did Kansas Mennonites, as a community, adapt to changing life in America? The process, which was well under way by the time the immigrants and homesteaders set foot on Kansas soil, spans many generations. Only the first generation had opportunity consciously to choose publicly to declare their American citizenship. The record of Mennonite naturalization proceedings, to which we now briefly turn, is a significant measure of Mennonite Americanization and an indication of what to expect in the political acculturation of the sons and daughters of Mennonite immigrants.

"*One learned to reckon with the fact that the young people here in America grow up with the consciousness of free citizens who can be elected to Congress. That creates most significant challenges for the Christian family and congregation*" (C. H. WEDEL, 1904).

CHAPTER 3

The Reluctant Citizens

IT WAS ONE THING FOR A MENNONITE TO DECIDE THAT AMERICA would be a good place to settle and another thing to sign a public statement of intention to become a citizen of the United States. Naturalization proceedings were an embarrassment and confusion for the new immigrant. How could one understand what the English-speaking public official was saying? Was it dangerous to sign a statement which one could not read? Would there be objections when one refused to swear the oath? Did naturalization entail any obligations for military service?

Most of these anxieties could be overcome through a trusted interpreter. More important, however, was the fact that one's signature on the naturalization papers symbolized a kind of commitment. Citizenship was a public sign of a personal decision and, as such, shared certain overtones with the decision to join the church through baptism. The document itself suggested more than a transfer of allegiance or change in physical location. One's civic status changed from subject to citizen:

. . . who being duly sworn, upon his oath declares that it is BONA FIDE his intention to become a citizen of the UNITED STATES OF NORTH AMER-ICA, and to renounce and adjure forever all allegiance and fidelity to every foreign power, prince, potentate, state and sovereignty whatever, and particularly to the . . . . of whom he was heretofore a subject.[1]

If, as one scholar suggests, in the modern national state "the secular registration of birth is the national rite of baptism,"[2] the Mennonites had an even more precise analogue to naturalization in their ritual of adult baptism. As such, the rate of naturalization may be one of the most important indexes of Mennonite Americanization.

The question of naturalization was too sensitive an issue for Mennonites to reach a collective decision on the matter. The first meeting of the Kansas Conference of Mennonites in December 1877 explicitly refused to "recommend or condemn in a onesided manner the aversion for or inclination to become a citizen." In the very same resolution, however, the conference advised Mennonites to set up public school districts in areas where they could control them.[3] Such action, left to the discretion of the individual congregations, required public elections and the completion of first citizenship papers. Jacob Buller, pastor of the Alexanderwohl congregation, counseled his members to take out first papers in order to wield influence in the establishment of public schools.[4] Some Mennonites took pride in being among the first to initiate naturalization proceedings.[5] Others felt it wise to hesitate for a time before taking such a serious step.[6]

One reason for Mennonite hesitation was that naturalization seemed so closely bound up with politics. As early as 1876, Republican politicians in Marion County made an effort to round up Mennonites who would take out first papers and vote a Republican ballot.[7] The stakes were even higher in railroad bond elections held in Marion and McPherson counties in December 1878 and February 1879 respectively. The Mennonites of McPherson County were a potential antirailroad force because the proposed road, a branch line of the Santa Fe, passed north of their territory. They had closer access to the Santa Fe main line at Newton and Halstead. Politicians on both sides went after the Mennonite vote and accused their opponents of unfair tactics. J. T. Moffatt, an antirailroad resident of Mound Township, claimed that someone in Lone Tree Township to the north had boasted "that the people of McPherson had raised $140 for him with which to naturalize the Mennonites of Lone Tree, and as they could not read the English language, and he could speak their language, he intended to vote them all for the proposition."[8] The McPherson *Freeman* meanwhile told its readers that Newton businessmen had raised $1,500 "in a short time" for use in McPherson County against the railroad.[9] The Newton *Kansan* saw this charge as evidence of "a few big liars" in McPherson, but it did admit that a Harvey County deputy official had been active in McPherson County writing out first naturalization papers for Mennonites in the days prior to the election.[10] The Mennonites themselves, said the *Kansan,* had hired the job done. Harvey County had a clean conscience.

There are no contemporary written records to indicate what Mennonites thought of the bond election controversy, whether they in fact did hire a Harvey County official to come over the line and write out first papers, or what their reaction was to the solicitations of uninvited politicians. The experience, however, must have left an indelible impression upon Mennonites as they considered the nature of American politics and its relationship to the process of becoming a citizen. David Goerz of the Halstead (Harvey County) *Zur Heimath,* who printed column after column of theological argument regarding church and state and political participation, remained safely silent when the constituency confronted politics as an immediate practical decision. The individual Mennonite farmer and his wife had little help from their church on what to do when the politician came around with palm grease and naturalization papers.

Mennonites did leave a permanent record of naturalization proceedings in the county clerk offices. These records show that the McPherson County bond election stimulated an unprecedented enrollment of Mennonites for citizenship. In 1879, the year of the election, 215 Mennonites took out first papers, more than twice as many as in any previous year. Of the eighty-five Mennonite applications in McPherson County, eighty-one were between February 15 and 25. The election was on the 25th. Harvey County records show fifty-one applications on February 24, which verifies the newspaper report that an official from Newton had crossed into McPherson to qualify Mennonites for votes against the proposition. The record in Marion County is less dramatic. Here there were fifty Mennonite first papers in 1878 (the election was held several months earlier in Marion County), and the correlation with the bond election was not as great. Four Mennonites from the Gnadenau community are registered for December 16, 1878, the date of the election in Risley Township.[11]

The bond issue succeeded in both Marion and McPherson counties. Opposition to the railroad increased in direct proportion to distance from the proposed route, which suggests that Mennonites voted according to their economic interests rather than to pay a debt of gratitude to the Santa Fe Railroad or to please politicians who sought their vote.[12]

Table 1: Mennonite First Naturalization Papers

Year	Harvey Co.	Reno Co.	McPherson Co.	Marion Co.	Total
1874	15	0	2	2	19
1875	10	0	3	19	32
1876	3	0	4	39	46
1877	31	0	37	29	97
1878	18	0	2	50	70
1879	111	7	85	12	215
1880	17	3	2	13	35
1881	25	23	16	20	84
1882	81	24	8	15	128
1883	14	12	13	14	53
1884	64	23	20	21	128
1885	21	2	22	193	238
1886	20	11	41	36	108
1887	43	11	19	11	84
1888	34	4	32	23	93
1889	7	3	9	9	28
1890	31	4	31	23	89
1891	13	4	16	6	49
1892	48	10	75	61	194
1893	48	17	35	20	120
1894	33	11	16	35	95
1895	4	0	0	2	6
1896	19	16	49	19	103
1897	6	3	2	1	12
1898	2	2	4	17	25
1899	6	0	1	1	8
1900	8	16	12	5	31
1901	10	6	9	5	30
1902	2	0	0	1	3
1903	2	3	9	2	16
1904	10	5	9	13	37
1905	2	5	5	10	22
1906	6	185	24	10	225

The records of first naturalization proceedings in Harvey, Reno, McPherson, and Marion counties reveal that, in spite of the 1879 flurry, many Mennonites who came in the mid-1870s waited a decade or more before taking out first papers (see table 1). Four years stood out as exceptional: 1879, 1885, 1892, and 1906. In 1879 and 1885 the Mennonites took out first papers in order to vote in railroad bond elections. In 1892 the increase was related to November state and national political elections.[13] A prospective change in the naturalization law, which made the process more complicated and time-consuming, accounted for a large number of first papers in 1906. Most of the enrollments in that year took place in Hutchinson where Peter J. Galle, a Mennonite native son who had made good in politics, served as district judge in charge of proceedings. The days set aside for naturalization in 1906 coincided with the state fair in Hutchinson, which may have proved a double attraction for Mennonites to come to the Reno County seat.

There exist no records of naturalizations as a percentage of immigrant population with which to make accurate comparison of the Mennonites with other immigrant groups. The records of McPherson County on nearly every election year show that a higher number of Swedes from the northern part of the county took out first papers than did Mennonites. It is not unusual, however, that about twenty or twenty-five Mennonites became naturalized in order to vote. As early as 1876, twenty-six Mennonites took out first papers between November 4 and 7. The following year a newspaper correspondent from Risley Township boasted shortly before elections, "Fifteen more Germans naturalized in this township."[14] In the elections of 1888 and 1890 about twenty Mennonites took out first papers in the week before elections in both McPherson and Harvey counties. Mennonite voting and interest in politics may have been limited, but it surely took place from the very beginning.

By the end of 1906 over twenty-five hundred Mennonites had overcome their inhibitions and reservations and had taken out first naturalization papers. The overall picture is one of reluctance, especially in comparison with other immigrant groups. Mennonites cannot be included in the generalization that the American immigrant "accepted the invitation to become naturalized as soon as the residence requirements permitted. . . ."[15] The ground for Mennonite caution included a history of experience with untrustworthy governments, a church-state doctrine which encouraged political noninvolvement, and fears that citizenship implied duties, such as military service, which could not be performed in good conscience. Many Mennonites went to their graves without the "saving benefit of civic baptism." It would be many more years before the Mennonites would completely lose their characteristic of being reluctant citizens.

"*We admit there is much that is fine and good to be said for free trade from an international standpoint, but the editor of the* Anzeiger *is an American in the egotistical sense of the word. America's interests are closer to our heart than those of Styria or Prussia*" (JOHN F. HARMS, 1888).

CHAPTER **4**

Political Orientations, 1870-1898

MENNONITE SOCIAL RELATIONSHIPS IN THE OLD WORLD STOOD ON three institutional legs—the village, the church congregation, and the family. The village was the center of local politics. On the open Kansas frontier, where abundant land was available, the village disintegrated. Only two of the immigrating Mennonite congregations even attempted to recreate the village, with its stretch of clustered dwellings between long strips of land on either side. The Gnadenau (KMB) congregation came from the Crimea in 1874 and established a village on section eleven of Risley Township in Marion County.[1] The Alexanderwohl (GC) congregation, emigrating as an almost intact community from the Molotschna colony in South Russia, settled in eight separate villages in the southwest corner of Marion County and the southeast corner of McPherson County.[2] The village pattern soon proved inefficient as larger separate landholdings were made possible and desirable by Mennonite prosperity, by the introduction of machinery, and by the extensive wheat culture on the subhumid Kansas land which was too dry for intensive farming. The disappearance of the Mennonite village meant the loss of certain political functions long performed by Mennonites, though these functions had not always been recognized as political. The governing committee of three men which had made village decisions regarding discipline, personal disputes, and public improvements no longer exercised authority when the community was broken up into individual homesteads. American institutions of local government, based upon arbitrary county and township boundaries, took over governing responsibilities formerly in village hands.   Not all Mennonites were willing to accept the shift from the Mennonite village to the township.   Township and county elections required naturalization, and worldly people were involved in these elections.   Elder Jacob A. Wiebe of Gnadenau was dubious about the transition in the early years.   "We did not want to become citizens as yet," he wrote.[3] The demise of the village shifted the focus of Mennonite social life upon the congregation and had the immediate effect of removing Mennonites from politics.

Only the most conservative Mennonites could maintain the moral distinction between officeholding in a Mennonite village and office-holding in a predominantly Mennonite township.   Some Mennonites became township officials soon after settlement.   The county court-house records of township elections are too incomplete for a full tabulation of Mennonite township officeholders, but Mennonite names appear on the roster of township officials as early as 1877.   In that year Jno. Fast and B. Unruh were elected road overseers in Risley Township, Marion County.   In 1878 Meridian Township, McPherson County, elected J. A. Holderman township clerk; and A. Wenger received votes for constable and road overseer.   Chris Ropp received eight votes for Mound Township treasurer but was not elected.   In Garden and Alta townships, Harvey County, for example, Mennonite names dominated the township roster in 1888: John Toevs, F. J. Adrian, John Regier, E. J. Heidbrch (Heidebrecht), J. P. Vogt, C. A. Lehman, D. E. Eyeman, and J. N. Krehbiel.   These names are characteristic of Russian Mennonites who later joined the General Conference Mennonite Church.   The more conservative congregations, especially the Krimmer Mennonite Brethren and the (Old) Mennonites, were less willing to accept township offices.

The boundary between religion and politics was most fuzzy in the question of education.   Mennonites recognized the power of education in perpetuating or destroying the values and traditions of the community.   Public schools might be condemned as corrupt and godless,[4] but Mennonites had more reason for establishing their own schools than just to preserve a religious and ethnic heritage: in Russia the Mennonite schools were the mark of their cultural superiority over the natives.   They could not be sure, in their first years on the Kansas frontier, that the general quality of the public schools would meet Mennonite desired standards.[5]   The first Kansas Conference of Mennonites in December 1877 considered the English language not as a threat to community solidarity but rather as a desired prerequisite for

social communication and Christian witnessing among their neighbors.[6]

Several patterns of coordinating public schools with Mennonite
German schools were attempted. Some districts conducted public and
German schools consecutively, each for part of the year. Others
taught Bible and German for a part of each day. Some German
schools taught the full state-required course, although the completely
separate German-Mennonite schools were not as widespread as might
have been expected.[7] County public school officials were well-im-
pressed with the quality of instruction by Mennonite teachers and in
several instances made available county money for strictly Mennonite
sectarian education.[8] After the first decade or two, the German elementary schools began to decline, and Mennonites focused more effort
upon preparatory schools. Mennonite German schools continued in
some form until the 1930s when the community shifted from the German to the English language in home and church.

The education problem, as well as questions of political involvement on other levels, became issues for discussion and resolution at
conference meetings of the various Kansas Mennonite church groups.
By 1880 the Kansas Conference (GC)[9] Mennonites had achieved a
sufficient consensus to allow the appointment of a trusted leader, Valentine Krehbiel, to write an essay on the question of participation in
elections.[10] Krehbiel's essay, printed in a March 1880 issue of *Zur
Heimath*, justified political participation on the grounds that Christians are to be the "salt of the earth" and the "light of the world."
Krehbiel found no specific scriptural command on the matter, however,
and suggested that the final decision would have to be left to the individual conscience. Although he conceded that there was always
"something worldly" about elections, Krehbiel pointed out that America can best achieve her goal of a government in the interests of the
people if the number of good voters is decisive. It is also possible, he
went on, to see the vote as an important means for "actual realization
and spread of evangelical peace principles on this earth."[11]

From the earliest years in Kansas, then, there were Mennonite
leaders who not only encouraged participation in politics, while carefully trying not to offend more conservative members, but who had
the kernel of a vision that politics may be an arena for the expression
of a Mennonite witness to the world. That witness seemed particularly
relevant to issues of war and peace.

The vision for political participation as a Christian witness seems to have been limited to the Mennonites of the Kansas Conference. The Mennonite Brethren Conference in 1878 adopted a resolution which forbade voting and political officeholding for church members. The resolution, proposed by the chairman, a Brother Loeppke of Marion County, was adopted unanimously. Since the Bible says that God has given the sword to the authorities for judgment, said the resolution, the church can enjoy the protection of the state even though church members do not engage directly in political behavior.[12]

Although such a conference resolution was supposed to be binding on all MB church members, it is not clear how faithfully or how long it was observed. No records of individual votes remain to verify when Mennonite Brethren members began voting. One old-time amateur MB historian in 1966 doubted that there ever was a time when the church prohibited voting by resolution.[13] The records of conference resolutions do not indicate that the 1878 resolution was ever formally rescinded or superseded. Only a decade later, however, the 1888 MB Conference in Reno County discussed the question of "whether a brother may allow himself to be elected as a national party delegate to a political convention."[14] The form of the question indicated reference to a specific case of a member who had achieved or contemplated such election, a type of political involvement considerably beyond the mere use of franchise which had been forbidden a decade earlier. The 1888 conference refused to adopt a resolution restricting the political-minded brother. Instead they admitted their dilemma with surprising candor: "We want to have a good government, but we also wish not to defile our consciences with political contentions."[15]

Two years later the MB Conference discussed Prohibition and resolved in revealingly negative language that church members not vote against Prohibition, that the peaceful casting of the vote not be condemned, and that members avoid partisan disputes and fights.[16] In spite of its negative formulation, this resolution was the only instance in Kansas Mennonite history when the community, as a conference, specifically instructed its members how to vote in a political election.

At the conference in 1893 the Mennonite Brethren resolved that its members not be allowed to hold the office of justice of the peace or constable, presumably because such offices involved the use of violent coercion. The office of notary public was not forbidden.[17] The 1893 resolution was the last time that the issue of political involvement was discussed and resolved upon in the Mennonite Brethren conferences. One explanation for this would be that there was general compliance in the policy of noninvolvement so the issue did not have to be discussed.[18] Another explanation would be that the Mennonite Brethren gradually began to take part in elections and to hold political office without sufficient opposition among their members to make it an issue worth discussing in conference sessions. In any case, one must account for the fact that Mennonite Brethren eventually did take part in politics to some degree, even though that participation was never officially sanctioned in conference resolutions.

The Krimmer Mennonite Brethren group was more conservative. At an 1885 church council meeting ("Bruderrat") the KMBs discussed the dangers of conformity to the world implicit in the political office of township road overseer. They agreed that their church members should avoid the office if at all possible.[19] Before the election of 1890 the KMBs suggested that their members keep out of the temperance movement in behalf of peace and love in the community and because of "the danger of division in political matters" ("die Gefahr der Verzweiung in politischen Dingen").[20] Although Mennonite conference resolutions occasionally conceal more than they reveal, there is reason to credit the KMB suggestion here that political involvements were feared primarily as a threat to the internal unity of the group. When church members lined up on opposing sides of political issues, both the myth and the reality of congregational unity or "oneness in Christ" were undermined.

The KMB congregations were more persistent and more explicit in their conference resolutions against political participation than were the Kansas Conference or the Mennonite Brethren churches. In a conference statement of 1896 they requested their constituents not to take part in political meetings and in voting. Another statement at the 1898 conference reconfirmed this position, with the exception of school elections. They added that members should not sit as judges or jury members. Guns were forbidden.[21] The 1898 resolution was upheld in conferences of 1907 and 1911.[22] The persistent conservatism of the KMB congregations was most evident during the First World War when they resolved, in a conference in late October 1917, to advise their young men not to report for military service unless they were given alternative service outside of the military camps. At the same time they appointed a committee to check into the possibilities of emigration.[23]

The Krimmer Mennonite Brethren conference resolutions were filled with concern over accommodation to the world (Gleichstellung der

Welt), but the traditional Anabaptist-Mennonite two-kingdom dualism was stated most explicitly in the proceedings of the Kansas-Nebraska (OM) conferences. At their first meeting in McPherson County in 1876 the OM*s* appealed both to the logic of nonresistance and to the authority of the Scriptures as they resolved,

That it is entirely inconsistent with the nonresistant doctrine to go to the polls to vote because if we are faithful followers of the Lord Jesus we then belong to His kingdom: and "my kingdom," He says, "is not of this world." Read John 18:36. We find the subjects of His kingdom are not to fight. If we then help to elect men in the kingdom of this world we are in duty bound to fight for them; hence the inconsistency and danger of laboring or taking part in both kingdoms. "No man can serve two masters." Matthew 6:24; Luke 16:13.[24]

At the same conference they advised members against accepting the office of Road Overseer "since such person is bound to enforce the law if necessary. . . ."[25] The meticulous concern of the Kansas-Nebraska (Old) Mennonites to keep separate from the kingdom of this world included not only rejection of lightning rods, insurance, and worldly amusements, but also the raising of the hand when rendering public affirmation in place of the oath. Some even had scruples against use of the words *solemnly* or *under the pain and penalty of the law* in the affirmation, for "the Savior had commanded to let your yea be yea, and no more."[26] They completely excluded jury service in any case. Although political offices were forbidden, the conference in 1890 opened the door a crack by allowing members to fill "in extreme cases, the place of School Director, Supervisor, Director of the Poor, and Post Master." Presumably the office of township road supervisor was still out of bounds, though it was not specifically mentioned.[27]

Like the Mennonite Brethren conferences, the Kansas-Nebraska (Old) Mennonite conferences found it necessary particularly in the first two decades, until about 1890, to articulate their attitudes toward the world of politics. Except for one brief reference to elections in 1898,[28] the (Old) Mennonites did not raise the questions of voting and officeholding around the turn of the century. Again it is unclear whether this is due to compliance with the rules or to indifference to violation of the rules. In the conference sermon of 1898, Brother S. C. Miller of Monitor, Kansas, rebuked his listeners for not taking the resolutions seriously. What good have the resolutions done if we have not "touched them with one of our fingers"?[29] The record does not specify whether he had reference to politics or to other forbidden forms of creeping worldliness.

Mennonites of all groups were more conservative in conference resolutions than they were in everyday practice. Resistance to political involvement was strongest among the smaller groups—(Old) Mennonites, Krimmer Mennonite Brethren, and Church of God in Christ (Holdeman)—which either had had no prior political experience or were under the influence of strong conservative leadership. The two largest bodies, the Mennonite Brethren and General Conference Mennonites, were more open to political participation. Their favorable experience with local government in the autonomous communities in Russia accounts largely for GC and MB relative receptivity. These two groups provided nearly all the Mennonite political action in Kansas until well into the twentieth century.

VOTES AND ISSUES

County government was already established in Kansas by the time the Mennonites arrived. The interval of five years which separated the bawling of longhorn cattle on the Chisholm Trail from the turning of that trail's sod by Mennonite ploughmen, sufficed for advance American pioneers to move into the territory, hold elections, and establish government. These hardy frontiersmen belonged to the party of Lincoln—the party which freed the slaves, built the railroads, and provided homestead land. Table 2 shows that they consistently returned Republican majorities in the elections prior to the Mennonite arrival.

Table 2: Republican Vote as Percentage of Total Vote in Central Kansas Counties 1868-1876[30]

	Harvey Co.	McPherson Co.	Marion Co.	Reno Co.
1868 presidential election	—	—	52.5%	—
1870 gubernatorial election	—	99.5%	50.0	—
1872 presidential election	75.1%	90.2	82.1	74.7%
1874 gubernatorial election	88.7	67.3	70.6	91.4
1876 presidential election	74.1	80.6	68.0	76.3

Given the ascendancy of the Republican party in the Mennonite area and given the fact that Mennonites had received their introduction to America from Republican-oriented railroads, it was natural for Mennonites to vote Republican. A son of one of the immigrants summed up his explanation of why his father, who later became a Populist and a Democrat, joined fellow-Mennonites in voting Republican in the early years: "They all wanted to be good citizens."[31]

Good citizenship in central Kansas entailed Republican politics in the 1870s. To vote Republican was to certify the authenticity of one's naturalization.

The Marion County Republican leaders were the first to see the potential in the Mennonite vote. The "Regular Risley Reporter" noted in the *Marion County Record* on November 10, 1876, that "it was a grand sight to see 40 or more of our Russian-German neighbors in solid phalanx, march up to the polls and vote for Hayes and Wheeler." Providing the German-speaking voters with instructions on how to mark the strange ballot were Republican leaders Charles Verling and E. Baxter.[32]

Whatever hopes county political leaders may have had for a "solid phalanx" of Mennonite Republican voters in the years after 1876, Mennonites tended to be more independent in their politics than they promised to be in their lineup for Hayes and Wheeler. Mennonite community solidarity did not result in simple Mennonite political uniformity. The editor of the McPherson *Republican* recognized this fact as early as 1882 when he wrote, "The German vote does not seem to cut so much of a figure as it did. Politicians are beginning to learn that Germans are just like other people and that they divide on public matters as much as native born Americans do."[33]

The voting records from selected townships in the area of Mennonite settlement do deviate somewhat from the Kansas average in comparative percentage for political parties. In the five gubernatorial elections between 1882 and 1890, the "Mennonite" Republican vote was several percentage points less (as much as 11.1 points less in 1890) than in Kansas.[34] (See Appendix D, page 163.) In the six gubernatorial elections between 1892 and 1900, the "Mennonite" Republican vote was several percentage points higher. The deviation from the Kansas norm in most of these elections was hardly enough to suggest that a Mennonite vote may have accounted for it. By way of contrast, the Swedish vote in northern McPherson County was significantly higher than the state average (as much as 26.0 points higher in 1886) throughout this entire period.

Of special interest is the third-party vote in the Mennonite townships. The third-party vote in the gubernatorial elections of 1880 (Greenback), 1882 (National Labor), 1888 (National Labor), and 1894 (Populist) was over 10 percent higher in the Mennonite townships than in the state of Kansas or in Chase County. The same trend held also in the presidential elections of 1880 and 1888. There is no way of knowing, however, how much of this third-party vote actually represented Mennonite ballots. There are no written records suggesting early Mennonite third-party interests. The minority represented by the third-party vote in each of these elections was small enough to be accounted for entirely by non-Mennonite residents in the "Mennonite" townships. At least it can be said that the political units in which Mennonites lived not only had a tradition of Republican domination of politics prior to the Mennonite arrival, but also that a third-party protest vote did appear in this area and therefore was an option for the Mennonites in their consideration of their own political attitudes and behavior.

Another protest movement which had an impact upon the Mennonite community was the drive for Prohibition. In 1880 Kansas became the first state in the union to adopt a Prohibition amendment to the state constitution. The Mennonites had come to Kansas with divided opinions on the alcohol question. Their communities in Russia and Prussia had known the profits and pleasures of brewing and imbibing as well as the annoyance and dissensions of a temperance movement.[35] The Mennonite Brethren and Krimmer Mennonite Brethren had developed a conscience against drinking alcoholic beverages,[36] but Mennonites who later joined the General Conference had fewer scruples on the issue. David Goerz attempted to keep the problem before the community through antialcohol material in *Zur Heimath*. The "Murphy movement" which swept Kansas in 1878 established a temperance club in Halstead which attracted the interest and possibly the membership of some Mennonites. Opponents of the movement believed that power against drunkenness should be sought within the church rather than outside of Christ in the "Murphy Clubs."[37]

The 1880 vote on the Prohibition amendment in Mennonite townships was inconclusive: 57.1 percent in favor and 42.9 percent opposed compared to 52.3 percent in favor and 47.7 percent opposed in the state at large. The voter turnout in Mennonite townships was not significantly larger than usual, indicating that no great numbers of normally nonvoting Mennonites turned out at this election to vote on this moral issue. Nor were the numbers of votes cast in the Prohibition election greater than the numbers of votes cast for the usual county and state candidates. Apparently very few, if any, normally nonvoting Mennonites took the position that it was justifiable to go to the polls when a moral issue was at stake. By 1934, when Kansas voted on Prohibition repeal, this situation had changed radically and Mennonites turned out in unprecedented numbers specifically to vote against repeal. (See pages 116-126 on voting patterns in chapter 8.) The variation within townships in 1880 was quite great and without observable pattern: Lone Tree Township in McPherson County voted 82.8 percent for the amendment; Liberty Township in Marion County voted 84.8 percent against. The turnout of only thirty-three voters in Liberty Township indicates a remarkable apathy during a crucial election and suggests that Mennonite temperance crusading was a later development.

Several Mennonites did pick up the temperance cause as a political issue. The most notable Mennonite Prohibitionist in the nineteenth century was J. J. Krehbiel, a lay leader in Harvey County who was a co-founder of Bethel College and chairman of its board of trustees for twenty years. Krehbiel ran on the Prohibition ticket three times for county commissioner and once for county treasurer between 1888 and 1904. He received totals of only sixteen, sixty-one, thirty-nine, and thirty-two votes.

The eventual wholesale Mennonite swing to the temperance movement was a kind of Americanization. Temperance had special appeal as a religious and moral crusade which involved the Mennonite conception of their own social status. Mennonites were not afraid to differ from society, but to reject the temperance movement would have been to contradict their belief in their own moral superiority. Christian Krehbiel, a progressive Mennonite patriarch who was no stranger to alcoholic beverages, announced his conversion to Prohibition before a ministers' meeting at the Alexanderwohl Church in these terms: "Brethren, we have made a name unto ourselves that stinks, and we must change our attitude if we want to keep the respect of our English-speaking Christians."[38] Krehbiel's reputation-conscious appeal had special import in Kansas where Prohibition was the law and where Germans had a name for tippling. It was time, he believed, for the Mennonites to reject alcohol, especially if they wanted to maintain an image of moral rectitude. The Mennonite shift to a doctrinal position of total abstinence was a kind of conformity to their world.

For advice on the wide range of public issues, from Murphy Clubs to local education, Mennonites looked to their own newspapers. The Americanizing function of David Goerz's *Zur Heimath* was most evident in the earlier years of its brief life in Kansas from 1875 to 1881. Practical questions of secular interest such as advice for new immigrants, instructions for naturalization proceedings, and debate on the public school question filled *Zur Heimath* pages in 1875, 1876, and 1877. When the crisis over the disputed Hayes-Tilden election in 1876 led Wilhelm Ewert, elder of the Bruderthal congregation in Marion County, to warn the Mennonite community of a possible violent revolution, Editor Goerz expressed confidence that a compromise would be reached and that the militia would not be called out.[39] Such basic guidance in the workings of American democracy seemed less necessary in succeeding years and *Zur Heimath* evolved into a religious, church-oriented periodical with little concern for secular or political events. In 1882 it merged with another paper to become the *Christlicher Bundesbote,* the official German paper of the General Conference.

For three years the central Kansas Mennonites lacked a secular newspaper of their own, but between 1885 and 1887 five German-language newspapers were founded to fill the vacuum: *Der Freundschafts-Kreis* (Hillsboro), edited by John W. Fast and Son; *Hillsboro Herald,* edited by John C. Fast; *McPherson Anzeiger* and *Marion County Anzeiger,* both edited by John F. Harms; and *Newton Anzeiger,* edited by Ulrich Hege. All of these newspapers initially professed nonpartisan political orientations, but all were willing to take positions on political issues and to endorse election candidates. Except for the *Hillsboro Herald,* all were friendly to the Republican Party.

Of these newspapers, only the *Marion County Anzeiger* (later changed to the *Hillsboro Anzeiger*) lasted more than five years. Editor John F. Harms was an 1878 immigrant from South Russia who had come to Marion County in 1884 after several years of publishing work in Indiana with the (Old) Mennonite leader John F. Funk. In Kansas, Harms became a noted editor, teacher, and preacher in the Mennonite Brethren Church. At the same time that he edited the *Anzeiger,* Harms also put out the *Zionsbote,* a religious publication which eventually became the official organ of the Mennonite Brethren Church. Those who knew Harms in his later years did not remember him as a man of strong political interests.[40] In the decade from 1887 to 1897, however, his controversial newspaper editorship was the most visible—and possibly the most significant—politicizing force among the Kansas Mennonites.

Harms ambitiously planned to blanket the Mennonite community with a triangular newspaper chain with centers in Hillsboro, McPherson, and Newton. Two of the paper's four pages were to be the same for each location, with the inside pages given to local news and correspondence.   Harms never got the Newton corner of his *Anzeiger* triangle off the ground, largely because of competition from an already established *Newton Anzeiger,* edited by Ulrich Hege, Harms' former associate.   When Harms began to put out a rival *Harvey County Anzeiger* in June 1888, he drew bitter fire from Hege[41] and set the stage for several politically-oriented insults later that year.

The central political issue in the national campaign of 1888 was defined by President Grover Cleveland's advocacy of protective tariff reduction.   Editor Harms was an outspoken protectionist who grounded his argument in an openly nationalistic point of view.   "We admit there is much that is fine and good to be said for free trade from an international standpoint," he wrote in reply to a correspondent in his pages who argued for lowered tariffs as a boon to international trade, "but the editor of the *Anzeiger* is an American in the egotistical sense of the word. . . . America's interests are closer to our heart than those of Styria or Prussia."[42]   Mennonite American patriotism could hardly be more explicit.

John J. Funk, a free-trade Democrat from Peabody, was aroused to combat by Harms' equation of protection and patriotism.   Funk challenged any opponent to a public debate on the issue.[43]   H. D. Penner of Hillsboro accepted the challenge, and the debate was held in a packed Hillsboro schoolhouse on September 10, 1888.   The spectacle of two Mennonites squaring off in public debate on the great political issues of the day is alone sufficient evidence to lay to rest the common notion that immigrant Mennonites were not interested in American politics.   The antagonists brought up the issues of Prohibition, political parties in general, and the tariff question.   Editor Harms generously refused to judge who won the debate, though in a later issue he printed some "Democratic Questions and Republican Answers" in which questions attributed to Funk were fully and satisfactorily answered by Penner.[44]

Harms advised his readers to vote a straight Republican ticket in the 1888 election.[45]   He did not even admit the possibility that a Democratic candidate of German background or of superior abilities would merit support.   Ulrich Hege of the *Newton Anzeiger* printed an article by "A Tariff Reformer" which accused Harms of supporting the "monopolists" and of backing the Republican platform which included reduced whiskey taxes as well as high tariffs.[46]   Harms replied that he had always been opposed to monopoly, that he supported the Republican ticket in this election because of Democratic free trade tendencies, and that he did not support the Republican platform in every detail.[47] Harms also wrote a letter to the English language Newton *Republican* discrediting the *Newton Anzeiger's* attempt "to scare the Mennonites from voting for the Republican party."[48] Hege in turn scoffed at Harms for acting as if he "carried the votes of the Mennonites in his vest pocket."[49]

The Democratic *Hillsboro Herald* provided Harms with more friendly campaign competition. Editor C. E. Schmidt of the *Herald*, who had replaced John C. Fast, was less thorough in his discussion of the issues than was Harms. Schmidt's editorial position emphasized tariff reduction, Cleveland's courage, and the need to hold the big money power in check. In the issue prior to the election, a letter from a "Volksfreund" imported a bit of corrupted German poetry into the campaign: "Lieb Vaterland kannst ruhig sein; Fest tritt das Volk fuer Cleveland ein."[50] In the issue after the election, Schmidt turned the symbol of the Democratic Party, a rooster, on its head and printed in bold type, "In spite of everything we remain faithful to our rooster."[51]

The voting results from Mennonite townships indicate that neither Harms nor Hege held the Mennonite vote in his pocket. The combined vote for incumbent Democratic President Cleveland and for Andrew J. Streeter of the National Union Labor third party was 54.1 percent; Republican candidate Benjamin Harrison received a plurality of only 44.7 percent as compared with 55.4 percent in the state of Kansas as a whole. Because the Mennonites were only about 55 percent to 60 percent of the population in these townships and because a smaller percentage of Mennonites voted than other citizens, it cannot be said definitely that these figures represent exact Mennonite percentages. The most solidly Mennonite townships (Menno and West Branch of the Alexanderwohl community in Marion County) turned in the strongest Republican vote.

The most surprising statistic from the 1888 voting returns in Mennonite townships is the 452 votes (27 percent) for the National Union Labor party. It is statistically possible, though quite unlikely, that none of these votes were cast by Mennonites. Harms himself, in spite of all his patriotic Republicanism, hardly had an alarmist view of the Union Labor party. Rather than sneering at their reform proposals, he suggested that the reforms called for—such as opposition to foreign absentee landowners and the demand for lower interest rates—could best be achieved by the Republican party.[52] The emergence of Populism later reduced Harm's toleration for reformers, but in 1888 he viewed the reform party more as a source of useful suggestions than as a threat to the established order. It is quite possible that some Mennonites, especially those who may have had experience with the lands of William Scully, an Irish absentee landlord with considerable holdings in Marion County, could have voted the Union Labor ticket. It was at least a respectable option in south central Kansas.

POPULISM

The Mennonites were better equipped than most of their neighboring American farmers to cope with the agrarian depression of the 1880s and 1890s which spawned the Farmers' Alliance and Populist movements. Their social creed combined firm belief in the Protestant ethic of individual hard work and a sense of mutual responsibility for the welfare of their families and congregations.[53] They helped each other in times of economic distress. Their innate caution against dangerous speculation and overinvestment reduced their vulnerability when farm prices plummeted and money sources evaporated. It would be an oversimplification, however, to say that Mennonites avoided Populism because they avoided the depression.

Speculation was not a Mennonite habit, but neither was it unknown in their communities. The most spectacular example was C. B. Funk, one time mayor of Hillsboro, whose plans and considerable investments in a proposed "Funk's City" near Durham were lost in 1887 when the anticipated Fort-Smith Railroad failed to materialize.[54] More direct victims of the depression were the hundreds of Mennonites who were sued for unpaid notes or had mortgages foreclosed. The Marion County court records (table 3) show that ordinary civil court cases involving Mennonites, most of whom had conscientious scruples against initiating court proceedings themselves, increased sharply in the depression period to a peak of ninety-three in 1888. During the decade from 1884 through 1893 Mennonites were involved in 445 cases, most of which, it may be assumed, were directly related to the depression. Also related to the depression were the delinquent tax notices which listed lands to be sold by the county in order to cover the taxes. The notice for 1896 in Marion County, for example, listed sixty-six plots of delinquent tax land in the "Mennonite" townships of Menno, West Branch, and Risley. Eighteen of the plots were quarter-sections of 160 acres. There was no immediately apparent difference between "Mennonite" and non-Mennonite townships in the amount of delinquent tax lands.[55] Statistics comparing

Table 3: Ordinary Civil Cases Involving Mennonites, Marion County, 1880-1900 (Excludes divorce and criminal cases)

Year	Cases	Year	Cases
1880	—	1891	37
1881	1	1892	22
1882	13	1893	19
1883	5	1894	12
1884	20	1895	10
1885	34	1896	13
1886	38	1897	11
1887	55	1898	7
1888	93	1899	7
1889	73	1900	4
1890	49		

Excerpted from chart based on the Civil and Criminal Docket, Marion County, Kansas, 1872-1924, in Cornelius Cicero Janzen, "A Social Study of the Mennonite Settlement in the Counties of Marion, McPherson, Harvey, Reno, and Butler, Kansas" (unpublished Ph.D. Dissertation, University of Chicago, 1926), p. 60.

the economic conditions in the Mennonite communities with Kansas in general are difficult to compile, especially because the Mennonites were not clustered in a single county for comparison with other counties. Available evidence indicates, however, that the Mennonites were hard enough hit by the depression to give ample reason for participation in the Populist revolt had there been no restraints against radical politics in the Mennonite ideology and social experience.

Some Mennonites did, in fact, join the reform crusade. One prime candidate for Mennonite Populism was Abraham Thiessen, a recent immigrant who had been banned from Russia for his social agitation in behalf of the underprivileged landless. Thiessen came to Kansas via Nebraska in October 1887 to be manager of the Peabody silk factory. Although he did manage to get involved in local controversies, Thiessen died in 1889 before he was able to establish himself as an agrarian reformer on the American scene.[56] Peter Loewen, a Republican farmer from near Hillsboro who lost a race for Register of Deeds in Marion County in 1891, decided to go over to the Populists when, in the words of his son, "the Republicans got to be so infernally crooked that he couldn't take it any longer."[57] Loewen eventually became a Democrat, again missing the Register of Deeds office in a 1910 campaign. Another Mennonite Republican who turned Populist was farmer-businessman Joseph C. Goering of McPherson County. Although Goering was "more of a businessman than he was a politician," he did run for clerk of the district court on the Populist ticket and, like Loewen, became a Democrat partisan in later years.[58]

The Mennonites produced an occasional Populist, but the mind of the community was spoken more clearly by John F. Harms of the *Anzeiger*. As the Farmers' Alliance grew and the Populist party emerged, Harms reacted with increasingly partisan Republicanism. Opposing viewpoints gradually disappeared from the Anzeiger pages. Harms saw the Alliance reforms as a kind of socialism, sharply distinguished from the Christian socialism of apostolic times. Just as a liar and hypocrite was struck dead at the hand of Peter in the early Christian community, Harms suggested that "if St. Peter would enter a convention of Farmers' Alliance presidents, a mass funeral would be the result, we reckon."[59] When the Alliance-Democrat coalition made election gains in 1890, Harms called up the specter of approaching Communism and claimed a good conscience for not having contributed to the disaster.[60] A year later Harms argued with the Populist Judge Frank Doster that the time for individual effort ("persoenliche Bestrebungen") was not past, that "personal effort, industry, and endurance" had made the Mennonite successful, and that "Doster's theories are highly dangerous and appear to point towards a state welfare-institution for all people."[61]

In spite of his occasional references to the convergence of Mennonite and Republican principles, Harms did not ground his politics in a systematic Mennonite ideology. He wrote no essays explaining the link between Mennonitism and Republicanism. His Republican orthodoxy was as much related to a desire for a reputation as it was related to any orthodox Mennonite beliefs. He believed that the "closed German settlements" in central Kansas had (in a period of widespread unrest) won credit for themselves in the eyes of the world by their faithfulness—"with a few exceptions"—to the Republican party "which represents morality, order, and justice."[62]

As he approached the end of his *Anzeiger* editorship in 1897, Harms seemed to lose his relish for politics. He felt betrayed by Governor E. N. Morrill who abandoned Prohibitionism after election in 1894 and went "to the side of the whiskey-element."[63] Harms withheld his support from Morrill in 1896 and thereby contributed to the election of fusionist candidate John W. Leedy. Harms stood firm for the protective tariff and sound money in the 1896 election, but his departure from editorship of the *Anzeiger* for greater attention to the church was symptomatic of a community easily disenchanted with the political world.

The most consistent voting trend in the "Mennonite" townships during the Populist period is the gradual increase in the Republican percentage of total votes for governor. The Republican gubernatorial candidate Lyman U. Humphrey received only 27.9 percent of the "Mennonite" vote in 1890, the lowest percentage a Republican candidate for that office has ever received in the community. By 1898 the Republican vote had increased to a majority of 60.8 percent. Trends in the Democratic vote for the same period cannot be observed because of the fluctuating relationship of the Democratic and Populist parties. The "Mennonite" Populist vote in 1890 was nearly 15 percent below the state figure; in 1892, with no Democratic candidate on the ballot, the "Mennonite" vote closely approximated the state vote; in 1894 the "Mennonite" Populist vote exceeded the state vote by some 20 percent; and in 1896 the "Mennonite" vote for a fusionist candidate was about 6 percent less than the state percentage. The lack of a conclusive trend in these figures is significant evidence in itself, however, for it tends to refute the commonly-accepted notion that the Mennonites remained firmly Republican throughout the Populist movement. The 560 votes in "Mennonite" townships in 1894 for the Populist candidate Lorenzo Lewelling were probably not all cast by non-Mennonites living in this area. Editor Harms' pride in Mennonite resistance to reform movements was not as completely warranted as he believed.

The "Mennonite" vote for presidential candidates in this period shows a gradual increase in the Republican percentage. This trend began with the 44.7 percent vote for Harrison in 1888 and continued toward a peak of 73.3 percent for Roosevelt in 1904. Although the "Mennonite" percentage was usually a few points higher than the state vote in this period, the disparity was never greater than 8 percent. This relatively slight difference likewise tends to break down the conception of traditional Mennonite bedrock Republicanism. The deviation of Mennonite voting patterns for the state pattern is not nearly as great as might be expected from a community which was so distinct from its environment in the more obvious matters of language, custom, and religious belief and practice.

Pockets of solid Mennonite Republicanism did emerge, however, and none was more united than the Alexanderwohl congregation spread through Menno and West Branch townships in Marion County. In 1892, for example, Menno Township turned in seventy-nine votes for the Republican candidate for governor, E. N. Morrill; two votes for Democrat David Overmyer; and none at all for Lorenzo Lewelling, the Populist candidate. In neighboring West Branch, the votes were sixty-two, one, and ten, respectively. William Jennings Bryan in 1896 got only nine votes in Menno (11 percent) and eleven votes in West Branch (10 percent). Menno and West Branch were never crossed by railroads and, therefore, never benefited directly from the alien influences of railroad transportation and the relative cosmopolitanism of small railroad towns. In the townships of Risley (with Hillsboro), Mound (Moundridge), and Superior (Inman), the Democratic and Populist votes were usually larger.

Mennonite political officeholders before 1900 were scarce. Not until 1887, more than a decade after arrival in Kansas, did the Mennonites place a representative in county office when Ferdinand J. Funk of Peabody was elected register of deeds. Even this breakthrough was threatened both before the election when some Republicans wanted to scratch Funk's name from the slate[64] and after the election when Funk's defeated opponent contested the results.[65] Funk went on to win two terms as clerk of the district court in 1890 and 1892, and a term in the state house of representatives in 1894. Governor E. W. Hoch of Marion made Funk his executive secretary in 1907, but Funk's main importance for Mennonites was his aid and assistance to the German Mennonites in the county courthouse and his enthusiastic campaigning for the Republican party among Mennonites in the Populist and Progressive eras. Peter J. Galle, though a less vocal campaigner, performed a somewhat similar service for the Mennonites of McPherson County. Galle, a teacher at the Halstead Mennonite Seminary in 1883-84, was elected a McPherson County attorney for four terms after 1888 and state representative in 1902 for one term. He later became a district judge for the area including Reno, McPherson, and Harvey counties.[66] For both Funk and Galle, the broader orbit of their political activities led them away from the Mennonite church.

The Mennonites were aware that they were underrepresented in county government. John W. Fast of the *Freundschafts-Kreis* blamed Marion County Republican party officials for the habit of treating Hillsboro "like a little stepmother (Stiefmuetterchen)." But the Mennonites had mainly their own political apathy to blame when they were ignored by county party organizations. Mennonite newspapers were often founded with the objective of assisting Mennonite political self-realization,[67] but the community consistently failed to get its share of the offices and the spoils. The Mennonites elected none of their own county officials before 1887, none in Marion County between 1894 and 1902, and none at all in Harvey County before the turn of the century.

CONCLUSION

Between the late 1870s and the Spanish-American War, the Mennonite strangers and pilgrims in the world established a home for themselves on the Kansas prairies. It was a German-American home, still more German than American. Contacts with the outside world, such as "the annual trip to the county seat to pay taxes and buy heavy suits,"[68] were few. The German language prevailed in home, church, and publications. The village system disintegrated on the Kansas frontier, and the very railroads which brought the Mennonites on their search for isolation and autonomy, in turn, imported American influences. But Americanization was a slow process. The Marion and McPherson railroad which cut through the Mennonite territory in 1879 was expected by some to be "the fatal wedge which would destroy their German nationality." Yet the railroad-spawned town of Hillsboro, foreseen as a center of Americanizing influence, soon became "almost a thorough German village."[69] Mennonite farmers, with their large families and successful operations, extended the consolidation process by purchasing land from their American neighbors. A local American newspaper found a dismal metaphor to describe what was happening: "One by one the roses fall and one by one the American farmers are selling out to the Russians. This time it was Warren Parker, the south half of section twelve. Consideration, $8,000."[70]

Economic prosperity was indeed the most impressive characteristic of the Mennonite community. This fact atoned for all the sins of delayed Americanization. The Mennonites added to local wealth and taxable property; their thrift stopped the drain of interest to outside moneylenders. One editor wrote:

The prosperity of the Mennonite communities in Kansas is wonderful. There are about 15,000 of these sturdy Russians in this state, chiefly in Marion and McPherson counties, and they now own between 15,000 and 20,000 acres of land. . . . Mennonites who went to Kansas six years ago with only a few hundred dollars each are now worth from $8,000 to $10,000 each, and are clearing from $1,000 to $2,000 annually on wheat alone.[71]

In politics the Mennonites were cautious. They were generally hesitant in taking out first naturalization papers and they voted in fewer numbers than did other Kansas citizens. Several of their conservative conference groups were on record throughout this period as forbidding voting and officeholding. Some Mennonites, however, were actively interested and involved in political affairs from the date of their arrival. Their voting patterns by political party did not differ markedly from the state as a whole. Even the presumed Mennonite resistance to the Populist movement is difficult to document on the basis of voting records. Mennonite newspaper editors were usually Republicans, but a handful of Mennonite Populists did emerge and the voting records indicate that they won at least some Mennonites to vote for reform. Mennonite "bedrock Republicanism" was not as solid as usually assumed and certainly less uniform than the Republicanism of their Swedish neighbors in north McPherson County. The Mennonite voter, outwardly distinctive in language and dress, was much less unique in actual voting.

The most significant aspect of Mennonite political acculturation in this period was the growing sense of identification with America. Characteristic of Mennonite immigrants leaving Russia was a warning to the czarist government that God would one day judge all worldly authorities.[72] But the American authorities were different. By 1888 a respected Mennonite leader could ground his political convictions in the unabashed claim "[I am] an American in the egotistical sense of the word."[73] The positive image of the American Government, which Mennonites began to adopt already in the process of immigration, was irreconcilable with the traditional Anabaptist dualistic view of church and world. The American Government was not merely God's instrument for maintaining order in an evil world, but the provider of freedom and a good life. Mennonites gradually came to accept a favorable image of the American Government. They came to value American democratic freedom, a new ideal which had different meanings from the traditional Mennonite ideal of the autonomous disciplined community. In this context the erosion of the old Anabaptist church-world dualism was inescapable.

Preoccupied with their economic and religious enterprises, the Mennonites did not take time for systematic reflection on their changing relationship to worldly authorities. Perhaps they did not want to think about this problem, for it contained a fundamental dilemma. At what point would the claims of Americanism contradict the principles of the Mennonite faith? Or was there no contradiction?

The Spanish-American War gave the Mennonites a chance to face this difficult question and to identify America's call to military service as the step of citizenship they were unwilling to take.

"We do not want to be regarded as people who are harmful to the public welfare" (WESTERN DISTRICT CONFERENCE, 1898).

CHAPTER 5

Mennonites and Imperialism

MENNONITES CAME TO KANSAS TOWARD THE BEGINNING OF THE longest interval of peace the United States ever experienced. The absence of war and conscription led Mennonites to ignore their doctrine of nonresistance. An isolated attempt to revive interest in the topic was Samuel S. Haury's speech at a Sunday school convention at the Alexanderwohl Church in 1894.[1] Haury said, "The principle of nonresistance is self-giving and self-sacrificing love, the essence of Christianity." On the personal level, he suggested, nonresistance pervades all of life—home, church, and business. On the political level, nonresistance implies that there is no such thing as a "Christian state." But Haury, who had been the first Mennonite missionary in America, spoke in generalizations and said nothing about how nonresistant Christians could properly influence public life, what the duty of the Christian was in wartime, or whether his expanded view of nonresistance related to the questions raised by the Populist movement. Haury's speech was printed in the Mennonite newspapers and in pamphlet form, to be revived nearly a quarter century later when the Mennonites faced a world war and desperately needed to know what nonresistance was all about.[2]

The coming of the Spanish-American War in April 1898 forced the Mennonites to think about nonresistance in specific terms. As America committed herself to rescue the oppressed Cubans, two concerns were uppermost in the Mennonite community: (1) to preserve military exemption, and (2) to maintain respectability as citizens. The second concern, it seems, was as urgent as the first.

The leaders of the Kansas Conference (GC) called a special session in Newton on May 17 to determine the position of the church on the war.[3]

The special conference adopted a short report which began with an affirmation of "our confession of nonresistance." Faced with criticism, the report went on, the Mennonites were willing to join in the nation's task in ways not involving warfare, such as "medical service in the army voluntarily under the Red Cross." The report claimed to prefer arbitration to war and expressed satisfaction that President McKinley had tried to avoid war "as long as possible." The Mennonites esteemed their privileges highly and hoped their members would not abuse them.[4]

A tone of embarrassment and defensiveness colored the entire statement. The Mennonites were answering criticism, apologizing in advance for abusing their privileges. They suddenly needed to tell each other and the world that they "would not like to be regarded as people injurious to the common welfare."

The reason for Mennonite embarrassment was obvious. America was at war and Mennonites could not go along. Mennonites were suddenly set apart from America. Their discomfiture was a measure of the degree to which they had begun to see themselves as American citizens. Had they remained in isolated sectarian communities for the previous twenty-five years, untouched by the requirements of nationalism, they could have watched the Spanish-American War come and go without embarrassment. But they had absorbed the American doctrine that it was natural and right for the country to expect special efforts and sacrifices from citizens in wartime. To claim exemption from military service at such a time was to invalidate one's own citizenship.

So the Mennonites proclaimed their willingness to assist the war effort in nonmilitary ways. They opened the way for their members "to render medical service in the army voluntarily under the Red Cross." This, in fact, would only be "Christian duty." It was more than mere coincidence that Mennonites felt the tug of "Christian duty" at the same time that the rest of America indulged in that combination of moral indignation and national self-righteousness which characterized emerging American imperialism. Christian duty was stimulated, if not defined, by the national community. Even the success of Mennonite collections for famine relief in India during the war, a benevolent project which won praise from outside the community,[5] was surely related to the current Mennonite need to engage in a moral equivalent to the war.

The statement's claim that Mennonites "as nonresistant Christians" favored "international arbitration" was likewise an awkward attempt to redeem an embarrassing situation. The Mennonites had heretofore given little indication that they understood the doctrine of nonresistance to have relevance for international politics. Samuel Haury had not mentioned this issue in his 1894 speech. The Mennonite newspapers had not viewed the approach of war with unusual alarm. The Mennonite-edited *Volksblatt und Anzeiger* had worked up no greater moral indignation than to find it "unfortunate" that the mood was for militancy rather than for peace.[6] A serious Mennonite attempt to find international political relevance in the nonresistant ethic did not come until after the community had been caught napping.

The Mennonites were wholesale dupes of the American myth that McKinley had delayed the war "as long as possible."[7] Many Mennonites had voted for McKinley. They lacked the critical frame of mind which might have doubted the altruism of the American war effort. If the history of Mennonite persecution and flight had once taught the Mennonites to be wary of official government pronouncements, the lesson did not affect their impulse to believe in the justice and good intent of American foreign policy. Their congratulations to McKinley for his attempts to avoid war may have been based upon trusted sources of information, but they were nonetheless strange coming from a nonresistant sect addressing a government which had just gone to war.

The *Volksblatt und Anzeiger* took a passive, almost neutral, position during the Spanish-American War. There was no criticism of the war on the grounds of Mennonite nonresistance; nor was there praise of the war as a Christian crusade in behalf of suffering Cubans. But news of the war came from American sources and there was little evidence that it went through a Mennonite editorial filter before reaching the pages of the *Volksblatt*: American military victories were occasions for rejoicing and Spanish defeats were counted gain. That Spaniards were barbaric and uncivilized fighters was an item of unquestioned American reportage.[8] The tone of the news, however, was not belligerent, superpatriotic, or excessively enthusiastic. In the issue that announced the triumphant end of the war, an editorial cautioned that the Roman Catholic population of the country would grow by about three million if Cuba and Puerto were annexed.[9]

On September 8 appeared the editorial suggestion that the Philippines be traded to England in exchange for her West Indian possessions plus Bermuda.[10] The Mennonites did not protest against the war, but they were ready to see that war victories were a mixed blessing.

When the splendid American victory in the Philippines turned into a bloody suppression of a native revolt for independence, some dissenters in the Mennonite community finally found their voices. H. O. Kruse, principal and natural science professor at Bethel College, became convinced that American expansionism in the Far East was leading toward a world war which would pit the East against the West. "Today," Kruse wrote in May 1899, "the American eagle pounces upon the Philippines and claims them as her prey"; tomorrow may well see "intervention" into "the continental parts of Asia." Kruse warned that the outcome of "the coming world conflict" depended upon the position of China.[11]

William Jennings Bryan's opposition to American imperialism in the Far East provided the Mennonites with their first clear-cut opportunity to apply the doctrine of nonresistance in a national political campaign. Henry Peter Krehbiel, a native Kansan who had taken theological training at Oberlin College, provided the forum for exchange of opinion in his monthly paper, *The Review*.[12] A reader stated the question in unmistakably clear terms in the September issue.

Is the doctrine of nonresistance compatible with the expansion policy of our present administration, and with the contents of the platform adopted by the Republican convention at Philadelphia? . . . What is the difference between indorsing such a policy by argument and the ballot and taking up arms to carry out this policy?[13]

Another writer in the next issue, J. J. Funk (who had been the first mayor of Hillsboro), not only agreed with the implied answer to this question but argued further that nonresistance was "the main distinguishing feature of our Mennonite faith," and therefore "if they vote for war . . . I shall have to conclude they care nothing for the nonresistant doctrine."[14] Replies to Funk either avoided the issue or got tangled in contradiction. Editor Krehbiel wrote that neither party believed in peace "according to the Mennonite conception of it," and therefore the peace issue was irrelevant.[15] P. H. Richert, a colleague of H. O. Kruse on the Bethel College faculty, argued that other religious questions were of more importance than nonresistance in this campaign—for example the "money question" (which was tied up with religion because it "has to do with honesty"), the candidates' personal character, and "Bryan's misuse of the Bible." Richert warned his Mennonite readers not to "confound religion with politics."[16]

J. J. Funk responded with a spirited challenge to debate Richert or anyone else "at any place in Kansas" on four propositions, the loser to provide twenty-five dollars per proposition "to a Mennonite educational or charitable institution." Richert declined the challenge and the controversy faded after the election.[17]

The confusion of Mennonite Republicans—challenged in their nonresistance—occasionally gave rise to indignation. C. Frey grumbled in the Hillsboro *Post* that the Democrats were trying to make political capital "out of the circumstance that we Mennonites are against war."[18] Ferdinand J. Funk, the leading Mennonite Republican politician, moved to the attack in an extended article charging that the Democrats not only favored the Spanish-American War in the first place, but also "provoked or at least encouraged" the Filipinos to revolt by opposing our government's policy there. A vote for Bryan was not a vote for peace, but a vote to delay the establishment of order in the Philippines.[19] Funk also refuted charges that vice-presidential candidate Theodore Roosevelt was anti-pacifistic by printing a letter from the hero of San Juan Hill affirming his respect for the consciences of religious objectors to war.[20]

The election results of 1900 confirmed the success of Funk, Richert, and other Republican party apologists in allaying Mennonite suspicions that there was a contradiction between the doctrines of Christian nonresistance and American imperialism. The "Mennonite" townships voted 57.6 percent for McKinley and 42.1 percent for Bryan. This was an increase of 2.6 percent over the "Mennonite" Republican vote four years earlier. The Mennonite Republican vote remained a few percentage points above the average in the state of Kansas. Menno and West Branch townships continued as a pocket of solid Republicanism with a 92 percent McKinley vote, but fairly strong Bryan support in McPherson County townships lowered the Republican overall percentage.

The lack of a strong Mennonite peace vote in 1900 suggested that Mennonites were not anxious to let their religious doctrines get in the way of their growing confidence in and commitment to America. The impulse to criticize was likely to be diminished at a time when Mennonites needed to protect their exemption from military service.

The brevity of the Spanish-American War spared the Mennonites from the dilemmas of a national conscription law. But they did not escape the temporary embarrassment of their apparent inability wholeheartedly to join their country in fighting the war. Their willingness to sanction noncombatant war work[21] and their contributions to famine relief in India helped to relieve this tension. The wartime strains on the Mennonite nonresistant conscience, however, did not fully disappear. Indeed, they may help explain why Mennonites were drawn to support the Progressive movement in the following years.

"*These various communities shall become examples to the world where the kingdom of Christ is working itself out in the economic, intellectual, physical, political, social, and religious life of country people*" (E. G. KAUFMAN, 1917).

CHAPTER 6

The Untroubled Generation

THE MENNONITE COMMUNITY BRIMMED WITH ECONOMIC SUCCESS, religious vitality, and social optimism during the Progressive era, 1900-1917. The spirit of the age was caught most vividly and comprehensively at its conclusion in a 1917 master's thesis by Edmund George Kaufman, "Social Problems and Opportunities of the Western District Conference Communities of the General Conference of Mennonites of North America."[1] A second-generation member of the Eden (GC) congregation west of Moundridge, Kaufman later became a missionary to China, a University of Chicago Ph.D. (1928), and Bethel College president (1932-1952). His master's thesis was a manifesto for a self-confident community.

The Mennonites, Kaufman believed, were wrestling with a series of challenges which together constituted "the rural problem." Economically the problem was to modernize and rationalize farming procedures. In politics they had to adjust from autocracy to democracy. The major social difficulty, in Kaufman's view, was inter-Mennonite differences in social customs. The moral problem grew from a "competitive state of mind."[2] None of these "problems" seemed insurmountable barriers to progress. Indeed, Kaufman's basic analytical image was the contrast between the benighted past and the enlightened present. Thus Mennonites in Kansas at first were hesitant about American politics and citizenship, but now "their attitude towards politics is quite liberal. All political parties are represented among them, and an intense interest is taken in political issues. . . . They soon learned that in a democracy each individual is in a degree responsible for the affairs of government." The adjustment from autocracy to democracy, Kaufman believed, was an almost completed process, except for some hesitancy on women's suffrage.[3]

Kaufman closed his thesis with a list of no less than sixteen Mennonite "Possible Contributions to American Christianity," two of which were marginally relevant to politics. One was rejection of the oath and the other was "the peace idea." "Their principle of non-resistance, or universal peace," Kaufman wrote as America entered the First World War, "is at present sweeping the world as an ideal. . . ." Optimism overflowed as Kaufman went to the future emphatic tense in his final paragraph: ". . . And in that way these various communities shall become examples to the world where the kingdom of Christ is working itself out in the economic, intellectual, physical, political, social, and religious life of country people."[4]

Kaufman wrote for the future, but his rhetoric belonged to the previous two decades. Here was that youthful, enthusiastic crusading which was characteristic of the Progressive movement. Here was the optimistic assumption (shared alike by Theodore Roosevelt, the muck-rakers, and *The New Republic*) that political reform and social justice flowed naturally from a forthright exposure of undesirable conditions and a dedicated effort of will to root out evil. Success also depended upon leadership, and Kaufman gave his thesis a peculiarly Mennonite twist in a fifteen-page section which emphasized the role of creative leaders in community development.[5]

"The Mennonites were a great people to follow the leader," said Kansas governor Walter A. Huxman, who grew up in a Mennonite community during the early Progressive years.[6] To explain adequately the origins of Mennonite political attitudes and behavior, suggested Huxman, one would have to write the biographies of the Mennonite patriarchs who dictated social and religious policy for their congregations. Although Huxman's judgment may be true, it was not until the Progressive era that politically-conscious Mennonite leaders emerged and left imprints conducive to a biographical approach in the understanding of Mennonites and politics. During this period, three Kansas Mennonite leaders, Jacob Gerhard Ewert (1874-1923), Henry Peter Krehbiel (1862-1946) and Abraham Schellenberg (1869-1941), articulated the Mennonite response to political events. These three men collectively represent patterns of Mennonite leadership reaction to trends in the Progressive era.[7]

Ewert, Krehbiel, and Schellenberg had much in common. They

all were sons of Mennonite immigrants and they all maintained a positive orientation toward their immigrant origins. None of them fell victim to the second-generation syndrome which, for many children of immigrants to America, resulted in attempted escape from evidences of foreign origin.[8] They were not greatly troubled by the problems of being Mennonite, German, and American, and they had unquestioning confidence that it was both possible and right to enjoy the fruits of American citizenship while preservng the German-Mennonite culture and religious heritage. The three leaders were also typical Mennonites in their mistrust of politics. Although Ewert saw hope in socialism, Krehbiel served a term in the Kansas House of Representatives, and Schellenberg wrote vigorously for Progressive reforms, they all expected the solution of human problems more from religion than from the political order. Although they favored more Mennonite involvement in politics, they laid out no specific program which Mennonite political action might help achieve. They were not politicians. They spoke the mind of an apolitical community.

JACOB GERHARD EWERT

Jacob Gerhard Ewert was easily the most remarkable personality among central Kansas Mennonites in the Progressive era. Born in Poland in 1874, Ewert came to Hillsboro with his family at the age of eight. As a bright young student he decided on a teaching career. He attended Bethel College from 1895 to 1897 where he specialized in languages and theology, taught some classes on his own, and found time to collect and classify nearly four hundred plants for the Bethel herbarium. Four months before completion of the college course, he contracted a paralytic disease which nearly killed him and turned him into a bedfast cripple for the remaining quarter century of his life.

Although his paralysis was almost total, Ewert's powers of speech and mind were unimpaired. He undertook private tutoring and teaching of classes; later he became a member of the Tabor College faculty. He wrote pamphlets of religious and social concern and newspaper articles on a variety of subjects. In 1909 he took over editorship of the Hillsboro *Journal* and, within two years, increased the circulation of the paper from about 1,250 to nearly 3,600.[9] Forced to give up his editorship because of physical and mental exhaustion and because of rheumatism in the fingers of his only mobile hand, Ewert continued writing, teaching, and corresponding with a worldwide circle of friends. By 1910 more than six thousand visitors had record-

ed their names in a book which he kept near his bed.[10]   During the
First World War, Ewert was the best informed man in the community
on the draft question and scores of Mennonite young men streamed
into his room for advice on how to fill out their registration papers.[11]
In the postwar period until his death in 1923, Ewert was active in
the organization and administration of the Mennonite relief program.

While other Mennonites were caught in the busy narrowness and
isolation imposed by the Mennonite version of the Protestant work
ethic, Ewert on his bed had time to read about the world, to consider
its wretched condition, and to imagine together with the great minds
of his age that there might be grand solutions to human problems.
He became the mediator of Karl Marx, Leo Tolstoy, and Walter
Rauschenbusch to an unreceptive community.   The cosmopolitan
spirit came to Hillsboro through the most obviously limited man in
town.

"Capitalism, militarism, and alcoholism," wrote Ewert in the wake
of William Howard Taft's election in 1908, are three of the greatest
enemies of civil peace and therefore also at the same time of practical
Christianity."[12]   The defeat of this demonic trilogy, Ewert believed,
would come through Christian socialism, Christian pacifism, and
Christian temperance.   True politics and true Christianity, far from
being antithetical, as many Mennonites seemed to assume, were the
members of a natural alliance for the achievement of Christ's prayer
"Thy will be done on earth as it is in heaven."   Ewert achieved an
integration of political views and religious doctrine which was unprecedented in the Mennonite community.   It was because he grounded his socialism, pacifism, and temperance in religious doctrine that
Ewert could get an audience in his community.

Ewert began as a typical Republican Mennonite and came to his
Socialist ideas after much reading and reflection.   His first publication after his illness was the allegorical tale of a courageous knight,
"Fides," who slew the giants "Indolence," "Selfishness," "Untruth-
fulness," "Hatred,"   and "Pride" in individualistic and unpacifistic
combat.[13]   The allegory reflected Ewert's struggle with his paralysis
as triumph of personal will against the onslaughts of evil and suffering,
but in succeeding years Ewert came to an understanding of how the
strivings of oppressed people might be aided through social cooperation.
He summed up his Christian Socialist credo in a 1909 pamphlet
Christianity and Socialism.[14]

Ewert's greatest concern was to demonstrate the harmony between socialism and Christianity. He quoted examples of social justice from Hebrew law and prophecy. He pointed to the community of goods in the early Christian community and suggested that the Socialist's call for the abolition of class distinctions conformed to Paul's statement that in Christ there is neither Jew nor Greek, bond nor free. To those who worried because Karl Marx and other Socialist leaders were Jews, Ewert wrote that "salvation cometh of the Jews."[15]

The rival Mennonite newspaper at Newton, *Der Herold,* edited and managed by the brothers C. E. and H. P. Krehbiel, could not let Ewert's socialism go unchallenged. H. P. Krehbiel claimed particular horror over what he saw as Ewert's defense of Eugene Debs' attack on the anti-Socialist clergy. Krehbiel could not understand how any true Christian could condone, much less defend, such a man as Debs. As for his personal objections to socialism, Krehbiel mentioned two: (1) the emphasis on "overthrow" (Umsturz) and (2) the nationalization of production. ". . . The first brings ruin and the second leads back to slavery. Man is made for freedom and not for personal or paternal slavery."[16] When Ewert was bold enough to charge that "capitalism is, in a certain sense, the antichrist," Krehbiel neglected to offer a full defense of capitalism but criticized the Socialists for trying to equate their program with Christianity.[17]

Ewert took great encouragement from the increases in the Socialist vote in the United States and other countries, but he had little to report of news about Mennonite conversions to socialism. The "Mennonite" vote for Socialist candidates in state and national elections never rose above 2 percent before the First World War. Mennonite wartime frustrations were expressed in the slightly larger vote for Socialist presidential candidates Allen L. Benson (6 percent in 1916) and Eugene V. Debs (9.3 percent in 1920), and in the vote for Socialist gubernatorial candidates E. N. Richardson (3.8 percent in 1916), George W. Kleihege (16.7 percent in 1918), and Roy Stanton (9.3 percent in 1920). Only five Mennonites ventured to run for county political office on the Socialist ticket. In Harvey County, G. B. Ruth ran for county superintendent of public instruction in 1906 and for county commissioner in 1912. In Marion County, Emilie Wedel and her brother Hugo of Hillsboro's First Mennonite Church ran for county superintendent in 1910 and 1912 respectively. John J. Janzen, a Mennonite farmer, ran three times for clerk of the district court and twice for register of deeds between 1910 and 1918. His nephew Ferd F. Janzen ran for county clerk in 1914, 1916, and

1918. None of these Socialist candidates received more than a handful of votes in Mennonite townships. Most Mennonite voters apparently were able to dismiss J. G. Ewert's Socialist appeals as easily as one
Hillsboro lady who commented, "Learning politics from a sickbed
is different from learning it in life."[18]

Ewert's campaign against alcohol was less radical and therefore
had greater community support than his opposition to capitalism.
Prohibition was an immedite political issue in Kansas and saloons were
to be found even in Hillsboro where Ewert wrote.

Although Ewert believed that the most important task of the Christian for temperance was the personal influence of his good example,[19]
he also believed that it was part of being one's "brother's keeper" to
forbid the sale of liquor through Prohibition laws.[20] He tempered his
Prohibition appeals, however, with the warning that drunkenness was
not the only evil to battle in this world and that finally "each should
follow his own conscience and knowledge (*Erkenntnis*)" in the matter. For several years he was general secretary of the Kansas Prohibition Movement.[21] In general elections he did not hesitate to
endorse *both* the Prohibition and the Democratic candidates, a position which confounded Republican politicians who saw Ewert's support for Bryan in the 1908 election as a betrayal of an earlier promise
to support the Prohibition candidate.[22] But Ewert saw no reason why
idealistic commitment to Socialist and Prohibitionist goals precluded
involvement in debate between the main party candidates. He was
realistic enough to realize that the Mennonite community had little
inclination to vote a third-party Prohibition ticket and that his political
voice would be most effective if directed to the real choice that voters
would make on election day.

Pacifism, for Ewert, came before socialism, but both ideologies were
incorporated into his scheme for the new social order. Already in
1899 he published a German translation of an exchange of letters
between pacifists Leo Tolstoy and Adin Ballou under the title *The
Christian Doctrine of Nonresistance*.[23] Later in his Socialist tract
he suggested that the elimination of a standing army and all unnecessary expenditures would not only be a step toward peace but would
also release money to compensate capitalists whose property would be
nationalized.[24]

In the 1908 election Ewert acclaimed William Jennings Bryan as
the peace candidate and William Howard Taft as the "Secretary of
War who was proposed as a candidate by the warlike Roosevelt."

The peace issue alone, Ewert wrote, should be decisive for Mennonites "who came to America because of European militarism."[25] Four years later Ewert reminded dissatisfied Republicans that he had warned them against Taft, and now he warned them against the Bull Moose Roosevelt as "the biggest incarnation of the war spirit in our country." He also resurrected the old charge of Roosevelt's public disdain for nonresistant groups.[26]   But the Mennonites were no more persuaded by the ideological appeal to nonresistance as a politically relevant doctrine in 1912 than they had been in 1900 when they ignored their chance to vote against McKinley and imperialism.   They gave a solid majority to Taft in 1908 and a strong plurality to Roosevelt in 1912.

The coming of World War I and the military draft forced Ewert's peace interests inward to a focus on the immediate problems of Mennonite drafted men.   Although his bedfast condition prevented him from taking an office on the church committees formed to deal with wartime Mennonite problems, Ewert was among the most active of Mennonite leaders in counseling young draftees, providing news about the war and the draft through the newspapers, and in defending the Mennonite position to government and to the public.   While the Progressive reform spirit in the United States was transformed and subverted by the Great War, Ewert's broader social vision was similarly narrowed by his new preoccupation with the problems of Mennonite wartime pacifism.   He had the consolation, however, of knowing that he had become more useful to his church than he had ever been before.

Ewert failed to carry the Mennonites with him into the Socialist camp, but this did not make him a loner in his own community.   His significance lay in the fact that he was accepted and loved in spite of his dissenting views.   It was a reflection of the Progressive era's optimism and self-confidence that the Mennonites in this period not only produced and accepted an outspoken Socialist, but also gave him the editorship of one of their leading newspapers, asked him to teach classes for one of their colleges, sent their young people to him for counsel, and had him instruct Saturday night classes for Sunday school teachers.   Ewert's acceptability in the community was aided by public sympathy for his physical condition, by his own good-naturedness and integrity, and by his unrefuted claim that his reform ideas were grounded in the Christian gospel.   The combination of imaginativeness and productivity which marked Ewert's life was a tribute to the man, the community, and the times.

HENRY PETER KREHBIEL

Henry Peter Krehbiel was the active, vigorous Mennonite leader that J. G. Ewert never had the chance to be. As the son of an immigrant to America in 1851 from South Germany, H. P. Krehbiel reflected the greater degree of acculturation undergone by the South German Mennonites as compared to Russian or Prussian Mennonites. His father, Christian Krehbiel (1832-1909), had vigorously assisted the settlement of Russian Mennonites in Kansas in the 1870s and became a prominent farmer, pastor, and leader in the establishment of institutions for Mennonite education and missions, Indian education, and medical care.[27] As a young farm boy, H. P. developed a deep appreciation for the values of rural life, but he did not consider farming as an occupation for himself. After tries at teaching, studying medicine, and running a hardware store, Krehbiel spent five years in theological training at Oberlin in preparation for the ministry. During his first pastorate at the Mennonite church in Canton, Ohio, he founded *The Review*, an English-language newspaper with which he hoped to promote the unity of separated branches of Mennonites. *The Review* became a lively forum for the exchange of differing Mennonite viewpoints (see chapter 5), but it only accented the differences between Mennonite branches. After Krehbiel moved to Newton, Kansas, he discontinued *The Review* and devoted his energies to German-language publications for the German-speaking community in Kansas, to a book and school supply store, and to his pastoral ministry and church work.

As a nonfarmer Mennonite who had left the community for his education, Krehbiel found it necessary to define for himself the values of the Mennonite community and the justification for maintaining peculiar Mennonite distinctiveness within American society. The spiritual vitality of the Kansas Mennonite churches, most obvious in the enthusiasm of young people in church work and in support for benevolent enterprises, impressed Krehbiel at the time of his decision to return to his home community.[28] The one Mennonite doctrine which interested Krehbiel most of all was that of nonresistance. On occasion he claimed that nonresistance was *the* key Mennonite doctrine. Of the Mennonites in Germany who had accepted military service Krehbiel wrote, "Having surrendered the doctrine of nonresistance it is difficult to see on what principles or doctrine these churches, calling themselves Mennonite, may claim the right of separate existence."[29]

Although Krehbiel affirmed the traditional Mennonite doctrine of nonresistance and scolded those who abandoned the doctrine, his broader political outlook on the world made him imagine implications for the Mennonite peace emphasis which his forebears had not dreamed of. The social optimism which Krehbiel shared with the Progressive movement was channeled less into the kinds of reforms suggested by J. G. Ewert's socialism and more into an interest in the possibilities of world peace. Krehbiel never did explain the precise relationship between Mennonite nonresistance and the world peace movement. It just seemed natural somehow to Krehbiel, as it did to C. H. Wedel (the first president of Bethel College, 1893-1910), that Mennonites who rejected personal participation in war should have common interests with those who rejected war for social and political reasons.[30]

A firm grounding in Mennonite nonresistant doctrine, which had a dim view of the prospects for peace in the unregenerate world, might have restrained Krehbiel from undue optimism regarding the world peace movement. As it was, Krehbiel saw international harmony around the next corner. The Hague Court of Arbitration, he believed, would probably be supplemented by "an international legislature." The world was not now ready for an international executive, Krehbiel thought, but "it is not beyond hope that extensive power can ultimately be added to such an international body which will enable it to enforce its decisions. When that has been accomplished we shall have a central government for the whole world. Thereafter international wars will be impossible."[31] Krehbiel read widely and accumulated a personal library of peace literature, but it was not until 1937, at seventy-five years of age, that he systematically presented his views on war and peace in book form.[32]

Throughout his life Krehbiel maintained an active interest in politics and encouraged Mennonites to increase their political involvements. He did not run for local or county offices, but in 1908 he was elected to the Kansas House of Representatives. He was never able, however, to integrate his overriding social concern—the peace movement—with his political opinions and activities. Like other peace-minded internationalists of the Progressive era, Krehbiel did not sufficiently comprehend the contradiction between the nationalism of the American political creed and the internationalism of his own peace principles. He did not suspect that his hero Theodore Roosevelt, who won the Nobel Peace Prize, also embodied a more potent self-righteous parochialism which subverted the broader ideal of international harmony. Nor was Krehbiel equipped to deal with the contradictory claims of nationalism versus internationalism, for he never understood that this was a fundamentally political problem which could not be transcended or solved outside the realm of politics.

Krehbiel's earliest and most clear-cut opportunity to vote his peace position was in the election of 1900 when William Jennings Bryan took a definite position against the United States' imperialist military adventure in the Philippines. Krehbiel voted for McKinley and dismissed the peace issue with the accurate but irrelevant statement that no one in the campaign proposed a truly Mennonite peace policy.[33] The fact was, of course, that if the Mennonites excluded the peace question as a significant consideration until the day when a presidential candidate ran on a platform of Mennonite nonresistance, the Mennonite peace doctrines would never become applicable in American electoral choices. Only when they would be willing to make a choice between candidates as more or less militaristic or pacifistic would they find a political application for their aversion to military service and war. Krehbiel undoubtedly spoke for most Mennonites when he argued that in 1900 other issues were more important than imperialism and militarism.

Criticism of American imperialism in the Philippines or of Theodore Roosevelt's Big Stick policies in Latin America would have thrust Krehbiel and the Mennonites into the role of dissenters in society. Such a role might have been consistent both with Anabaptist heritage of social dissent and with the contemporary Mennonite emphasis on nonconformity to the world. But Mennonite nonconformity apparently did not apply to politics, except for those who stayed entirely aloof from politics. Most Mennonites who did become interested and involved in politics were conformists to what they considered to be the mainstream American political tradition; they resisted the suggestion that any distinctive Mennonite doctrine—even a doctrine believed essential and central to the Mennonite faith such as nonresistance—might require their dissent.

The Mennonites, therefore, usually found themselves on the winning side in American politics. H. P. Krehbiel's "lifelong sympathy for the underdog"[34] was not reflected in his political attitudes. He consistently took the side of management in labor disputes. During the 1902 strikes in Chicago transportation and Pennsylvania coal mines, he observed that the greedy workers always strike for higher wages and never for lower wages, whereas the generous managements

"not infrequently increase unnecessary wages."[35]   Whatever concern
that Krehbiel shared in the Progressive movement for control of the
trusts and reform of machine politics was hardly motivated by sympathy for the little man against the big oppressors.   The trusts deserve
opposition, Krehbiel believed, because their abuses cost money and
undermine the confidence which is the cement of trade and business.[36]
Corrupt machine politics must be eliminated primarily because they
are corrupt.[37]   Krehbiel's moral concerns were invariably popular
moral concerns which conformed to the temperament of the political
establishment.   The unsatisfactory results of Amercian imperialist
policy sorely tried Krehbiel's faith in the American Progressive establishment.   His expectations were great.   The granting of independence
to Cuba he had acclaimed as "a triumph of Christianity. . . . For such
a deed the world is obliged to the ennobling influence of the teachings
of Jesus Christ.   It is a sign that the time is approaching when justice
instead of power will rule in the world."[38]   Four years later he was
ready to admit that the American policy had failed to solve the Cuba
problem although he still had "great faith in our President Roosevelt
and in his weighty Secretary of War Taft."[39]   The Philippines were
even more frustrating, especially when there was talk of increasing
the American fleet for the protection against other powers.   Rather
"sell the Philippines to the Japanese," said Krehbiel, for he was beginning to see what had remained strangely obscure at the time of
the Spanish-American War—the delicious fruits of American imperialism came at the price of increasing American militarism.   This
realization led Krehbiel so far as to put in a good word for William
Jennings Bryan as an ambassador for international peace,[40] though
in the election of 1908 his *Post und Volksblatt* got in line for the
Republican candidate Taft and disparaged Bryan's "phoenix-like
theories."[41]

The Mennonite reaction to Theodore Roosevelt is at once the
most puzzling and illuminating indicator of Mennonite political
attitudes and behavior during the Progressive period.   For although
the vigorous and militant Roosevelt projected an image which directly
contradicted the presumed Mennonite virtues of passivity and un-
demonstrativeness, Roosevelt became an immensely popular president
in the Mennonite community.   In 1904 Roosevelt received 73.3
percent of the vote in "Mennonite" townships, the largest Republican
vote up to that time and 8.5 percent higher than the Republican
vote in Kansas for that year.   Nor could the 1904 Roosevelt vote

be credited simply to Mennonite adherence to the Republican party, for the Mennonites endorsed Roosevelt with a 47.9 percent vote in 1912 when he bolted the Republican party and ran on a Progressive third-party ticket. The "Mennonite" Roosevelt vote again exceeded the state vote in 1912, this time by 7.7 percent.

Mennonites who liked Roosevelt could not claim ignorance of his militancy. Roosevelt's personal distaste for pacifists, which he had expressed clearly in print, became an issue among Mennonites already in the 1900 election.[42] In later campaigns J. G. Ewert kept this issue before the community.[43] In the view of H. P. Krehbiel, however, Roosevelt's personal characteristics and religious convictions outweighed all other consideration. After the 1904 election Krehbiel hailed the victor as a "clean, courageous, honorable man" who was liked for his "straight forward and manly ways." Furthermore, said Krehbiel, Roosevelt "is a devout Christian and in all his deeds he has been actuated and tempered by the high ideals of the Nazarene." His victory was "a tribute to integrity, and manly courage of conviction, both of which grow best in Christian soil."[44]

The Mennonite enthusiasm for Roosevelt is surely a measure of political acculturation. Although they continued to speak and read the German language and although their homes and churches would have seemed strange to the average American, they were happy to accept as their leader a nationalistic war hero and to believe that his vigorous crusading was what the country needed. It may be that support for Roosevelt was one way for Mennonites to reassure themselves that they were good Americans in spite of their obvious social distinctiveness. Mennonites, especially such leaders as H. P. Krehbiel, could conveniently ignore their nonresistant doctrines and inclinations if their politics brought them the benefits of the good feeling that they were solid American citizens.

But the Mennonite support for Roosevelt may have had even deeper roots in Mennonite tradition and social attitude. Throughout their history in Europe as a sectarian group, the Mennonites often exhibited a remarkable capacity to place confidence in a strong political ruler, whether he was the king of Prussia or the czar of Russia.[45] This trust had the sanction of the New Testament's command to be subject to the higher powers and the support of a patriarchal model in the Mennonite family.[46] The habit of deference to political authority was not a lobbying tactic by which Mennonites attempted to win special privileges; rather it was an expression of their understanding of the obedient and suffering church in its proper relationship to the powers ordained by God. In America this attitude showed up in special Mennonite conference declarations recognizing political authority as well as individual cases such as the Mennonite minister who kept a portrait of President McKinley on his living-room wall for several decades into the twentieth century.[47] The Mennonite support for Roosevelt, then, was related to the fact that he was the strongest political leader that America had known since their immigration.

As the Harvey County representative in the 1909 Kansas legislature, Krehbiel served on five committees: education, temperance, federal relations (chairman), state historical, and congressional apportionment. Of the eight bills he introduced, only the measure outlawing Sunday baseball came close to passage. The bill survived a three-hour filibuster but failed by three votes to get a constitutional majority.[48] Krehbiel's other bills against nonintoxicating alcoholic beverages and against pool halls suggest that his contribution to politics lay in the attempt to legislate statewide the kind of morality which Mennonite parents attempted to enforce in their own homes. The most significant legislation supported by Krehbiel was a bill for the guarantee of deposits in state banks; a bill similar to his was passed and signed into law.[49]

Krehbiel felt the frustrations of a freshman legislator and confessed that it would take several terms before one could really apply the knowledge learned. Although he relished "the touch with the strong men,"[50] he decided not to make a career out of politics. The brevity of Krehbiel's dip into politics and his retirement to publishing and church work was a characteristic Mennonite act—the rejection of politics.

ABRAHAM L. SCHELLENBERG

A latecomer to the scene of Mennonite editorial commentary in the Progressive era was Abraham L. Schellenberg, editor of Mennonite Brethren Church publications from 1907 to 1919.[51] As the first of his father's twenty children, Schellenberg came from a larger family than did H. P. Krehbiel who could count only fifteen brothers and sisters. The vocational careers of the two men ran in a roughly similar pattern from teaching to editing to preaching. Schellenberg shared with Krehbiel a huge capacity for work, an impulsiveness of spirit, and an unyielding will which occasionally involved him in unlovely quarrels with his church and community.

Schellenberg was different, however, in the thread of skepticism which ran throughout his life. He delayed joining the church until his twenty-eighth year, and even then his decision was the result of an extended struggle rather than a sudden conversion such as was preferred in the Mennonite Brethren Church. Though he later became a conference officer and a church minister, his children remembered his solemn quotation from the words of Solomon that "he who increases knowledge increases sorrow."[52] In his writing, Schellenberg seldom showed enthusiasm for any particular religious doctrine. The task of defending the faith he left to other writers in the papers he edited.

If the spark of certainty and concern was missing in Schellenberg's religious life, it was written all over his interpretive reports of news from the local community and around the world. The clue to his social and political interests was in the names he gave to his sons: Henry George, Theodore Roosevelt, and Abraham Lincoln. He did not find a suitable instrument for getting his political views in print until 1913, however, when the Mennonite Brethren Church purchased *Vorwaerts*, the Hillsboro newspaper which had been edited by J. G. Ewert from 1909 to 1911. Schellenberg took over the editorship with the issue of February 13, 1914.[53] He had no inclinations to change the name of the newspaper but rather announced that "the *Forward* is the Progressive paper for Germans of the Western States and Canada." On the masthead appeared the slogan, "The golden rule overcomes the power of gold."[54]

Schellenberg outlined his view of the priorities of the Progressive program in his second issue as editor. The Progressives, he said, stood for Prohibition, women's suffrage, minimum wage and maximum hours labor legislation, initiative, referendum, recall, railroad reforms, "and similar Progressive ideas."[55] Schellenberg, more than most Mennonite editors, took a partisan position in state and local politics. He supported Progressive candidates Victor Murdock and Henry Allen for national senator and state governor in 1914. (Republican gubernatorial candidate Arthur Capper was "an able businessman for whom everything that brings money is right.")[56] But the Progressive party was feeble in Kansas in 1914 and the candidates got small minorities. In local politics Schellenberg usually endorsed German candidates, although he made an exception by casting his vote for the incumbent American Republican county superintendent of public instruction rather than for P. C. Hiebert, a Progressive-minded professor at Tabor College who ran on the Democratic ticket.[57]

One of Schellenberg's sons remembered him as an adherent to the typical Mennonite viewpoint that "that government is best which governs least."[58]   The published record does not support such a judgment either for the Mennonite community or for Editor Schellenberg.   The Mennonites had no tradition of opposition to strong, authoritative government in Europe or America; nor did they ever reason that a limitation of government power would help preserve their own special privileges.   In the 1908 presidential campaign, Ferdinand Funk (one of the few genuine Mennonite politicians) argued against William Jennings Bryan before a Mennonite audience on the grounds that the Democrats stood for "the bitterest pill of all . . . weakening of the courts and of the government."[59]

The World War destroyed Schellenberg's Progressive hopes before he had opportunity to clarify and develop them.   From the outset of the European conflict he became the most outspoken defender of Germany and critic of the Anglophiles in the Mennonite community. Unlike Ewert and Krehbiel, Schellenberg had shown little interest in the Mennonite doctrine of nonresistance which might have helped temper his approval of Prussian militarism.   The pacific tenor of most Mennonite commentary was lacking when Schellenberg saw the style of an "old grandmother" in Wilson's indulgent policy toward Mexico and also when the editor proudly acclaimed the German military advance.[60]   Symptomatic of the pro-Germanism which dominated Schellenberg's political views after the outbreak of war was his opposition to Arthur Capper for governor in 1914 on the grounds that Capper was anti-German.[61]   When Ewert and Krehbiel responded to the wartime draft with a flurry of activity on behalf of Mennonite drafted men, Schellenberg reacted negatively with persistent criticism of the American Government.[62]   His frustrated but courageous position earned him both local abuse and a federal investigation during the war; but the greater tragedy lay in the war's narrowing of his earlier more generous social and political impulses.   He resigned his editorial job in 1919 and moved to a farm in Texas.[63]

Ewert, Krehbiel, and Schellenberg all supported a Prohibition movement which entailed extended government control over social life. They all were, to some degree, willing to legislate not only morality but also certain Progressive reforms of the economy and government. If their hopes and plans for effective government were limited, it came not from any kinship with Jeffersonian political theory but from the Mennonite understanding of church and state. It was the church, in the final analysis, which generated and extended the fundamental values of human life; it was to the church that one looked for the fulfillment of Christ's kingdom. Therefore the mission of the church had a greater attraction for these men than did the untrustworthy and ephemeral business of politics. Schellenberg and Krehbiel continued preaching long after they gave up editorial work; Ewert's last great work was in the administration of church relief funds.

As moderately articulate spokesmen for specific particular political ideas, Ewert, Krehbiel, and Schellenberg differed from Mennonites who, for reasons of inertia and doctrine, abstained from political interests and from voting. Ewert and Krehbiel were from General Conference churches; Schellenberg was from the Mennonite Brethren. Their political preferences cannot be held as fully representative of the more conservative (Old) Mennonite, Krimmer Mennonite Brethren, or Church of God in Christ Mennonite (Holdeman) congregations. Even among these smaller groups, however (who were a minority of Kansas Mennonites), one could find involvement in local politics. The (Old) Mennonites, for example, discouraged voting in elections. But one of their most distinguished leaders, T. M. Erb (business manager at Hesston College from 1909 to 1929), served for a time as president of the Hesston town council. Even so, among all branches of Mennonites there were members who had religious reservations against politics.

Despite persistent Mennonite political aloofness, a tradition of Mennonite representation in the McPherson and Marion County courthouses was fully established in the Progressive period. Mennonites had Jacob A. Unruh in the Marion County commissioner's office from 1906 to 1918 and Jacob W. Wiens from 1918 to 1920. In McPherson County the succession of John C. Goering, Peter H. Schroeder, and J. J. Krehbiel held down a commissioner's position from 1898 to 1920. In Harvey County the Mennonites were a smaller minority, and local politicians did not need to take them so seriously. H. P. Krehbiel's 1908 election to the state house of representatives depended upon non-Mennonite support. Krehbiel was the third Mennonite to achieve that office but first genuine Mennonite churchman in the Kansas legislature. Ferdinand J. Funk (Marion County, 1894) and Peter J. Galle (McPherson County, 1902) also served only one term each but had no deep commitments to the

Mennonite church. Despite their limited political success, however, the Mennonites continued to be underrepresented in local politics in proportion to their actual growing numbers and wealth, a fact which Mennonite editors did not fail to point out to their readers.[64]

For the perceptive observer of the Mennonite community it was clear that Mennonite political behavior was only one aspect in a broader pattern of Americanization. H. O. Kruse, professor at Bethel College from 1898 to 1902, summed up the process in a paper presented before a Modern Languages Association meeting in 1910.[65] Although "the Mennonites have preserved their fundamental characteristics and their religious views and have high regard for the preserved customs of their fathers," wrote Kruse, their Americanization continued slowly and steadily. Marriages outside the community were rare but were expected to increase. German was still the language of home and church but in a few of the congregations many of the young people speak better English than German, an issue already taken into account in the selection of preachers. Mennonites were mostly farmers but increasing numbers were taking up other occupations—craftsmen, millers, businessmen. Americanization influenced the church through the Sunday schools, lighter church choir music, Thanksgiving celebration, and the reduction of other church celebrations. In the homes one could find American clothing, food (pie and ice cream), musical instruments (organ, guitar, and piano), and American first names for the children. Mennonites were quick to modernize farm machinery and to replace buggies with automobiles without hesitation.[66]

The picture of the Mennonite community was one of confidence and well-being. Change was abundantly evident, but change seemed under control. The natural stresses and tragedies of human life were ever present, but the disruptions of the immigration experience and the rough edges of the first frontier years had been quickly forgotten in the flush of prosperity and rapid expansion. The children of the Mennonite immigrants, compared to their parents before them and World War I experience ahead of them, qualify as the Untroubled Generation. The genuinely satisfying years which preceded the war made that tragedy doubly bitter.

As members of the Untroubled Generation before the World War, Ewert, Krehbiel, and Schellenberg were not impelled by that sense of status revolution frustration or alienation from middle-class values which some authors cite as the motivational mainspring of much of

the Progressive movement.[67]   The Mennonites seemed incapable of
getting thoroughly indignant about anything.   Ewert's Christian
socialism was more notable for its generous impulses than for criticism
of social ills, and Schellenberg's occasional digs at the plutocrats
were redeemed by a clever wit which made political commentary seem
as much like a playful game as like serious business.   A crusading
Mennonite muckraker is unimaginable.   Mennonites shared the
Progressive optimism, but not its anger.

   The politically articulate Mennonites in the Progressive era, for
all their desire that their community become more aware of and
involved in politics, were prime exhibits of antipolitical tendencies of
their community.   Although they raised no objections to the vigorous
use of governmental power and authority, they were attracted to
Progressivism because it represented a challenge to the unsavory aspects of the political process.   Schellenberg liked Henry Allen for governor precisely because Allen was contemptuous of regular party
affiliations and his aspirations for political office were not so blatantly
obvious as other candidates.[68]   J. G. Ewert looked forward to the
elimination of the national senate and the direct responsibility of the
people for government.[69]   And H. P. Krehbiel drew back from a
potentially active career in the Kansas legislature because prospects for
building the kingdom seemed greater within the church than within
politics.

   The political acculturation of Mennonites in the Progressive era
was as notable for its limitations as for its advances.   Despite the increasing political interest, the enthusiasm for Roosevelt as a great
Christian leader, and the relatively informed commentary by Mennonite newspaper editors, the pitch of political excitement did not become
intense.   Numbers of voters remained relatively low, and social expectations from the church exceeded expectations from politics.
Although the community remained attached to its German language
and culture, the Mennonites grew in commitment to American national ideals and enterprises—a fact most evident in ready Mennonite
acceptance of the new expansive American foreign policy.   But American foreign policy took some new turns after 1914 which the Mennonites could not endorse.   The Untroubled Generation faced its Time
of Troubles.

J. G. Ewert, c. 1897 (1874-1923), was a General Conference Mennonite, a socialist, pacifist, and temperance crusader.

A. L. Schellenberg, 1924 (1869-1941), was a Mennonite Brethren leader and editor of Hillsboro Vorwaerts from 1913 to 1929.

John F. Harms, c. 1923 (1855-1945), was editor of the Marion County Anzeiger (1888-1897), notable Mennonite Brethren leader, and defender of the Republican party.

H. P. Krehbiel, 1898 (1862-1940), was a General Conference Mennonite editor and church worker; he was elected to the Kansas State Legislature in 1909.

HILLSBORO

Vorwärts.

Die goldene Regel überwindet die Macht des Goldes.

Hillsboro, Kansas, Freitag, den 9. April, 1915.

„Wir fürchten Gott und sonst nichts in der Welt."—Bismark.

VORWAERTS *for April 9, 1915, proclaimed, "We fear God and nothing else in the world." The picture on the front page of the Hillsboro paper suggested Mennonite pro-German sympathies in the early years of World War I.*

Vorwärts.

Die goldene Regel überwindet die Macht des Goldes.

Hillsboro, Kansas, Freitag, den 28. Juni, 1918.

und Brie-
für nüch-
sozialen

reitag in
nuty und

Vor
Vor
Wohl
Dies
Weil

„Wi
neue Erde
rechtigkeit

d noch heute in dem Gepräge jener
it erhalten ist, zusammen, aus 53
präsentanten bestehend, darunter
ashington, Lee, Henry, Samuel und
hn Adams, Roger Sherman, John
v. Peyton Randolph von Virgi-
r wurde zum Sprecher gewählt,
n am 22. Oktober Henry Middle-
t von South Carolina im Amte
gte.

Das Staats-Haus — Indepen-
ce Hall — war dem ersten Kon-
sse zum Sitzungssaale angeboten
rden, aber die Repräsentanten war-
schon damals um die Volksgunst
schieden sich für die von den Schrei-
n ihnen gemachte Offerte und
hlten Carpenters' Hall. Auch der
eite Kongreß tagte noch da.

über das Gebet, oder vielmehr die
age, ob die Sitzungen mit einer An-
ung Gottes eröffnet werden sollten,
n es zur ersten Debatte unter den
präsentanten. Samuel Adams
te den Vorschlag gemacht, der New
rker John Jay opponierte. Epis-
alen, Quäker, Baptisten, Presby-
ianer und Kongregationalisten sei-
da versammelt und würden kaum
vereinigen können zu gemein-
aftlicher Andacht, hob Jay hervor.
er Adams drang mit seiner Be-
uptung durch, jeder Patriot könne
n von einem Manne, dessen Fröm-
gkeit und Gottseligkeit bekannt und
zugleich auch ein Patriot sei, ein
bet anhören. Er hatte den Epis-
alprediger Duché von Philadelphia
neint, und dieser wurde denn nun
n Kaplan gewählt. Er waltete
igere Zeit seines Amts, als aber
Briten Philadelphia einnahmen,
leugnete er seinen Patriotismus
d hatte sogar die Unverschämtheit
einen Briefe Washington zum Ver
aufzufordern.

Vertilgt die Ratten.

Dieses wurde uns von der Regie-
ng zugesandt und sie muß für die
hlen garantieren: In Kansas sind

Sterne und Streifen.

Im Morgenwind, in der Sonne Gold,
Der Freiheit heiliges Banner rollt;
Sein Rauschen tönet wie Adlerflug
Um Alpenhäupter im Siegeszug.
Es klingt wie das Rauschen im Urwaldsdom,
Es klingt wie das Plätschern im Waldesstrom,
Es klingt wie die Brandung am Klippenstrand,
Von See zu See und von Land zu Land.
Freiheit, Freiheit!

Wie die ewigen Sterne vom Himmelszelt
Herniedergrüßen zur träumenden Welt,
Wie im blauen Aether ihr Licht erglüht,
Erfreuend erhebend des Menschen Gemüt,
So grüßen die Sterne des Banners, wenn hold
Es den staunenden Blicken der Völker entrollt,
So kündet ihr Anblick vom heiligen Hort
Dem Lande der freien das herrliche Wort:
Freiheit, Freiheit!

Jahrhunderte lang in gutem Zusta
de erhalten. In vielen Fällen wi
es mittelst der modernen Erfindu
gen und Errungenschaften auf diese
Gebiete möglich sein, wenig besch
digte Schiffe in ihrer Gänze zu hebe
wie z. B. der genannte Admiralität
bericht die erfolgreiche Hebung ein
großen Kohlenschiffes meldet, das
72 Fuß Tiefe lag und zur Anwe
dung von Maschinen, Kranen us
nötigte, die eine Last von 3,500 To
nen heben konnten. In anderen Fä
len wird man sich begnügen müsse
bloß die Ladung oder auch nur ein
Teil derselben zu bergen, je nach i
rem Zustande und der Höhe der Be
gungskosten.

Außerdem sind auch vor der N
tur selber der Bergung von Schiff
oder Ladung verhältnismäßig en
Grenzen gezogen, denn die Wassert
fe, in welcher selbst ein mit den m
dernsten Apparaten ausgestattet
Taucher noch mit Erfolg seinen B
ruf ausüben kann, beträgt nur ung
fähr sechzig Meter; tiefer hinab wir
dann der Druck der Wassersäule, d
von 10 zu 10 Meter um etwa eine A
mosphäre wächst, zu gewaltig. Do
auch Lage und Beschaffenheit des
Schiffes, vor allem aber die des Me
resbodens, der das Schiff gar oft i
Schlamm und Sand begräbt, vere
teln häufig alle Mühen.

Was weiter aus gesunkenen Schi
fen wird, hängt nicht zum wenigste
auch von dem zum Bau verwendete
Material und von dem Zustande a
in dem die Schiffe sich auf den Grun
betten. Außer den Wunden, die Tor
pedos, Minen oder schwere Artiller
dem Schiffsleib schlugen, kann d
Art und Weise des Versinkens weiter
Schäden bringen. Ein leicht belad
ner Holzkutter wird beispielswei
langsam untergehen und sich dann ol
ne schweren Stoß aufsetzen, währen
das Panzerschiff, die schwimmende F
stung aus Stahl und Eisen, jäh ab
stürzend auf hartem Fels zerschell
Wohl kann der Wogenprall, der da
gestrandete Wrack zerschlägt, schon i
geringer Tiefe nicht mehr wirker

VORWAERTS *for June 28, 1918, featured the "Stars and Stripes." Mennonite newspapers, pressed by American wartime patriotism, shifted from honoring Bismark to acclaiming the American flag, here called "the holy banner of freedom."*

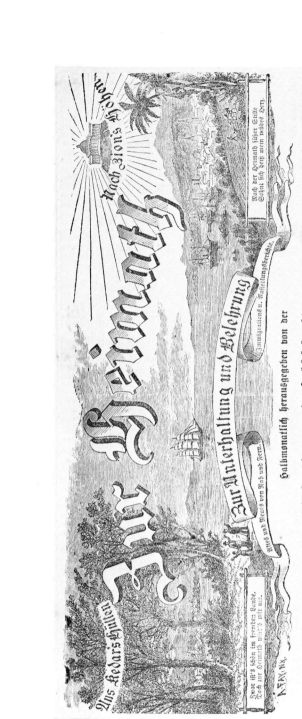

ZUR HEIMATH, the Mennonite immigration newspaper, was edited by David Goerz from 1875 to 1881. The masthead depicted the transition from the old country to a new homeland, which was rooted in the soil (lower right) and exalted "to the heights of Zion" (upper right).

John F. Funk (1835-1930) was an American Mennonite (OM) publisher and church leader of Elkhart, Indiana; he assisted the immigrants to Kansas in the 1870s.

Bernhard Warkentin (1847-1908) was a Mennonite imigrant miller of Halstead and Newton and a promoter of Turkey Red wheat in Kansas.

P. C. Hiebert (1878-1963) was president of Tabor College, first chairman of Mennonite Central Committee, and unsuccessful candidate for Marion County Superintendent of Public Instruction in 1914.

John "Kricke-Hannes" Schrag (1861-1953) was a Mennonite farmer who was persecuted in Burrton for his refusal to buy war bonds in 1918. Incidents of mob violence against Mennonites took place also near McPherson, Canton, and Moundridge during this war.

S. S. Haury (1847-1929), first American Mennonite missionary, is pictured with his wife, Susie Hirschler, and their children, Walter, Dora, and Elsa. They worked among the Arapahoe Indians in Indian Territory (Oklahoma) from 1880 to 1887.

The Bethel College administration building near Newton stood uncompleted from 1888 to 1893 as declining farm prices stalled fund-raising efforts.

The first Tabor College building was built in Hillsboro in 1908 and destroyed by fire in 1918.

Green Gables, built in 1909, was the first building at Hesston College, Hesston, Kansas. It continues to serve a variety of uses.

Mennonite young men drafted into military service in 1918 were placed in a separate detention camp at Camp Funston. Here, along the Kaw River, they gather for a meeting led by visiting Mennonite preachers.

Mennonites were not agreed on how far to cooperate with the military system in 1918. These young men peeling potatoes were willing to take up non-combatant work at Camp Funston. Others refused any work at all inside the camp.

"The Mennonites will now be purified by fire. What will become of us in the heat?" (H. P. KREHBIEL, 1918).

CHAPTER **7**

Crisis of Citizenship: Mennonites in the World War

WAR IN EUROPE

THE MENNONITES LACKED ANY SENSE OF IMPENDING TRAGEDY PRIOR to the outbreak of World War I. They had good reason for optimism. America had dealt kindly with them. America had given them rich land, abundant sunshine, and ready markets and had watched with open admiration as the Mennonites converted a patch of the great American desert into the breadbasket of the country. America had given them a free environment and had reaped the social reward as the Mennonites developed their private institutions, their schools, colleges, hospitals, insurance companies, churches, and Sunday schools.

The Mennonites saw no reason for viewing their thriving community as a political achievement. God's good earth and man's hard labor were responsible—not the will or the activity of governments. "A good harvest profits us more than a change of administration can help us in ten years," wrote Editor Abraham L. Schellenberg in *Vorwaerts,* the most publicized of Mennonite newspapers, "and a bad harvest can't be replaced by even the best government." At the outset of the year which brought the Great War, Mennonites took comfort in the irrelevance of politics. The uncertainties of governments would not upset the solid unities of Mennonite community life. "In this sense, then, we don't believe," wrote Schellenberg, "there is anything special in store for us."[1]

The Mennonites in central Kansas in 1914 still constituted a relatively closed German-American rural community. News of the outside political world reached Mennonites through the filter of Mennonite editorship in German-language semireligious newspapers. The Hillsboro *Vorwaerts* and the Newton *Der Herold*, German Mennonite newspapers with circulations of about two thousand each, had close connections with the conferences and colleges of the Mennonite Brethren Church and the General Conference Church respectively. Editor Schellenberg of *Vorwaerts* was for eight years the secretary of the Mennonite Brethren General Conference. The brothers C. E. and H. P. Krehbiel of *Der Herold* were respected leaders in the General Conference Mennonite Church. The free mixture of religious and secular news and opinion in *Vorwaerts* and *Der Herold*, not found in official Mennonite church publications, made them agents of the world's influence as well as barometers of the vitality of sectarian distinctiveness. These two newspapers both reflected and influenced Mennonite political attitudes and behavior.[2]

Fire raged through the Newton business district on the week that the European powers plunged into the Great War. The editors of *Der Herold*, who lost their entire plant and equipment in the fire, did not miss the portent. "The fire in Newton was bad," they wrote, "but a conflagration is breaking out in Europe which makes the whole world quake."[3]

Unlike the mysteriously caused Newton fire, the war in Europe could be blamed upon known evildoers. The Mennonites did not believe that Germany was at fault. Editor Schellenberg of *Vorwaerts* ridiculed the Anglo-American reports which pictured France as an innocent lamb molested by the Teutonic wolf. This lamb, he said, has been continually crying "revenge" these last forty-three years and even entered a humiliating alliance with Russia to promote this purpose. The lamb has a lion's courage and now attempts to swallow the wolf. Keep your heads, wrote Schellenberg. After all, the first reports in 1870—the beginning of the Franco-Prussian war—were equally unfavorable for Germany.[4] The initial successes of the German army confirmed Schellenberg's suspicion that Europe was replaying this war. On September 11 he announced that the Germans had taken Amiens, Reims, Maubeuge, "and probably Verdun." The news of "something conclusive" which Schellenberg expected shortly was delayed by the Battle of the Marne. French fighting men received no credit in *Vorwaerts* for the German retreat. Heavy rains had snarled German supply lines; victory would take somewhat longer than originally anticipated.[5]

Mennonite readers of *Der Herold* received a somewhat less frankly partisan view of the war. Editor C. E. Krehbiel willingly admitted that the German newspapers might be lying as blatantly as the English newspapers.[6] But Krehbiel printed numerous letters from friends in Germany or from patriotic German-Americans who were still moved by the defensive reassurance of Heinrich Heine's famous lines, "Lieb Vaterland magst ruhig sein. Fest stecht und treu die Wacht am Rhein."[7] While the rest of America was circulating stories of German soldiers violating Belgian nuns, the Mennonites read on the front page of *Der Herold*: "The treatment of the Germans in France and Belgium is flatly horrible according to all known reports."[8] And a month later: "The causes of the present war are the expansionism and lust of power of barbaric and despotic Russia, the desire for revenge of France, and the economic jealousy of England."[9]

In answer to critics who discerned a pro-German editorial bias, Krehbiel argued that editorial neutrality was not violated by printing letters from Germany, since readers could make allowances for the bias of the correspondents. On the same page appeared an advertisement for the book *Germany and the Next War* by the German general Friedrich von Bernhardi.[10] This book, available for thirty-five cents from the Herald Book Store, was a candid glorification of war as a political, biological, and moral necessity. The promotion and distribution of Bernhardi's book in Mennonite circles was convincing refutation of any disavowal of a pro-German bias.[11]

The war injected a new issue into the gubernatorial election of 1914. Articles in *Vorwaerts* counseled Mennonites to vote for Henry J. Allen, the Progressive candidate who was billed as a friend of the Germans. Arthur Capper, the Republican candidate, was said to have slandered the whole German people with his charge that the Kaiser is "war mad." Editor Schellenberg's tone was surprisingly moderate, however, for a seasoned crusader for Progressivism. One would "not go wrong," he wrote, to vote for Allen.[12]

Der Herold avoided political commentary in the 1914 election. Krehbiel did, however, reprint a letter from Capper to a local citizen in answer to the charges that he was anti-German. "As a matter of fact," wrote Capper patronizingly, "some of my most intimate friends are Germans."[13]

The question of attitude toward Germany had little apparent

effect on the election results. The Mennonites voted much like their neighbors. The predominantly Mennonite townships voted 28 percent for Allen (Progressive), 37 percent for Hodges (incumbent Democrat), and 30 percent for Capper (Republican). Schellenberg exulted over the large Progressive vote, since this was the first time that party had been on the ticket.[14] But Allen got a larger vote among the Swedes in north McPherson County than he did among the Mennonites, his presumed friendliness to the Germans notwithstanding. The election results proved little in terms of specific issues, although they did confirm something evident already in the 1912 presidential elections: the Mennonite Republicans were willing to abandon their party to switch over to third-party Progressive candidates—and they did so in about the same proportion as the average voters in the state of Kansas.[15]

Although the Mennonite newspapers often printed articles and editorials from the non-Mennonite German-American press in support of Germany in the war, Mennonites on the whole were less enthusiastic in support of Germany than were most German-Americans. The huge rallies, celebrations, propaganda campaigns, and watchdog committees for the press and cinema established by the National German-American Alliance had no counterparts among Mennonites of central Kansas.[16] The Mennonites were a sober, hardworking, conservative folk, not given to sudden enthusiasms of any type. More importantly, the Mennonites were believers in nonresistance. War to them was an evil. The Christian had no call to stand cheering on the sidelines.

The important question is why a nonresistant people supported the war at all. The answer is that they were not only Mennonites but also Germans, and there were nonresistant ways of supporting war.[17] Both *Der Herold* and *Vorwaerts* served as collecting centers for funds for the German Red Cross and periodically published the names of contributors. The lists indicated that support for Germany was a community enterprise, for the largest contributions came through church collections.[18] By December 18, 1914, *Vorwaerts* announced that contributions had exceeded one thousand dollars.[19] All these gifts were sent to the German ambassador in Washington, D.C.

The coming of the war and the growing threat of American intervention stimulated an unprecedented awareness of politics on the part of Mennonites. Mennonite leaders who would have abhorred the very notion of a Mennonite lobby now became active in attempts to

influence national public policy. Cornelius C. Wedel, pastor of the
large Alexanderwohl congregation and leader in conference activities,
appealed to readers of *Der Herold* to write letters to President Wilson
to keep the United States out of the war. "Use the right of petition,"
Wedel wrote. "Tell the president to use the power given him by Congress to stop the export of war materials from our country." Wedel
worried that the rising wartime grain prices would seduce the Mennonites from their duty of prophetic witness to government against the
war. He invited the readers to turn to the story of Naaman to dis-
cover the merciless judgment that awaits seekers of self-advantage who
disregard their fellowmen.[20]

The unprecedented Mennonite exhibition of interest in the political
world aroused the cynical comment of G. B. Ruth who surveyed the
apolitical history of the Mennonite immigrant:

For half a century and more one busied oneself with the settlement of the new
territories. One troubled oneself little over what happened in the 'world.' The
striving to achieve prosperity laid claim to the entire power of spirit and
body. . . .[21]

Suddenly, the Mennonites were caught up in the whirlwind of
political debate. The new awareness of the world, Ruth wrote, did
not result from the achievement of a measure of prosperity, nor from
a recovery of the sixteenth-century Anabaptist spirit which so upset
the political powers of that day. Far from becoming left-wing threats
to the state, the Mennonites had taken up German patriotism.

Ruth's criticism was too sophisticated to be comprehended by the
community he had left. His immediate warning was that Mennonites
were abandoning their religious heritage for an incompatible German
patriotism. His more fundamental message was that the radical social
implications of left-wing Reformation Anabaptism could be a basis
for left-wing political reform in the twentieth century. But Anabaptism had been long since domesticated. Nationalism was safe and
socialism was dangerous. Krehbiel's editorial comment after Ruth's
article implied that "Mennonite" and "Socialist" were mutually ex-
clusive categories.[22]

The war eventually forced Mennonites to confront the question
of the meaning of their traditional doctrine of nonresistance. But as
long as the war remained in Europe, this confrontation did not occur.
Most Mennonites saw no contradiction between their religious belief
in the gospel of peace and their cultural commitment to the advance of

the German nation through war. Schellenberg of *Vorwaerts* was far enough detached from Mennonite pacifism to go out of his way to point out the cultural benefits of the war. He reprinted an article from the Cologne *Volkszeitung* which acclaimed the moral improvement generated by the war. The war, it claimed, has called forth love of the fatherland, raised respect for high ideals, encouraged brotherly unity, strengthened love of God and mankind, renewed the upbuilding and purifying purposes of art and literature. Schellenberg agreed that the war has reversed the prewar deterioration of culture. "War is probably like a storm that is, to be true, horrible and often brings great destruction, but which also purifies the air of many damaging influences, relieves the breath, and refreshes the body."[23]

Until the United States' entry into the war, *Der Herold* and *Vorwaerts* provided Mennonite readers with a weekly fare of apologies for the fatherland from German correspondents and from the German-American press. Schellenberg was most outspoken in rallying to the cause. Much of the campaign was summed up in the April 9, 1915, issue of *Vorwaerts*. There on the front page was a nine-inch picture of Bismarck with spiked helmet, bushy eyebrows, stern countenance, prominent paunch, and the quotation, "We fear God and nothing else in the world." Underneath the picture was a poetic tribute to the iron chancellor by Karl Gundlach, promising that Germans far from home would stand with heart and hand for the fatherland as long as German blood beat in German hearts. (See picture section.)

The following issue of *Vorwaerts* commemorated the fiftieth anniversary of the death of Lincoln. But Lincoln rated neither picture nor poetry. The article mentioned that Lincoln was a nonsmoker but said nothing about his freeing the slaves. Both Bismarck and Lincoln were incongruous as Mennonite heroes. But in 1915 Bismarck got top billing.[24]

The reactions of *Vorwaerts* and *Der Herold* to the sinking of the *Lusitania* illustrated a growing difference in editorial policy between the papers. Schellenberg was bitter. The *Lusitania* incident, he wrote, was the natural result of munitions deliveries to the allies despite American professions of neutrality. As for the loss of American lives, "he who sits on a powder keg is in danger of being blown into the air when he comes to a place where sparks fly through the air."[25] A *Vorwaerts* front-page article of May 21, 1915, noted that New York newspapers were crying for war. But the *Lusitania* incident was only their excuse, the article said. The real reason for the war lust was that New York financiers had loaned millions of dollars to the allies and now wanted the people of the United States to save their investment.[26]

C. E. Krehbiel was conciliatory. It was time to weigh words carefully, he wrote, and especially the German papers in America should be moderate. All parties in the *Lusitania* tragedy were guilty —the English for transporting munitions on a passenger ship, the Americans for traveling on such a ship, and the Germans for having done the destructive deed. Krehbiel agreed with what he understood to be President Wilson's position—avoid war but maintain respect for the rights of neutrals.[27]

The war issue dominated Mennonite attention in the presidential election of 1916. J. G. Ewert entered the fray in March 1916 with an article on the Socialist candidates Benson and Kirkpatrick. Their prime qualification, in Ewert's view, was their opposition to war. He mentioned a Benson proposal that if war was to be declared, it should be done by popular vote and only those who voted for it should be required to go to the front and fight.[28] In the antiwar platform, Ewert had a more promising basis for his Socialist appeal to the Mennonites than he had had during the Progressive era. He hoped that the election of 1916 would give the Mennonites an opportunity to vote their nonresistant doctrine by voting Socialist.

Throughout 1915 and 1916 Schellenberg had covered the front pages of *Vorwaerts* with anti-Wilson articles from the German-American press.[29] A front-page article on September 22, for example, condemned Wilson's preelection peace proposals as a political maneuver. Wilson, in fact, "has prolonged the war for more than a year through the support of the allies with American money and munitions. . . . If peace comes it will be through the arms of the central powers, never through Wilson."[30]

Krehbiel was generally quite skimpy with war news and comment, but he was attracted to Wilson's idealistic rhetoric. The third *Lusitania* note, which was virtually an ultimatum to Germany, Krehbiel judged to be "the most significant document written since the outset of the war because it stood so clearly for justice and humanity."[31] Krehbiel believed he was steering a middle course. "If we believe in nonresistance," he had written earlier, "we will not prescribe for the good Lord to whom He must give the victory in order to be 'neutral.' "[32] Krehbiel balanced his call for an end to American munitions shipments with a denunciation of German submarine warfare.

The influence of Theodore Roosevelt in the Republican party prevented unqualified enthusiasm on the part of Mennonites for the GOP ticket. Roosevelt's popularity among Mennonites, so strikingly evident in their large Bull Moose vote of 1912, evaporated rapidly as he took up the war cry against Germany and condemned German-American pacifists as traitors. Traditional Republican voters had to come to terms with the prospect that Roosevelt might become secretary of state in a Republican administration. J. D. Fast, columnist in *Vorwaerts,* expressed amazement at the popularity of Roosevelt's warmongering, for only a few months before, 90 percent of the people had opposed war preparations. "The best explanation," Fast wrote, "is probably that the American people are mentally lazy (denkfaul)."[33] Fast questioned the meaning of the freedom to vote when there was no real choice. Mennonites would soon have new reasons for questioning the meaningfulness of American freedoms.

J. G. Ewert, sensing that the Socialists had no appeal for Mennonites even in wartime, shifted his energies to support for Wilson.[34] Hughes, Ewert wrote, refused to take a stand on the burning domestic issues such as the income tax, railroad rates, and women's suffrage. Hughes did say he was "in complete accord" with Roosevelt regarding American foreign policy. Ewert knew the hearts of his readers: "German citizens of America, consider what you owe to your Germanhood (Deutschtum) and that especially in this time when your vote will help decide whether we shall have war or peace in the next four years in our dear new fatherland."[35]

Although Schellenberg seemed to be leaning toward Hughes in his editorial comments in preelection issues ("it is to be expected that he will be more neutral"),[36] the November 3 issue of *Vorwaerts* carried a full front-page advertisement for the Democrats. "Vote for Wilson and you vote for continuation of peace and prosperity. When you vote for Hughes you vote for war and Roosevelt, the enemy of all Germans." In the postelection issue Schellenberg said he had voted for Wilson because of the slogan "He kept us out of war." Now we can hold him responsible. Schellenberg admitted he would have been equally happy to see either Hughes or Wilson lose, for neither sincerely opposed the drift toward war.[37]

C. E. Krehbiel shared Schellenberg's indifference regarding election results. With the outcome still in doubt he wrote, "We are satisfied with the election. Hurrah for Hughes or Wilson." After the result

was sure, "school children who have to memorize the names of the
presidents will be happy that the list is not one name longer."[38]

Mennonite indifference to the election results was fed not only by
the lack of choice between opposing major candidates but also by the
traditional Mennonite antipathy toward politics. The official German
periodical of the General Conference observed the dangers of the
national election campaign. We who have a dual citizenship, the
editor wrote, are in danger of losing our vision of the heavenly
kingdom in our enthusiasm for our earthly fatherland. We may
alienate our neighbors and friends. And we may be dissatisfied with
the result of the election and begin to doubt that God directs and rules
in what happens. "Be not dissatisfied with your government" was the
Mennonite editor's contradictory position, "even though she deserves
the punishment of God through war for her enormous munitions
deliveries and financial aid for the allies."[39]

Tradition in the Kansas Mennonite community has long held that
Wilson's appeal as a peacemaker shook many Mennonites loose from
their traditional Republican vote in 1916. Gerhard Zerger, Democratic party worker, remembered that Mennonite voters around Moundridge went fairly solidly for Wilson. Zerger believed that the "more
intelligent Republicans" in the Inman-Buhler area crossed party
lines in this election.[40] D. C. Wedel remembered that his father,
pastor of the large Alexanderwohl Church in Menno Township,
abandoned his customary Republicanism and counseled his neighbors
to vote for Wilson.[41] Gerhard Dalke of Hillsboro wrote that many
Mennonites voted Democratic for the first time in 1916 because William Jennings Bryan had told them that a vote for Wilson was a vote
for peace.[42]

The voting records from Mennonite townships give the lie to the
common belief that many Mennonites switched to Wilson in 1916.
In fourteen concentrated Mennonite townships, Wilson received only
33.6 percent of the vote and Hughes, 59.3 percent. This was a drop
of 5.8 percent for Wilson from the 1912 election, when he had
competition for the Progressive vote from Theodore Roosevelt. The
Mennonite vote of 33.6 percent for Wilson compared to 51.6 percent
for Wilson in Chase County and to 50 percent in the state of Kansas.

The pattern of votes by township is interesting. C. C. Wedel
of the Alexanderwohl Church took almost no voters with him into the
Democratic side, for Wilson got only 8 of 142 (5.6 percent) votes in
Menno Township and 8 of 276 (2.9 percent) in West Branch Town-

ship. Not only was the rejection of Wilson almost total in Menno
and West Branch townships, but the number who came out to vote
was larger than usual. In Menno and West Branch together there
were 230 more voters in 1916 than in 1912, and 168 more voters in
1916 than in 1920.

Mennonites in McPherson County were less like-minded. Wilson
got majorities in Little Valley, Lone Tree, and Superior townships
and strong minorities in Mound and Turkey Creek townships. Most
of the McPherson County townships also had significantly higher
turnout in 1916 than in 1912 and 1920, a pattern shared with Chase
County and with the state of Kansas in general.

The voting statistics should warn against generalizing about the
Mennonite vote as a whole. There obviously were significant differences between Turkey Creek Township with its majority for Wilson
and West Branch Township with less than 3 percent for Wilson.
Nonetheless, it can be said that there was no large swing to Wilson
in the Mennonite community in the 1916 election, and that the community as a whole found no stronger reason to vote for Wilson in 1916
than it had found in 1912. The large turnout indicated that Mennonites considered the vote of particular importance, but not that
the community had an opportunity to express itself clearly through a
choice of political candidates.

The Mennonite vote for Socialist national candidates was not
significantly different than the Kansas norm. Local Socialist candidates usually received fewer votes than national Socialist candidates.
Alta Township in Harvey County, for example, turned in twenty
votes for presidential candidate Allen L. Benson but no more than
twelve votes for local Socialist candidates.

The lack of a doctrinally acceptable political alternative in the
1916 elections made it impossible for Mennonites to express their
distinctive religious teachings through the ballot. Mennonite voting
patterns did not deviate significantly from a non-Mennonite or nonimmigrant norm. The Mennonites expressed little discomfiture at
the lack of a bridge between religious doctrine and political behavior.
Religion and politics were complacently compartmentalized.

Mennonites might have seen the war as particularly reprehensible
from the viewpoint of nonresistance. As long as their ethnic sympathies
found satisfaction in German victories, however, editors Schellenberg
and Krehbiel had little impulse to pronounce the judgment of God
upon the war or to question the participation of so-called Christians

in the war. Their opposition to the United States' entanglement in the war reflected an ethnic bias rather than a religious conviction.

When the United States mobilized for war and made demands upon individuals in the Mennonite communities, the Mennonites were forced to give doctrinal answers to political questions. The religious person and the political person could no longer conveniently be separated. One measure of this phenomenon was the new significance of J. G. Ewert's article in *Vorwaerts*. Ewert held no conference office, but unlike the politically secularized Schellenberg, Ewert saw his policies as an outgrowth of his religious convictions. He justified socialism in Christian terms, and he opposed war because he believed in nonresistance. Schellenberg lost momentum when the war dissolved the two main planks of his political platform—Progressive reforms at home and pro-Germanism in the foreign war. Ewert exhibited a new potency as he turned to the Mennonite religious heritage to help guide the community through the difficult days of World War I.

WAR AT HOME

Within a week of the United States' declaration of war, the Western District Conference (GC) held a special session in Newton. Representatives of the Mennonite Brethren, Krimmer Mennonite Brethren, Holdeman, Defenseless Mennonite, and several independent congregations attended the meeting. Two topics were up for discussion: "1. In what way can we give expression to our loyalty to our country in case of war without violating our doctrine of nonresistance? 2. Would it be advisable to send a delegation to Washington together with our other district conferences and other branches of our fellowship in order to represent our position on military service there?"[43]

The conference answered the second question by electing a committee of seven leaders to keep in contact with Washington and with other Mennonite groups.[44] The first question—how to be both loyal and nonresistant—was less easily answered. After extended debate, the conference adopted part of the resolution which had been adopted nineteen years earlier in a similar session regarding the Spanish-American War.[45] That resolution had been highly equivocal and had seemed as much interested in preserving an image of respectability as in being true to traditional doctrine. A key phrase was stated negatively: "The conference cannot dissuade those who would be glad to render medical service in the army voluntarily under the Red Cross."[46] The statement did not answer the important questions.

Would Mennonite boys answer the draft calls or would they render service only voluntarily? Would Mennonites serve under army administration or only under Red Cross administration? To what extent would Mennonites at home participate in the war effort? Instead of answering these questions directly, the resolution concluded four paragraphs of ambiguous generalizations with the statement that "although we cannot participate in inflicting wounds with the weapons of war in hand, we nevertheless regard it a Christian duty to help with the healing of wounds."[47] The adoption of this 1898 resolution by a 1917 conference was symptomatic; Mennonites had done virtually nothing in the intervening years to make possible specific expression of their sense of Christian wartime civic responsibilities.

The conference report for the American press showed the Mennonites on the defensive. It was more expedient to talk of loyalty than of nonresistance. The headlines came out: "Pledge Loyalty to Government." The Mennonite conference, said the article, did not discuss "international relations or the present state of war" but rather affirmed their appreciation of American liberties and their desire to be true to America in the present crisis. They were so loyal, in fact, that they adjourned their conference at 4:00 P.M. "so as not to seem indifferent" to the plans for Newton's Loyalty Day that same afternoon.[48]

Newton's Loyalty Day exhibited the same revival spirit which swept across America after the war declaration.[49] In Kansas, opposition to the war turned into enthusiastic support of the war. This reversal was "unpredictable and abrupt."[50] Across the nation, pacifists became militarists, isolationists became interventionists, and Socialists became patriots. Opponents of war watched in confusion and dismay as their ranks thinned and their popular orators gave prowar speeches.[51] Committees for all conceivable wartime functions sprang to life throughout the country. Mennonites had to beware of the American Protective League of Kansas, entrusted with the sacred task of exposing alien disloyal spirits who refused to join the war-crusading bandwagon.

The most immediate concern of the Mennonites was that the war should not change their exemption from military service. H. P. Krehbiel, former state representative and interpreter of laws for Mennonites, had reassured the constituency in March 1916 that the congressional law passed in 1903 put the exemption of Mennonites from military service "beyond doubt," even if the United States would adopt universal military service.[52]

The National Defense Act of 1916, however, made several important changes which seriously threatened the Mennonite exemption.[53] H. P. Krehbiel reviewed the changes in the *Herold* of March 15, 1917: In the new law it was the religious belief of the individual, rather than his adherence to a nonresistant group, which was the decisive criterion for determining eligibility for exemption. Furthermore, the law left it to the president to prescribe regulations to determine who actually was nonresistant, and even those who were judged nonresistant would be required to do noncombatant service. There would be no exemption from military service in general.[54]

Mennonites saw compulsory military service as a deviation from American promises and American ideals. C. E. Krehbiel attacked compulsory military service not only as a denial of freedom—possibly a form of "involuntary servitude" outlawed by the thirteenth amendment—but also as a kind of militarism which would be as reprehensible in America as it was in Germany and England.[55] When the Selective Service Act of 1917 instituted compulsory military service, Krehbiel exclaimed with a sense of betrayal which spoke for the entire Mennonite community, "We did not believe that that was possible in the United States."[56]

The Mennonites were not organized to speak with unity regarding the draft. There was no central committee of Mennonite groups to make denominational policy. At least five important conference groups in Kansas (GC, MB, KMB, OM, and Holdeman) reserved the right to make separate decisions, and each group had internal differences of opinion. On several points, however, there was general agreement: all groups desired complete exemption from military service but eventually proved willing to engage in alternative service under nonmilitary direction; all were agreed that the young men should register and report to the military camps as called.[57]

The decision to report to camp meant that Mennonite conflict with legal authority on the draft question was removed from the local community and from the processes of civil law. The burden of disobeying the government was put upon the conscripted young men whose refusal to join military service would take place away from home in the military camps, where disobedience was punished by military law. Thus the Mennonite decision to register and report to camp, even though the military law under which they registered made no provision for noncombatant service outside the military establishment, proved to be of tremendous significance for the Mennonite relationship to the state during the war.

Beyond the areas of general agreement, the Mennonite churches divided into two separate groups in their attitude toward military service and in their view of the proper tactics for negotiating with the government. The first group, which included the GCs, MBs, and KMBs —a strong majority of the Kansas Mennonites—tended to be conciliatory. Leaders of this group attempted to win the goodwill of the government by making it very clear that they had no objections to serving the country in time of war and that they were willing to negotiate for alternatives, possibly within the undefined area of noncombatant service.

By June 22, 1917, representatives from these three conferences had agreed upon a plan of descending priorities in approaching the government.[58] If the authorities would not grant the first preference of total exemption, they would ask for agricultural work in lieu of military service. If this was denied, they would request the alternative service under the Red Cross. And if this failed, they would negotiate for possible kinds of noncombatant work and advise the brotherhood accordingly.

The first step in this plan was a visit to Washington and a letter from the three groups to Secretary of War Newton D. Baker requesting "service in an agricultural capacity."[59] Secretary Baker granted the group a personal interview as requested in the letter. Part of the interview, preserved in the committee's records, shows Baker asking questions, H. P. Krehbiel answering fully, and Baker apparently concluding that arrangements would have to be made:

Baker: You can do quartermaster service?

Krehbiel: No, we could not do anything hostile to the enemy for it is against Scripture.

Baker: But, you pay the war tax?

Krehbiel: Yes, but we do it on the scriptural ground, Give unto caesar what is caesar's, and unto the Lord what is the Lord's.

Baker: What would you do if your young men would be drafted into military service?

Krehbiel: Many would do what they have done in former years, leave the country for religious liberty, as our people already have done.

Baker: That would be a sad, sad affair and it shall never happen.[60]

Baker requested that the Mennonites submit a list of kinds of work which their young men would be willing to do. The list, in a letter to Provost Marshal General E. H. Crowder on July 2, 1917, suggested two categories of work. Under the "general Government" the committee was open to irrigation projects, farming of public lands, drainage projects, bridge building, and river and harbor work. Under the "American Red Cross within the United States" they found acceptable various kinds of relief work both at home and abroad. The decisive point was "we can render any service, outside the military establishment, which aims to support and save life: but we cannot participate in any work which will result in personal injury or loss of life."[61]

The commission returned to Kansas in full confidence that they had won their case with the government by tempering their refusal of military service with open willingness to do nonmilitary wartime work in lieu of military service.[62] In late July the Western District (GC) committee printed a booklet of information for drafted men, saying that until July 21, 1917, the President "had not declared what is non-combatant service. Non-resistants will probably not be called upon for service until after such a declaration."[63] They clearly expected the matter to be settled shortly in a manner agreeable to the Mennonites. They had badly misjudged the government.

The (Old) Mennonites, a small group in Kansas but the largest Mennonite group in the country, took a more uncompromising position. They believed a conciliatory offer for work in agriculture or in the Red Cross would only encourage the government to draft the men into military service. "It seems to me you offer after all a compromise to engage under military direction," wrote T. M. Erb, OM leader of Hesston, Kansas, to P. H. Unruh of the Western District (GC) committee. "My sentiments are (and I think I am voicing the sentiments of our church as a whole) that we will not engage or offer ourselves in any service whatsoever. I think, if we are straight forward and come right out with our position we will be exempted for some time to come."[64]

The OMs were joined in this uncompromising stance by the Holdeman, Old Order Amish, and Conservative Amish groups.[65] Eastern OM leaders took the initiative with a position statement adopted at a conference near Goshen, Indiana, on August 29, 1917. The statement quoted the section on nonresistance from the Dortrecht Confession of Faith of 1632, expressed appreciation for past favors from the state and hoped for future exemption "when the powers that be fully understand our position," and counseled the congregations to firmness and meekness, to refuse any kind of service under the military arm of the government, but to submit "to any penalty the government may see fit to inflict."[66]   Seven Kansas Mennonites were on the list of 199 church leaders who signed the statement.

The dealings of Secretary of War Baker and the War Department with the Mennonites were a triumph of deceptive public relations. Although the Selective Service law had made no provision for service outside of the military organization by drafted men, Baker had led Mennonites of both conciliatory and uncompromising inclinations to conclude that it was best to register in the draft, to report for duty, and to await an order from the president or War Department defining "noncombatant service" in a way which would make it possible for them to work in good conscience.   Baker had achieved his first most important objective—to get the Mennonites into the camps along with everybody else.

Contrary to the Mennonite impressions,[67] Baker had not been convinced that the Mennonites would remain firm in their refusal of military service.   He believed that after a little exposure to life in a military camp, the conscientious objectors would see the light and join the army.   In early October, after a visit to Camp Meade where he saw several of the objectors in camp, Baker wrote to President Wilson: ". . . If it gets no worse than it is at Camp Meade, I am pretty sure that no harm will come in allowing these people to stay at the camps, separated from the life of the camp but close enough to come gradually to understand.   The effect of that I think quite certainly would be that a substantial number of them would withdraw their objection and make fairly good soldiers."[68]

Baker's intention of converting the conscientious objectors was implicit in a confidential War Department order of October 10, 1917, to commanding generals of the military camps.   The order directed that conscientious objectors be segregated and placed under "supervision of instructors who shall be specially selected with a view of insuring that these men will be handled with tact and consideration and that their questions will be answered fully and frankly."   The objective of such considerate treatment was not that it was lawful nor that the objectors deserved it, but that it might be successful in winning them to military service, as it already had been "in one of our divisions."   Camp commanders were to report on the success of this procedure.[69]

The delay of the executive order defining noncombatant service was confusing and disappointing to the Mennonites.   When the War

Department officially announced that members of nonresistant religious organizations were to be concentrated in mobilization camps, H. P. Krehbiel sent a telegram to E. H. Crowder, Provost Marshal General, asking "whether it is the ntern [sic] of the War Department to concentrate members of nonresistant religious organization drafted into service in the general mobilization camps for military exercises and service or in separate mobilization camps for civilian service." Crowder replied with the official dodge: there would be no exemption from noncombatant service, but it was up to the President to define what noncombatant service will be.[70]

President Wilson's order in conformity with the War Department's policy of giving time for "instruction" of the conscientious objectors in camp, was delayed until March 20, 1918, nearly six months after the first men were called into military camps. In the absence of a clarified policy, each camp commander had wide latitude to determine his own policies for separating the conscientious objector from the regular men and for persuading him to reconsider his position.

The Mennonite young men entering camp were confused and afraid. Their church leaders had been reassured that the conscripts would not be required to do anything against their consciences,[71] but who was to determine what was against conscience? Years later, one drafted conscientious objector said flatly, "We wasn't instructed of the church."[72] It was, in fact, both dangerous and futile to lay down specific rules for all situations. When should the declaration of nonresistance be made? What kinds of statements should one sign? Should one wear the uniform? Obey orders? Salute officers? Engage in drill? Accept KP duty? Organize with like-minded objectors? Sign the payroll?

Without exception the Mennonite men in camp reported that officers showed more interest in getting them to accept military service than in respecting their consciences.[73] When the draftee could not be won for military service through intimidation or persuasion, the officers resorted to more subtle tactics of drawing them into simple innocuous kinds of work and arguing that a step further made no difference in terms of military activity.[74]

The Mennonites were remarkably slow in discovering the government's intention to make soldiers out of their boys. H. P. Krehbiel's report of his September 26-28 visit to Camp Funston, near Fort Riley, Kansas, where most of the Mennonite men were called, was thoroughly positive. The draftees, he said, were not forced to wear the uniform or to participate in military exercises. They were doing such work as washing floors, kitchen duty, transportation, and building stairs. As a visitor Krehbiel was treated cordially by the officers. They even discussed the possibility of a permanent Mennonite chaplain in the camp.[75]

The euphoria lasted less than a month. By middle and late October 1917, Mennonite leaders were threatened with denial of visiting privileges in camp,[76] and reports were circulating that some boys had been beaten.[77] The delay of the government's definition of noncombatant service now made initial compromises on work in the camps seem inadvisable. The Western District Conference of October 24-25, 1917, adopted a resolution which signified retrenchment: ". . . We can do such work as is at present assigned to non-combatants in Camp Funston and Camp Travis, Texas, only under protest, because to us it appears that such service virtually constitutes military service, since the work is required by the military authorities and must be done within the military establishment."[78]

The official resolution to work in the camps only "under protest" indicated how far such decisions were out of the hands of conference leaders and up to the draftees in camp based on their own relationships with the officers. At Camp Funston a group of (Old) Mennonite draftees took the initiative in stopping all work entirely and several men from the other groups came along later in behalf of a unified front.[79] The Western District Exemption Committee was divided on the matter. The Reverend P. H. Unruh advised laying down the work rather than continuing under protest. J. W. Kliewer was uncertain what to do.[80] By early December, H. P. Krehbiel conceded privately what the Mennonites so long refused to admit: there was some reason to fear, Krehbiel wrote, "a concealed but definite purpose on the part of the military authorities to gradually draw our men into the net and hold them for military service anyway."[81]

The long-awaited presidential order defining noncombatant service, issued on March 20, 1918, failed to make the provision for service outside the military organization so optimistically hoped for by the Mennonites. The order listed categories of service in the medical corps, the quartermaster corps, and the engineer service as noncombatant. Persons with religious scruples against such noncombatant military service were to be segregated and dealt with fairly according to instructions from the Secretary of War.[82]

A total of about 315 Kansas Mennonites were drafted in World

War I, according to the best compilation.[83]   Of these, 141 (45 percent) refused service of any kind; 151 (48 percent) accepted noncombatant service; and 23 (7 percent) accepted regular army service. On the whole, boys from General Conference churches were more disposed to accept some form of military service than were boys from the more conservative churches.[84]

Most of the Kansas Mennonite draftees were sent to Camp Funston, near Fort Riley, Kansas, where they received better treatment than the Mennonites at Camp Travis, Texas.   Forty-five men at Camp Travis were court-martialled and sentenced to dishonorable discharge, loss of pay, and hard labor for life for their disobedience to an officer's order to wear the military uniform.[85]   The commanding officer reduced most of the sentences to twenty-five years; the men were eventually released after the war.[86]   In June 1918 the War Department set up a civilian Board of Inquiry to visit the camps and sort out the genuine conscientious objectors from the slackers.   Those who passed this reverse muster were granted furloughs for farm work or overseas relief service.[87]

While the War Department was pragmatically negotiating its way toward a settlement of the Mennonite conscientious objector problem, certain attorneys in the Justice Department were demanding tougher and more spectacular approach. United States Attorney Edwin S. Wertz of Cleveland, Ohio, projected a role for himself as star prosecutor in a mass trial of Mennonite leaders.   On August 20, 1918, Wertz wired the Justice Department, "I am ready to present grand jury indictment against one hundred eighty-one bishops, ministers, deacons of the Mennonite church for conspiring to violate espionage act...."[88]   Exhibit "A" for the prosecution was the statement of position on military service adopted by the Mennonite General Conference (OM), August 29, 1917, with the names of signing bishops, ministers, and deacons.   The names of seven Kansas Mennonite leaders were on the list, including T. M. Erb and D. H. Bender of Hesston.[89]   Wertz, caught up in the enthusiasm of his work on the Eugene V. Debs case, was sure that he would get a conviction and possibly pleas of guilty.   The crux of the case was the Mennonite refusal of noncombatant service.   Wertz said this was both a deviation from traditional Mennonite teaching and a violation of United States law.

Justice Department officials in Washington were less eager than Wertz for a mass Mennonite trial.   They had known about the official Mennonite position on military service long before Wertz brought it to their attention; indeed, their accumulated material constituted "a very much bigger case than Wertz has prepared."[90] But they were unwilling to undertake a prosecution of the Mennonites, partly because the case against the Mennonites was not entirely clear but primarily because the War Department was negotiating with the Mennonites and anticipated a satisfactory solution of the problem. The Justice Department put the leash on Wertz, but asked him to continue gathering evidence so all may be ready "in case it is decided to advise you at any time in the future to go ahead with the prosecution."[91] The war came to an end without a mass trial of Mennonite leaders, to the immense chagrin of Attorney Wertz who saw no sense in allowing the Mennonites "to defy the laws of the country." Three years after the war, Mennonites were still trying to retrieve some official church documents which Wertz had acquired in his hunt for lawbreakers.[92]

While the problem of the military draft forced Mennonites to reconsider their relationship to the government in specific terms, the Mennonite community as a whole had to reevaluate its place in the American community. For when America went to war against Germany, it became a requirement of acceptable citizenship to support the war and to hate things German. The Mennonites made agonizing concessions on both counts, but they finally failed to escape the intolerant wrath of their American neighbors.

The war bond drives became a second test of loyal support for the war. Faced with the persuasion and intimidation of local Loyalty Leagues, some Mennonites reconciled their nonresistance with the purchase of the bonds. After all, reasoned H. P. Krehbiel, a war bond is a kind of tax, and Jesus told us to pay taxes.[93] But not all the Mennonites agreed with Krehbiel, especially those among the more conservative OMs and Holdeman groups. The Holdeman conference of October 29-November 3, 1917, unanimously adopted a resolution against participation in Liberty Loan drives.[94]

Use of the American language became the test of one's emancipation from pro-Germanism during the war. Prominent signs in business places exhorted Mennonites to "Talk the American Language in This Place," attempts were made to eliminate German in church worship services, and watchdog patriots strove to purge public and private schools of the alien German tongue.[95] In Marion County the superintendent of schools came to the vigorous defense of the Mennonite-area public schools after they were attacked in the

Topeka *Capital,* the *Kansas Teacher,* and the *Marion County Review.*[96] But in Newton the local Loyalty League forced the discontinuance of German language instruction at Bethel College.[97]

While Mennonites were stung deeply by verbal and printed attacks, several incidents of mob violence against individuals symbolized most dramatically the Mennonite crisis of citizenship. The war bond issue was usually the pretext for the tar-and-feather or yellow-paint ceremonies.[98]

The celebrations of mob violence reached a climax in the public persecution of one John Schrag on the streets of Burrton on Armistice Day, November 11, 1918. Schrag was a member of the Hoffnungsfeld (GC) congregation and had become wealthy in pursuit of the durable Mennonite virtues of hard work, simple living, and wise investment. Forced by the leading Burrton citizens to come to town on Armistice Day, Schrag again refused to buy war bonds but wrote out a check for $200 for the Red Cross and Salvation Army. When he balked at their demand that he salute the flag and carry it at the head of their parade, Schrag was given a coat of yellow paint, rubbed into his scalp and beard until he resembled "a big cheese or yellow squash or pumpkin after the autumnal ripening."[99] The Harvey County sheriff rescued Schrag from his tormentors and took him to jail in Newton for cleaning and safekeeping. Reports on the incident in the Burrton *Graphic* and the Hutchinson *News* tended to take the side of the mob.[100]

Emboldened by community support for their open brutality, the Burrton patriots attempted to convict Schrag in federal court for violation of the Espionage Act. Five citizens presented fifty typewritten pages of evidence to prove Schrag's disloyalty and desecration of the flag before a United States Commissioner in Wichita on December 9. The decision, handed down two weeks later, was that although Schrag "could not have gone closer to a violation of the espionage act if he had had a hundred lawyers at his side to advise him,"[101] he should not be bound over for trial. Nothing in the Espionage Act required salute of the flag, and Schrag's words which supposedly slandered the flag had been spoken in German so that none of the monolingual plaintiffs could prove any guilt. The Newton *Evening Kansan-Republican,* frustrated by the acquittal of this "bull-headed" man, suggested that the case "should certainly make plain to any thinking person the viciousness that exists in the encouragement of the German language as a means of communication in America. . . . The melting pot cannot exercise its proper functions when such things are allowed.”[102]

If the Mennonites had anticipated that the American melting pot would come to such a vigorous boil in World War I, they might have considered emigration. But it all happened so suddenly. It was already July 1918 when H. P. Krehbiel and P. H. Unruh of the Western District Exemption Committee checked with the Argentine and Canadian consuls in Washington, D.C., regarding settlement possibilities. A few Mennonite families did migrate to Canada during the war, and some young men went north to escape the draft, but it was an informal and disorganized movement of anxious and harassed families and individuals.[103]

The crucial problem of Mennonites in World War I was not the physical threat of mob violence but rather the moral agony of discovering that they were not acceptable as American citizens. There were ways to alleviate this agony, but none of them was satisfactory. One way was to validate one’s citizenship by joining the patriotic crusade.[104] The Mennonites were great wheat raisers and it was possible, though not necessary, for them to see their grain production as a part of the war effort. Before the United States entered the war, C. E. Krehbiel of *Der Herold* glanced at skyrocketing grain prices and warned Mennonites against imagining that there was a great difference between providing food for civilians and bullets for soldiers in wartime. “It is a fact that soldiers eat first.”[105] But after he heard Wilson’s appeal to farmers to join the great crusade by providing food, Krehbiel’s antiwar conscience retreated. “Certainly no good citizen will have scruples on this point. All should respond to the appeal as it is possible.”[106] Mennonites found other ways to help their country. Many bought war bonds;[107] some contributed generously to the Red Cross; the Mennonite newspapers printed the government’s appeals to eat potatoes instead of flour, to drink coffee without sugar, and to write letters to servicemen. On July 4, 1918, *Der Herold* carried on the front page a patriotic message which was rankest heresy from the point of view of Mennonite nonresistance, for it identified the government with God: “Now is the hour for unquestioning loyalty to constituted authority, doing what it orders, obeying what it requests. . . . To authority in these days, as unto God, the inquiry, the only inquiry of the right-thinking American should be, Lord, what wilt Thou have me to do?”[108]

By the end of the war H. P. Krehbiel was organizing a project for the Mennonites to build and operate a hospital for disabled veterans in central Kansas. The armistice stopped the plans, but the mere dream of a Mennonite veterans' hospital symbolizes the incongruities of nonresistant Mennonite attempts to validate their citizenship in the World War.[109]

The great danger facing those who undertook to defend the Mennonites during the war was that the defense often tended to accept the standards of American nationalism and to abandon the case for Mennonite distinctiveness in its own right. C. B. Schmidt appealed for Mennonite exemption from military service on the grounds that their agricultural production was an essential contribution to the war.[110] Thus he put Mennonites in the position of needing nationalist excuses for obeying what they understood to be the Christian ethic. The secularization implicit in the Mennonite reconceptualization of their own social identity in response to wartime attacks was most obvious in the case of Gerhard Dalke, a Hillsboro evangelical pamphleteer whose prewar tracts were invariably on such religious themes as *Where Do You Want to Spend Your Eternity?* or *The Lost and Found-Again Paradise.* But when Dalke turned his amateur energies to a defense of the Mennonites in late 1917, he abandoned religious doctrine and spoke in the secular terms called for by the situation.[111] Dalke reminded his readers that the Mennonites came to Kansas only upon the invitation of and the promise of toleration by the government. Now this promise was betrayed by political leaders whom the Mennonites trusted, such as Roosevelt and Wilson. That Mennonites were "worthy of their citizenship" Dalke demonstrated by pointing to their prewar record of generous relief for the needy in disaster areas; their creation of institutions such as schools, colleges, and hospitals; and their work for world peace "by international law based on the Bible.[112]

Every argument in Dalke's defense might have been persuasive for Americans before the Great War. But citizenship in the context of the Great American Crusade had to be defined in terms of the crusade itself, and not merely in terms of social contribution to a peaceful world. Dalke claimed more for the Mennonites than was actually true, for they knew nothing about "international law" and had done little for world peace. A totally convincing defense of the Mennonite civic role during World War I was, in fact, impossible. Any defense at all was bound to draw Mennonites into the political world, for the tendency was to use the standards of that world in making the defense.

J. G. Ewert saw that the moral dilemma of war was that it forced people to choose between two polarized sides engaged in deadly combat. Neither choice was acceptable. Ewert defended the legitimacy of "a third way, the Christian way of reconciliation and understanding . . . of loving one's enemies." The Mennonites were loyal to the noblest aims of the country, said Ewert, but they would not approve of the current means to achieve those aims.[113] If true Americanism meant taking sides and entering the combat, then Mennonites clearly could not be true Americans. One problem with Ewert's argument was that Mennonites could not offer a "third way" of any political relevance. Their opposition to war was of a piece with their apolitical heritage.

Between the German declaration of war in August 1914 and the German humiliation at Versailles in June 1919 the German Mennonites of Kansas went through two stages, both of which frustrated their desire to be accepted as American citizens.

The effect of the first stage, which lasted until the spring of 1917 (when it became clear that the United States would enter the war against Germany), was to emphasize the national identity of the community as Germanic. The Kansas Mennonites identified with Germany in its great struggle and offered both moral and material support in the defense of German honor and integrity. The frustration of Mennonite pretensions to American citizenship came with the realization that it was increasingly unacceptable in America to hope, pray, and work for a German victory in the European war.

The effect of the second stage, which lasted beyond the end of the war, was to emphasize the religious identity of the community as Mennonite. For the Anabaptist-Mennonite tradition of nonresistance dictated a refusal to participate directly in the war which suddenly became the Great American Crusade. The Mennonite young man who was true to his faith could not fight alongside other Americans. The desire to be an American citizen was thwarted by the necessity of fidelity to the Mennonite religion.

It was the sequence of these stages which made the war experience such an overwhelming tragedy for the Mennonite community. Identification with Germany in a European war would not have caused insuperable difficulties for Kansas Mennonites had the war been settled without American intervention. And Mennonites would have been accepted had they been able to validate their citizenship by direct participation in the American war against Germany; the sin of having originally favored Germany in the European conflict could have been atoned for by young Mennonites fighting and dying for America on the front lines and by their families at home rallying to the cause.

But the Mennonite alienation from America through identification with the German nation was followed by a more serious alienation from America through refusal to fight in the war against Germany. With two strikes against them, the Mennonites could hardly expect to have their sectarian position understood by America, or even have their position accepted once it was understood. For there was a fundamental contradiction between the peculiar Mennonite distinctiveness and the demands of American nationalism. When Americans fought and died for their country, the Mennonites could not avoid looking like parasites who laid claim to extraordinary freedom at the very moment when freedom must be limited in order that it be made secure.

In retrospect, one sees that Mennonites might have challenged the myth of the Great American Crusade, for the course of events in the twentieth century has cast doubts on whether the American contribution to the First World War constituted an advancement of human freedom either at home or abroad. But the Mennonites would not have had the political sophistication to challenge the assumptions of the war-making country, even if they had had extraordinary foresight. The Mennonites were not self-conscious critics of the political world no matter how much their wartime suffering might have been a reproach to society.

In many respects, the war showed the Mennonites at their worst. Their sympathy for Germany in the European war exposed an ethnic bias which did not mesh with their religious doctrine of nonresistance. Their frantic attempts to secure exemption from military service were selfish. Their precarious definitions which balked at noncombatant military service but did not question raising the wheat which fed the armies smacked of legalism.

But the war was not an unqualified disaster for the Mennonites. For the first time in several generations the Mennonite community had living examples of Christian heroism in the face of persecution, a strong reminder of the tradition of martyrdom for conscience' sake in the Anabaptist tradition. The Mennonites of different branches drew together in closer cooperation as they faced common wartime problems. And the war stimulated creative search for a new social identity for Mennonites, a search which resulted in a remarkable voluntary relief program in the years following the war.

Recovery from the war experience of alienation was not so simple for Mennonites as for those German-Americans who were able to make a choice between America and Germany and thus to abandon the hyphen in their self-identity.[114] The Mennonites emerged from the war without having made a choice. They were still Germans, still Mennonites, and still Americans. Never again would those who had been through the fire assume that it would be easy to bridge the contradictions in these conflicting identities.

"There was little satisfaction in just maintaining a negative position toward war. What was needed was an opportunity to disprove the charges of cowardice and selfishness made against the conscientious objectors, and to express in a positive, concrete way the principles of peace and goodwill" (P. C. HIEBERT, 1929).

CHAPTER **8**

Era of Readjustment

FOR THE MENNONITES, EVEN MORE THAN FOR THE REST OF THE country, life during the twenties and thirties was shaped by the world wars which began and ended this period. The prosperity of the twenties and the depression of the thirties had a less apparent effect upon the Mennonite communities' political acculturation than did the immediate problems of adjusting to conditions created by the past experience and future prospect of war. In the first part of the interwar period, the community struggled to rediscover its purpose and mission in the light of the First World War. In the latter part of the period, the community prepared itself for another crisis.

MENNONITE BENEVOLENCE AND CIVIC IDENTITY

It was not possible for a Mennonite to survive the war with a clean conscience, for there was no way to fulfill one's responsibilities to both God and country. The community could not fully overcome this crisis of conscience without some visible means of expiation. There must be some community act which engaged the attention and effort of the entire membership to reestablish their worth as citizens, Christians, and human beings. The political realm offered no opportunity for such a community act; there was no political instrument or institution at hand whereby an embattled minority group could assert itself by a contribution to the public welfare. The Mennonites had been politically alienated through their stand on the war, and the prospects for their involvement in politics had been dimmed by their wartime difficulties with the broader political community.

Private channels for community action, however, remained open. As religious objectors to war, the Mennonites were especially sensitive to wartime destruction and suffering as they sought to reestablish a new civic identity. The characteristic Mennonite response was giving. They gave money so generously for war relief that their church conference officials had to scramble to find sufficient acceptable ways for disbursement. Between 1917 and 1920 the General Conference Emergency Relief Commission received 427 gifts from Kansas amounting to nearly $40,000, mostly designated for war sufferers. Only two of the contributions from individuals were above $200, which indicates that Mennonite relief was a broadly based grassroots program from the outset. Less than one-fifth of the contributions were designated specifically for Mennonite war victims.[1]

Mennonite benevolence went into its takeoff stage in 1920 when news arrived of the disastrous civil war and famine which threatened the existence of large populations in South Russia, including Mennonite communities to which many Kansas Mennonites traced their origins. The different Mennonite relief agencies across the country joined into a Mennonite Central Committee which coordinated a relief program to meet this need. Official agreements were made with the Soviet Government and with American relief agencies. Distribution centers were established. A flood of money, food, clothing, and farm equipment flowed from Mennonite America to Russia. The combined total of Mennonite wartime and postwar benevolence has been conservatively estimated at three million dollars.[2] The Mennonite Central Committee, after a relatively inactive period from 1925 to 1930, engaged in colonization efforts for Mennonite refugees in the 1930s and emerged as a major worldwide relief organization during and after the Second World War.[3]

The relationship of Mennonite benevolence to the problems of Mennonite political acculturation has frequently gone unobserved by scholars who have addressed themselves to the question of the sources of Mennonite giving. Most of the accounts of the development of MCC are descriptive rather than analytical; they are satisfied to see Mennonite relief programs simply as a natural outgrowth of Christian concern, "stemming out of the love of God and the love of neighbor. . . ."[4] An analysis by three leading Mennonite scholars in 1954 substantially affirmed the traditional view that Mennonite benevolence (or "altruism") was an expression of the historical religious principles of the group. From Anabaptist days onward, "the conscious cultivation of a disciplined brotherhood way of life rooted in a Biblical ethic" has resulted in altruistic mutual aid first within the body of Mennonites and then also among other needy persons.[5]

Leland Harder's 1962 dissertation continued the Mennonite reluctance to see their relief programs as a kind of acculturation. Although Harder dealt only briefly with Mennonite benevolence in his study of social change in the General Conference Mennonite Church, he fit the phenomenon into his general thesis that social change in the sect is accounted for not by theories of cultural contact but by an internal disequilibrium of norms within the sect. The Mennonites, he wrote, were committed both to the positive norm of peacemaking and to the negative norm of withdrawal or nonconformity. The Mennonite Central Committee "became a mechanism for restoring equilibrium" between the internal positive and negative norms.[6] Thus Mennonite relief appears as the fruitful product of internal sectarian contradictions and the attempt to overcome them. The impact of outside society is secondary.

Against the background of Mennonite experiences during the First World War, there is reason to reexamine the possibility that the root of Mennonite relief was a kind of acculturation, the result of contacts and pressures from American culture. What, after all, was the source of the positive impulse which created the Mennonite relief program? Why were Mennonites impelled to action at this particular time? And why were Mennonites enabled to sustain a remarkable program of benevolence in the succeeding decades of the twentieth century?

These questions cannot be answered adequately without reference to the fact that the war radically changed the Mennonite understanding of its relationship to the American community—the fact that the war forced Mennonites to accommodate to the nature of twentieth-century nationalism. World War I, as no previous war, established the right and responsibility of nations to mobilize the energies of their entire populations and to demand unconditional commitments and sacrifices for the achievement of national goals. For those who shared fully in the experience, it was an exhilarating enterprise which resolved personal doubts and confirmed the meaning of human existence. The stresses of war were compensated by the strengthening of belief in American political ideology. The war was a great act of community commitment.[7]

To their utmost discomfiture, the Mennonites could not participate in the invigorating national crusade. Their felt need for some corresponding positive act through which they, like their fellow Americans, could stand up among people without shame was at the core of their postwar behavior. P. C. Hiebert of Hillsboro, the first chairman of the Mennonite Central Committee, put it this way: "There was little satisfaction in just maintaining a negative position toward war. What was needed was an opportunity to disprove the charges of cowardice and selfishness made against the conscientious objectors, and to express in a positive, concrete way the principles of peace and goodwill. . . ."[8]

Not everyone agreed with Hiebert that the motivations of Mennonite relief programs were a credit to the community. One Mennonite scholar, Payson Miller of Indiana, raised the embarrassing question, "Did we do relief work because of actual concern for the needy, or to save our own faces?" Miller criticized this Mennonite "penance in the form of charity" and doubted whether Mennonite relief efforts would have been as successful had they not been directed in such a large degree to other suffering Mennonites.[9] Miller perhaps drew the dichotomy too strongly. Mennonite relief giving was *neither* disinterested Christian benevolence *nor* selfish penance. Both elements were present, and both were related to the process of Mennonite acculturation.

The acculturation of most German-Americans could be measured by their acceptance of the American call to wartime activity and sacrifice. The Mennonite response, however different, was likewise a step in acculturation. The form of Mennonite action—its expression as Christian benevolence rationalized in the terms of biblical discipleship, and its concentration upon inter-Mennonite assistance conceived as another event in the long history of mutual aid within the brotherhood—was a product of the internal ideology and unique historical experience of the community. The stimulus to Mennonite action—the urge to find a counterpart for the energies of nationalism—was a product of the communities' Americanization. In Harder's terms of the disequilibrium between the norms of positive peacemaking and negative withdrawal, the dynamic content of the positive norm came primarily from outside the Mennonite community. In succeeding, years, Mennonites faced the question of whether they could generate their own peace activities or whether their positive efforts for peace would remain a response to personal sacrifices demanded by American nationalism.[10]

VOTING PATTERNS AND OFFICEHOLDING, 1918-1940

Politics remained a peripheral interest in the Mennonite community throughout the twenties and thirties, perhaps because the Mennonites had found satisfactory substitutes for the expression of their social concerns, but also because the Mennonites' experience of what the political world had done for them was so thoroughly disillusioning. The Mennonite community, for whatever reason, remained as aloof from politics as it had been before the war. To all appearances, indeed, their political interests and involvements had diminished.

The unpopularity of politics among Mennonites was reflected in the fact that the community failed to produce replacements for J. G. Ewert, H. P. Krehbiel, and A. L. Schellenberg in these two decades. Before the war, these three men had provided the community with a fairly reliable diet of comment and counsel on leading political questions of the day. After World War I, the function of Mennonite political commentators gradually faded away or found other channels for expression. Ewert died in 1923, having burned out his incredible energies in the work of processing food and clothing remittances for the Mennonite relief program.[11] Krehbiel continued active church leadership and newspaper editorship in the twenties and thirties, but his political interests waned. He now gave greater attention to projects for Mennonite colonization, to an antipolitical formulation of the peace position, and to the preservation of Mennonite education from the evils of higher criticism and the theory of evolution. Schellenberg returned as *Vorwaerts* editor between 1923 and 1930, but his former political zeal showed only an occasional spark, as in the flicker of hope for a revival of Progressivism with the LaFollette candidacy in 1924. When Mennonite publishing interests fell into new hands, it was invariably taken up by men of narrower political interests and knowledge than that of the three editors of the Untroubled Generation.

The decline of politics as a topic in Mennonite newspapers may also have reflected the increasing ability of Mennonites to get what political information they wanted from non-Mennonite sources. The English-language press and radio found their way into increasing numbers of Mennonite homes as the gradual shift from German to English took place. The "critical year" of language change (i.e., the year in which most families with growing children ceased habitual use of German) was about 1935,[12] but English-language periodicals had long had a place in many Mennonite homes and had served as a source of information about the American political scene.[13] The Herald Publishing Company attempted to hold its share of the Mennonite reading market by initiating the English language

Mennonite Weekly Review in 1923, but the dependence of Mennonites upon outside American publications for secular news continued its steady increase.

The succession of Mennonite elected officials in county offices nearly died out after the war. In 1921 and 1922 the only Mennonite in county political office was Jacob J. Wiens, Marion County commissioner, who had been elected during the war in 1918 by a predominantly Mennonite district. Between 1920 and 1932 neither McPherson nor Harvey counties elected Mennonite county commissioners, although I. A. Toevs was elected clerk of the district court in McPherson in 1922 and J. J. Heidebrecht began a twenty-four year stint as probate judge for McPherson County in 1926. The numbers of Mennonites in county offices increased somewhat in the 1930s as wartime bitterness wore off. They never were able, however, to establish themselves in Harvey County politics. The claim that Mennonites were not getting their fair share of political representation continued to be true, but it also remained true that the Mennonites—with their distaste for politics—had primarily themselves to blame.

The predominant fact of Mennonite voting trends in national elections during the 1920s was their disaffection from the Democratic party. Percentage of Democratic votes in "Mennonite" townships in the elections of 1920, 1924, and 1928 dipped below 20 percent for the first time since 1880. James M. Cox, Democratic presidential candidate in 1920, got 17.5 percent; John W. Davis in 1924 got 14.8 percent; Alfred E. Smith in 1928 got 16 percent. These votes were less than the state Democratic vote by 15, 8.8, and 11.1 percentage points respectively. The small Mennonite Democratic vote, reduced from 33.6 percent for Woodrow Wilson in 1916, may have represented Mennonite reaction to the party in power when the United States went to war against Germany. The anti-Democratic reaction had been present already in the gubernatorial election of 1918 when the Socialist candidate for governor, George W. Kleihege, polled 16.7 percent of the Mennonite vote. In Risley Township (excluding the Hillsboro precinct) Kleihege got a strong majority, and in Menno Township (a Republican stronghold) he got 29.4 percent. It may be that some of the seventy-six Mennonites in Menno and West Branch townships who voted Socialist in 1918 were encouraged to do so by the thought that J. G. Ewert's Christian socialism was right after all. The Socialists were the only political people around who shared the Mennonite antipathy to the war. In this perspective, it is surprising that the Socialist vote among Mennonites in 1918 was so small, even though it was a state election.

A second fact that stands out on a chart of the Mennonite presidential votes in the 1920s is the strong vote for Robert LaFollette, the Progressive candidate, in 1924. LaFollette received a surprising 32.8 percent which was 17.9 percentage points higher than his percentage in Kansas as a whole. LaFollette's support came from normally Republican voters, for the Democratic Mennonite vote in 1920, 1924, and 1928 deviated less than three percentage points. What was the appeal of LaFollette among Mennonites?

LaFollette's Progressive platform for agrarian and industrial reforms swung little weight with Mennonites in a prosperous decade; the historical record yields no evidence at all that the LaFollette vote was an incipient Mennonite swing to the left. But LaFollette held the ultimate in political credentials as far as Mennonites were concerned. When the rest of America had betrayed the Mennonites by going to war against Germany, LaFollette had been a lonely, courageous opponent to the preparedness campaign and to the war resolution. The Mennonites had not forgotten. A. L. Schellenberg, again editor of *Vorwaerts,* supported LaFollette on the grounds that he was the candidate most friendly to the Germans.[14]

The Progressives got another assist in Kansas from the gubernatorial candidacy of William Allen White on an anti-Ku Klux Klan platform. After White aroused and entertained a Newton audience with a hard-hitting campaign speech, even the faithful Republican H. P. Krehbiel was led to endorse his candidacy and accept White's confident claim that he would be elected.[15] With the blessings of the two large Mennonite newspapers, White ran a shade behind LaFollette in the Mennonite townships and received 29.3 percent of the vote, about six percentage points higher than the average White vote in the state of Kansas.

By 1928 the political choices open to Mennonites had narrowed, and a degree of uniformity in political preferences had been achieved. The Democratic candidate of 1928 Alfred E. Smith got 16 percent of the vote in Mennonite townships, an increase of 1.2 percentage points over John W. Davis (the Democratic candidate of 1924) and only 1.5 percentage points less than James M. Cox (the Democratic candidate of 1920). Smith's Roman Catholicism apparently was no issue at all among Mennonites. None of the Mennonite newspapers rejected Smith for religious reasons. H. P. Krehbiel of *Der Herold* and Ferdinand J. Wiens of the *Mennonite Weekly Review* agreed that Prohibition was the main issue.[16] A. L. Schellenberg of *Vorwaerts* had run out of crusading steam. He endorsed neither candidate. With the Democrats demoralized and the Progressives no longer offering a third-party option, the Mennonites apparently had cast their lot with the Republican party.

The depression of the 1930s shattered whatever stability had been achieved in Mennonite political preferences. Although the conservative Mennonites lost no speculative financial empires in the stock market crash, they suffered together with the rest of rural America when farm prices dropped and sources of money to cover debts and operating losses disappeared. The local economy was helped somewhat, however, by two oil strikes in McPherson County. Some Mennonites, who owned land under which oil was found, benefited directly. Others had job opportunities on the oil fields and in the refineries built in McPherson. Between 1929 and 1935 the population of Turkey Creek Township, an entirely rural Mennonite area, grew from 525 to 1,028. For this section of the Mennonite central Kansas settlement, at least, the oil boom moderated the effects of the depression.[17]

The shocks of the depression were bound to produce less political differentiation of Mennonites from their American environment than did the shocks of World War I, for the Mennonites had no distinctive religious doctrine to govern their response. Mennonite religious directives regarding economic life were much less specific and compelling than the doctrine of nonresistance which prompted Mennonite nonconformity in the face of military service and domestic wartime requirements. To be sure, the Mennonites prized the values of industriousness, thrift, honesty, and individual effort. But they also carried a long tradition of mutual aid and assistance for the needy. The Mennonite mixture of individualism and mutuality was not specifically adapted to provide a doctrinal platform for ideological support either of the prevailing economic system or of New Deal innovations. The Mennonites simply knew they were pinched and they reacted much the same as everyone else, without regard for doctrine or ideology.

The depression brought to Kansas a political storm which made a shambles of all ideologies and forced politicians to reconsider their role as servants of the people. The name of the storm was the name of a man—Dr. John R. Brinkley. Brinkley was a quack doctor who built a millionaire's medical empire in Milford, Kansas, with the aid of a spectacular sex-rejuvenating operation which involved the transplant of goat glands into the human body. From his powerful radio station, KFKB (in Milford), Brinkley advertised his $750 operation and prescribed his drugs for ailing listeners on the basis of their letters. Vested interests were resentful. The *Kansas City Star* (suffering the loss of advertising revenues to KFKB) and the medical profession (suffering the loss of clientele) together mounted an overwhelming attack upon the flamboyant doctor and succeeded in revoking his licenses to practice medicine and to operate a radio station in Kansas. Then Brinkley decided to run for governor.

The regular party candidates in 1930 were unimaginative, unmarried, and unexciting—Republican Frank Haucke (a farmer-legislator) and Democrat Harry H. Woodring (a Neodesha banker). Neither understood the frustrations which were finding focus as Brinkley hopped across the state in his private airplane to promise the people free school textbooks, a lake in every county, lower taxes, medical care at cost, and an end to corrupt political machines. On election day, only six weeks after the doctor had announced his write-in candidacy, the people of Kansas gave him 183,278 votes, only 34,000 less than the borderline Democrat winner, Woodring. Most observers believed that enough write-in Brinkley ballots had been invalidated by party poll-counters to make up the difference. Everyone agreed that Brinkley would have been elected had his name been printed on the ballot. In Mennonite precincts Brinkley won decisively with 42.3 percent of the vote, over ten percentage points more than Haucke.

The Brinkley vote was a jolt to all who assumed the existence of a sane and sober electorate. William Allen White was moved to write of "a moronic underworld which cannot be civilized."[18] More to the point were reflections about a very civilized Kansas contempt for the ineffectual machinations of party politics. W. G. Clugston believed the Brinkley vote was an uprising of democracy against "tyrannical" pretensions of political parties.[19] P. H. Berg, the Mennonite editor of *Vorwaerts*, agreed. Brinkley was a man, he said, "who cares about the welfare and woes of the common people. We would advise future candidates to learn a lesson from this result and get busy in the service of the people. . . ."[20]

Only 9 of the 105 Kansas counties returned a higher percentage for the doctor than did the Mennonites. The Mennonites simply reflected to a greater degree the same characteristics that accounted for the surprising Brinkley vote in the state at large. Brinkley's rich radio voice, flamboyant personality, religious overtones, underdog appeal, and promises to do something for people hit by the depression contributed to his success among Mennonites as among other Kansans. But Mennonites may have had a special motive which was rooted in their mistrust of politics and politicians. Even the Progressive Mennonites, who were supposedly emancipated from the church-world dualism which dictated complete political withdrawal, continued to reflect their heritage by voting a protest against politics when given a clear opportunity. The Brinkley campaign, fundamentally a protest against politics in a time when politicians seemed unable to mend the ripping seams of the American economic and social order, attracted the Mennonite vote.

The political establishment was prepared by the time of Brinkley's second campaign for governor in 1932. A heavy mixture of ridicule and slander took its toll on Brinkley's respectability, and he fell short of election again by about 34,000 votes. He had had a longer campaign and his name was printed on the ballot this time; he did manage to garner 30 percent of the vote. The Mennonite vote for Brinkley dropped from 42.3 percent to 30.1 percent, about the state average. The Mennonites were fed up and restless, but apparently no more so than other Kansans, and at least not enough to place trust in a man who was looking more and more like a crackpot.[21]

In the 1930s the numbers of Mennonites running for local offices picked up somewhat and actually exceeded the numbers involved in campaigns during the Progressive era. In the election of 1934, for example, six Mennonites were elected or reelected to McPherson and Marion County offices, four Mennonites failed in campaign attempts, and one incumbent was not up for reelection. All but one of these candidates were Republicans. In that same year P. A. Hiebert (a Republican of Marion County) failed, and J. A. Schowalter (a Harvey County Democrat) succeeded in elections for state representative. The numbers of Mennonites running for offices fell off sharply during the Second World War.

Schowalter and Leon H. Harms, a Hillsboro merchant who served a single term in 1937, were the two Mennonites who were elected to the Kansas House of Representatives between the wars. A wealthy bachelor-farmer, Schowalter wore a red tie on the house floor and wrote notes for speeches on the backs of envelopes in order to save paper.[22] His three-term legislative career was somewhat less distinguished than his money-making investments, which made him a millionaire. A depression Democrat from a Republican constituency in a Republican legislature, Schowalter introduced a total of six bills, none of which were enacted into law. Three of the bills dealt with financial matters, particularly the legal relationship of landlord and renter.[23] There is little evidence that Schowalter found specific ways of realizing his high ideal to "put more Christianity into our political life." Unlike those Mennonites for whom the political life led away from adherence to distinctive Mennonite doctrines, Schowalter retained his simple and rough-hewn belief in nonresistance. "To *Reform* with a *Gun is redigulas!*" he wrote in notes for a speech. He appealed to the church to come out of "seclution" and apply its saving message for world peace. He willed his million-dollar estate to three Mennonite conferences for church work, including the cause of peace.[24]

In 1934 a state vote to repeal the Prohibition law gave Kansas voters an opportunity for an unambiguous vote on a question which frequently complicated multi-issue campaigns in the 1920s and 1930s. Kansas voters rejected Prohibition repeal decisively by a vote of 436,688 (55.7 percent) to 347,644 (44.3 percent). In predominately Mennonite precincts it was no contest: 3,013 (75.3 percent) against repeal to 989 (24.7 percent) in favor.

The opportunity to vote on a clear-cut moral issue brought to the polls Mennonites who had never voted before and who, even in this election, refused to cast a "political vote." The Mennonite voter turnout in 1934 was higher than in any nonpresidential election year before or since, and 312 of those voters who cast an anti-repeal ballot did not vote for governor.

The Mennonites were not alone in their high voter turnout in 1934, for more Kansans in general voted in that election (70.3 percent of eligible voters)[25] than in any previous nonpresidential election year. The Prohibition issue undoubtedly accounted for the large vote, because Alfred M. Landon's successful bid for a second term as governor did not generate extraordinary political interest. Over four thousand more votes were cast for governor than on the Prohibition question, which indicates that there were few, if any, Kansans who joined Mennonites in marking "No" to Prohibition repeal on an otherwise blank ballot.

The high Mennonite vote against repeal neither proves nor dis-
proves political acculturation. The Swedes in northern McPherson
County also voted over 70 percent against repeal, and this was over
two decades after the Swedish party vote in state and national elections had begun to approximate the Kansas norm.[26] What was
distinctive among Mennonites was the conservative traditionalist
minority who voted on Prohibition but not for political candidates.
The persistence of Mennonite nonvoting in regular elections indicated that this minority was a significant element in Mennonite
community political behavior.

The 1932 presidential election saw Kansans, including the Mennonites, deserting traditional Republicanism to vote for Franklin D.
Roosevelt. The aging H. P. Krehbiel, editorializing for the last time
in a presidential campaign, tried to stem the tide with warnings
against the repeal of Prohibition and against political experiments to
deal with the "temporary" depression.[27] P. H. Berg of *Vorwaerts*,
who endorsed a mixed list of Democrats and Republicans for state
and local offices, could not bring himself to recommend either
Hoover or Roosevelt. Hoover was a defender of capitalists who
vainly tried to help the country by making more debts. Roosevelt's
platform was "dripping wet" and *Vorwaerts* would never support
liquor.[28] Thoroughly dissatisfied with both presidential candidates,
Mennonites nevertheless joined fellow Kansans in a record voter
turnout and an unprecedented Democratic vote. The percentages
for Roosevelt were almost exactly the same: Mennonites, 53.3 percent; Kansas, 53.6 percent. In West Branch Township, the number
of Democratic votes increased tenfold from 1928 (from 4 to 40), but
Roosevelt still received only 16.3 percent in this shaken Republican
stronghold. Mound Township in McPherson County meanwhile
gave 66 percent for Roosevelt. Roosevelt swept along Democratic
gubernatorial candidate Woodring in Mennonite precincts. Woodring got 40.7 percent, whereas the Republican, Alf Landon, ran
behind Brinkley with 28.8 percent. The Mennonites, like their state
and nation, were ready to give the Democrats a chance.

It is not possible to reconstruct the attitude of Mennonites toward
Roosevelt and the New Deal on the basis of their editorial political
commentary, simply because they refrained from comment. The
chart of Mennonite voting tells a clearer story. The break in Mennonite voting patterns came in 1940. From 1932 to 1936 the Mennonite Roosevelt vote dipped somewhat, from 53.3 percent to 44.5

percent, while the Kansas Roosevelt vote remained about the same. But in 1940 the Mennonites dropped Roosevelt with a thud. They gave him a mere 17.6 percent (less than 3 percent in Menno and West Branch townships) compared to 81 percent for Willkie. Four years later Roosevelt's Mennonite vote dropped below 15 percent.

The chart for state gubernatorial elections gives the same picture. In 1936 and 1938 the Mennonite vote for Republican candidates Will G. West and Payne Ratner hovered around 50 percent, about the same as the Kansas average. But suddenly in 1940 the Mennonite vote (Payne Ratner for second term) shot up to 70.5 percent, over twenty percentage points more than the Kansas average. Throughout the 1940s, this Republican margin in Mennonite gubernatorial election votes was maintained. The Kansas Mennonites, as never before in their history, became a distinctively Republican-voting community.

That 1940 began a new era in Kansas Mennonite voting behavior is abundantly evident. There is little reason to believe that the 1940 Mennonite flight from the Democrats was a negative ideological reaction to the New Deal on grounds of Mennonite beliefs in individual enterprise, honest budget-balancing, or some such conservative doctrine. Had this been the case, Roosevelt would not have come within 5.6 percent of a majority among Mennonites in 1936. The 1940 switch was probably not economically motivated, for farm prices were higher in 1940 than they had been in years. There is more evidence that Mennonites feared the implications of the third term. Menno Schrag, editor of the *Mennonite Weekly Review* which usually avoided political comment, obliquely connected the third-term issue with "the totalitarian trends which have been set in motion all over the world." This trend, said Schrag, "is all important." [29] Mennonite fear of Roosevelt's increasing power may have been reinforced by the influence of Gerald B. Winrod, a fundamentalist evangelist who linked Roosevelt with the Jewish-Communist conspiracy and who had a considerable following among Mennonites.

The overriding issue for the Mennonite community in the election of 1940 was the Second World War. The war really began for Mennonites not with the German blitz of Poland in September 1939, nor with the Japanese attack on Pearl Harbor in December 1941, but rather with the passage of the Burke-Wadsworth Bill for universal compulsory military training on September 16, 1940. America was preparing for war and Mennonites again were forced into the awful situation of public declaration that they could not join America in the undertaking. True, the Mennonites in 1940 had the legal option of an alternative to military service, but the community which watched its young men register for the draft just two weeks before election now saw its hopes for peace and for an unquestioned claim to the rights of American citizenship going down the drain. America was heading for war, and Mennonites again were strangers and pilgrims in the world. And it happened under a Democratic administration which had promised better, just as in 1917.

The Mennonites' public articulation of their fear and anger was scarcely audible, perhaps because they hoped it was not really true. But their votes said they saw war coming, even if they did not admit it otherwise. At Bethel College, where students coming into draft age apprehended an uncertain future, Roosevelt in a straw vote polled only 16.6 percent, and Norman Thomas, the antiwar Socialist candidate, polled 25.3 percent. It mattered little that Willkie's campaign foreign policy was hardly distinguishable from Roosevelt's. For Mennonites, war was an emotional issue. The Mennonite vote of 1940 was a negative reaction to an undesirable political course. That vote clearly set a pattern of Mennonite deviation from the state norm for 2½ decades to come. Mennonite voting by political party abruptly became more distinctive than it ever had been before.

INTERWAR PACIFISM

The experiences of the First World War blunted the sanguine hopes of Mennonites who had expected the approach of a warless world. The Mennonite interest in pacifism, nevertheless, remained a predominant, if chastened, concern of the community in the post-World War I period. The difference was that Mennonites after the war were more insistent that world peace could come only through Christianity. Humanitarian pacifists who sought peace "outside Christ" were suspect. The political details of a world order based on Christian principles were unclear, but the kernel of optimism that such an order was possible remained to encourage Mennonite pacifists.

John W. Kliewer, president of Bethel College from 1911 to 1920 and from 1925 to 1932, outlined his position in a "Sermon on Christian After War Questions" on January 5, 1919, less than two months after the armistice declaration.[30] Kliewer, whose forthright peace campaigning had earlier included a pacifist address to a local Grand

Army of the Republic (G.A.R.) post, was both urgent and optimistic.[31] "We must Christianize our international thinking," he said,
"or our international thinking will paganize our Christianity." With
the smoke of battle still drifting over Europe, with Mennonite draftees still in federal prison for refusing the uniform, and with the John
Schrag espionage case a fresh memory, President Kliewer stubbornly
insisted that Christianization of the international order was a live
possibility.

The evils to be overcome in future years, Kliewer said, were four-
fold: war, militarism, selfish nationalism, and spiritual indifference.
Hidden in his sermon text were several political issues upon which
Christians should take a stand: support for the League of Nations,
inclusion of Germany in the league, disarmament, and resistance to
universal military training. More specific than this the Mennonites
in succeeding years would not get. Their interwar pacifism was a
generalized moral appeal which was conspicuous for the absence of
definite political proposals. Kliewer's 1919 sermon, filled with dis-
gust for war and with continued hope for peace, set a tone for Mennonite pacifism in the interwar period.

C. E. Krehbiel, editor of *Der Herold*, shared Kliewer's interest in
the League of Nations. Although his coverage of national and international news was scanty, Krehbiel hailed the league's constitution as
a document of "epochmaking importance." He filled the entire front
page of *Der Herold* with the text of the constitution. Where Kliewer
was all urgency, Krehbiel was hesitant and a bit plaintive, but no
less encouraging. "Is it not true in the light of this," he asked,
"despite present isolated propaganda here against the conscientious
objectors, that one can view the future hopefully?"[32]

The election of 1920, which President Wilson had hoped would
become a national referendum on the League of Nations, did not
give the Mennonites or the country an opportunity for clear expression of approval or disapproval of the U.S. Senate's vote against the
league. Domestic concerns pushed international issues off the state,
and the Democratic candidate (James M. Cox) was ineffectual
against the popular appeal of Warren G. Harding's comforting call
for a return to normalcy. When C. E. Krehbiel reviewed the campaign he failed to include the league among the three most important
issues: militarism, Prohibition, and the labor question.[33] J. G. Ewert,
participating in his last presidential campaign, said the two main
issues in 1920 were militarism and capitalism; he detailed Harding's

bad Senate record on both counts.[34] As if to balance Ewert's anti-Republicanism, Editor J. D. Fast of *Vorwaerts* printed an unsigned front-page preelection article which condemned Cox as an enemy of German-speaking people for his wartime opposition to German classes in Ohio schools.[35] It was not difficult for Mennonites to find arguments *against* political candidates in 1920.

As was so often true, H. P. Krehbiel came closest to laying his finger on the central issue regarding the League of Nations. The heart of the matter, he wrote, lies in the league's power to use force in suppression of belligerent nations. Such exercise of military power —the attempt to drive out war with more war ("Krieg mit Gegenkrieg zu beseitigen")—contradicted Krehbiel's pacifist principles. "Whoever really wants to take a position according to the teachings of Jesus," Krehbiel wrote, "cannot therefore consistently speak in favor of Article X."[36] Krehbiel voted for Harding in 1920 because Cox favored a League of Nations which proposed to enforce peace by military means.

The average Mennonite farmer knew very little about the League of Nations and what United States membership in such an international organization might imply. More significant was the fact that the Democratic Administration was identified with a war which was exceedingly unpopular among Mennonites. The Mennonite vote for Harding in 1920 was 73.2 percent, almost exactly the same percentage as the Roosevelt vote of 1904, and 8.4 percentage points above the Kansas Harding vote.

The peace interest among Mennonites in the postwar years came to be expressed most often and most clearly on the college campuses. With the exception of H. P. Krehbiel's personal writing on the peace question, the colleges at Hesston, Hillsboro, and North Newton seemed to have a corner on the articulation of Mennonite concerns for world peace. This, of course, was no accident, for the colleges were the communities' contact with the world, the places where Mennonite young people became acquainted with ideas and events beyond ethnic circles, and the channel for many a young person's escape from the community and entry into American society. Bethel College at North Newton was the Mennonite college most academically advanced, most secularized, most afflicted with the modernist-fundamentalist split, and also most aware of national and international peace problems.

Prior to the Washington Armament Conference of 1921 the Bethel

College students and faculty adopted a resolution expressing appreciation to President Harding for calling the conference. The resolution illustrated perfectly the Mennonite tendency to place hopes for peace in the universal acceptance of an overarching peace principle rather than in the working out of political details for disarmament and the administration of a new world order. The resolution called for not only the limited aim of "reduction of armaments" but also for the conference to "lead the world toward permanent peace by the adjustment of international problems on a basis of cooperation and goodwill and by a declaration that war should be outlawed and made an international crime. . . ."[37] The expectation that the nations of the world would suddenly transcend the ambiguities of international politics and order their affairs according to some great moral declaration was, of course, characteristic not only of the Mennonites but of the entire peace movement in the interwar period. A nationwide peace oration contest, organized with eliminations on the campus and state levels, provided opportunity for bright Bethel students to wax eloquent on prospects for a warless world. Many of the students who participated in the peace oration contests later became leaders in the peace interests of Mennonites. "The spirit of cooperation is fast permeating all human society," said Philip A. Wedel in his prize-winning oration of 1923. "The age of provincialism is past."[38] The 1925 winner, Albert J. Penner, took second place in the national contest with an oratorical denunciation of nationalism and imperialism and with his appeal to the principle of love. "We have tried man's way—selfishness—and we have utterly failed; and God's way—LOVE—it has never been tried."[39]

Bethel was proud of her orators. The *Bethel College Monthly*, edited by German and Bible Professor Abraham Warkentin, said, "Bethelites have a right to be proud to feel that their institution, which is a living evidence of their sacred principle of peace, should have representatives who can so ably present her ideals."[40] Throughout the twenties and thirties Bethel College promoted peace interests through continuing series of prominent peace speakers, celebration of special occasions such as "World Court Week,"[41] student participation in YMCA-YWCA peace conferences,[42] and continued interest in the broader peace movement throughout the country.[43]

Occasional straw votes at national election time revealed that the Bethel faculty and student body expressed this peace interest in socialist votes. Among the twenty-one faculty straw voters in 1928, nine

(44.4 percent) voted for Socialist Norman Thomas. Senior class members, showing the greater influence of their liberal teachers, also voted over 40 percent for Thomas, while the student body as a whole reflected popular Republican Mennonite sentiment with 75.5 percent for Hoover.[44]

The peace interests of Bethel College received a special boost in 1933 when Dr. Emmet L. Harshbarger of Ohio joined the faculty as professor of history. A stimulating teacher and public lecturer on contemporary social and political topics, Harshbarger gathered around himself a following of students charged with the liberal reform vision. "We had adequate solutions to man's three big problems," remembered one of Harshbarger's students of the late '30s, Esko Loewen. "We had socialism to solve the political problem, the cooperative movement to solve the economic problem, and pacifism to solve the religious problem." The rise of Hitler and Mussolini seemed no insuperable obstacle to this optimistic liberal mind. Dictatorships and democracies alike would respond positively if only the Christian way were tried in national and international politics.[45]

Harshbarger's most ambitious and most successful peace promotion project was his deanship of the Kansas Institute of International Relations hosted by Bethel College from 1936 through 1940. The ten-day June institutes were designed as adult education programs and attempted to involve Mennonite church and community leaders with peace-minded people of different denominations throughout Kansas. Sponsorship by the American Friends Service Committee enabled the institutes to obtain as speakers such internationally known figures as Dr. Eduard Benes, former president of Czechoslovakia; Dr. Sidney B. Fay, Harvard professor and expert on the origins of World War I, and Clarence Streit, New York *Times* correspondent and advocate of a North Atlantic federal union. Harshbarger sold the program to the churches as an opportunity for peace propagandizing: ". . . The Institute gives the Mennonites the very best way to carry their message directly to non-Mennonite church, community, and educational leaders who would not otherwise come into contact with this Mennonite principle."[46]

The institute enlisted the support and participation of the surrounding community, including the Mennonite constituency, in various ways. Institute stationery claimed as "sponsors" a long list of prominant Kansans including Governor Henry J. Allen, Editor William Allen White, and Kansas University Chancellor E. H.

Lindley. The Newton Chamber of Commerce, nearly two decades removed from the First World War when Mennonite pacifism was anathema downtown, unanimously pledged support for the first institute in 1936.[47] Financial support to cover the $2,000 costs not covered by institute tuition was solicited from church groups, businessmen, peace societies, and individual Mennonites. When the 1937 institute came up $200 short of meeting its budget, Harshbarger wrote to Senator Arthur Capper in Washington asking him to make up the difference.[48]

Full-time enrollment at the institutes ranged from 135 to 89, but the open sessions with prominent speakers occasionally drew over a thousand guests. Local Mennonite ministers from the area were among the considerable group of part-time participants. Although there was some criticism about "the neighboring preachers who love to sleep late" and therefore often arrived "too late to hear the best lectures on the program,"[49] the institute programs provided Mennonites with their closest personal acquaintance with the issues, attitudes, and personalities in the peace movement.

The negative reaction of certain quarters of the Mennonite community to the institute was as revealing about Mennonite peace attitudes as was the fact that the community was willing to attend and support the program for five years. The Reverend P. H. Richert was disturbed by the rumor (which turned out to be false) that the Japanese Christian Kagawa, "an extreme evolutionist," would be an institute speaker. "I am afraid that his appearance on the program will hurt our school even in Newton," wrote Richert. "If Christ is a product of evolution, then he is not the Son of God nor the Saviour."[50] M. Horsch, a Mennonite minister of Beatrice, Nebraska, had a more relevant complaint in his criticism of "the commonly accepted popular pacifist idea that *we* can bring about a warless world by human effort." A participant in the 1936 institute, Horsch detected "a subtle perhaps unconscious intolerance" against those who rejected this premise of humanitarian pacifism.[51] Criticism of another type came from a Bethel faculty member, J. R. Thierstein, who was disturbed by the anti-German bias of the institute, especially one British speaker. "Get a Nazi from Germany to tell the other side of that country," suggested Thierstein. "Englishmen are Englishmen. Let's hear from a real German."[52]

When the institute of 1940 met, Europe was at war and President Roosevelt was urging American preparedness. Criticism of the institute mounted on all sides. Former sponsors Henry Allen and William Allen White were counted among the critics of the institute.[53] Funds were harder to raise for peace education. The Bethel College administration had second thoughts about the wisdom of connections with such a peace witness if they jeopardized public relations. Mennonite criticism increased yearly until in 1939 reports were circulated that Dr. Benes, the highlighted speaker of that year, was "friendly to Communism and . . . therefore a dangerous man."[54] After 1940 Bethel College cut off its connection with the institute. The pretext for dropping the program was doctrinal. "The position of Bethel College and the constituency was that . . . peace can be built only on a positively Christian basis. . . ."[55] The coming of the war was the primary problem, however. It was safer to avoid discussion of pacifism and international relations and to focus upon the narrower question of religious conscientious objection and refusal of military service.

Harshbarger's assumption that there was, in fact, a Mennonite peace witness which could be transmitted through the international relations institute movement was, of course, open to question. In a general sense the Mennonites had cultivated a special peace concern which might be communicated to other Americans. And on a specific individual level there was the tradition of conscientious objection to military service which might interest non-Mennonite peace enthusiasts. But there was no body of Mennonite thought which had anything at all specific to say about political or diplomatic decisions facing national governments. The Mennonites had more to learn than to teach about international relations.

Competing against the rise of secular peace interests among Kansas Mennonites throughout the interwar period was the impact of the fundamentalist movement. Fundamentalism had its beginnings among Kansas Mennonites already before the First World War, but it gained its genuine toehold in the immediate postwar years in a fight against modernism and evolution. The fundamentalist-modernist controversy dealt a severe blow to the prewar consensus in Mennonite social and political attitudes. Prominent Mennonite leaders fearfully speculated that their already splintered denomination faced another division.[56]

Neither fundamentalism nor modernism was a native Mennonite product. The Mennonites failed to produce representatives who would conform to either the fundamentalist or the modernist stereotype. Mennonite fundamentalists usually retained a potentially radical belief in nonresistance which sharply distinguished them from their American fundamentalist friends. Mennonite modernists remained quite traditional in their basic Christian convictions—there was no Mennonite Clarence Darrow. But some Mennonite scholars had been off to graduate schools such as the University of Chicago where they were taught to come to terms with the theories of modern science, including higher biblical criticism and the theory of evolution. Some of them returned to teach at Bethel College. Other older Mennonites of more limited education and acquaintance outside of the Mennonite community had read conservative religious periodicals which warned against the new evils which were undermining the Christian faith. Such men held control of the Bethel College board of directors. A conflict was inevitable.

The tension between the Bethel faculty and board came to a head in 1919 when the board forced the resignations of two faculty members, Samuel Burkhard (acting dean) and Cornelius C. Regier (history and social sciences), on grounds of their unorthodox religious beliefs. A mass faculty resignation in support of Burkhard and Regier was narrowly averted as indignant professors protested the board's action.[57] The Bethel board of directors won the day and the college was restored, at least for a time, to safety and orthodoxy. Prospective liberal teachers knew they were not wanted; professors who did not like the fundamentalist straitjacket left quietly; the Mennonite churches through the Western District Conference (GC) established closer control over the college. Throughout the twenties and thirties, a science or Bible teacher at Bethel College (or Hesston and Tabor) could not openly and safely declare acceptance of the theory of evolution or seek natural causes for biblical miracles.[58]

The paradox of Mennonite fundamentalism was that although it paraded as an attempt to preserve time-honored community traditions and beliefs, it actually represented a quite new and characteristically American set of attitudes. It was from their American fundamentalist friends and not from their Anabaptist forebears that Kansas Mennonites around 1920 learned to make biblical literalism an end in itself, to worry over the details of millenialism, to suspect higher learning, and to hang the significance of Jesus on the question of His virgin birth. Fundamentalism, therefore, was as decisive— though less obviously—a product of Mennonite acculturation as was the modernist scientific heresy which made its way into the community by way of higher education.[59]

One major barrier that stood in the way of full Mennonite conversion to the fundamentalist movement was the doctrine of nonresistance. Some of the most fundamentalistically inclined of Mennonite leaders, including H. P. Krehbiel and P. H. Richert, could never
quite come to terms with the fundamentalist movement because it
was not nonresistant. The fundamentalists' unquestioning acceptance of nationalistic militarism became a special problem for Men-
onites at the approach of the Second World War. P. H. Richert,
after two decades of friendly attitudes toward the fundamentalist
schools, wrote to a fundamentalist Mennonite friend in 1940, "You
mention Wheaton and Moody schools. They justify war, and it is
almost impossible to separate war from hate. John says, 'Whoso
hateth his brother is a murderer, and ye know that no murderer
hath eternal life abiding in him.' "[60] H. P. Krehbiel remained
equally true to Mennonite nonresistance in the crisis and equally
dismayed by the failure of American fundamentalists to understand
that participation in war contradicted the commands of Jesus and
the will of God.

There is something instructive in Richert's proof-text condem-
nation of fundamentalist schools; it shows how Richert had adopted
the typical fundamentalist method of biblical literalism even while
rejecting fundamentalist unconcern with nonresistance. Traditional
Mennonite nonresistance was based on a biblically grounded ethic of
love as a way of life.[61] Under the influence of fundamentalism, the
biblical grounding became a matter of strict literal interpretations of
specific texts. The Mennonite fundamentalist mind was impelled to
explain the "difficult Scripture passages" throughout the Bible which
contradicted nonresistance. P. H. Richert agonized long over
troublesome Bible verses which had been of no bother to earlier
Mennonites who were not bound by the necessity to justify every
biblical word as literally true.[62]

The impact of fundamentalism as a form of acculturation was
only marginally relevant to the question of Mennonite political acculturation. The fundamentalist influence certainly gave the Mennonites
no encouragement to become more politically involved, for fundamentalists disdained the social gospel movement which sought the
salvation of humanity outside of the redemptive blood of Christ.
Fundamentalism did serve to shake a few Mennonites and congregations loose from their traditional doctrine of nonresistance. The work

of fundamentalist-patriot Gerald B. Winrod among Mennonites eventually became a genuine political temptation for many Mennonites. In ways not easily definable or measurable, the impact of fundamentalism was to further acclimate Mennonites to the American political community, especially to one set of nationalistic ideals or values which saw America as a last bastion of Christian fundamental beliefs in a world beset by international socialism, Communism, and atheism.

The impact of fundamentalism was particularly interesting in the thought of H. P. Krehbiel, who summed up his pacifist convictions in 1937 in a 350-page privately published book, *War, Peace, Amity.* The book was Krehbiel's personal capstone to a career of undiminished interest in peace and his plea to the world for positive action to end the scourge of war. Unfortunately, the book lacked the stylistic unity and ideological consistency necessary for a lasting influence. But more importantly, Krehbiel foundered on a monumental contradiction which he could only solve through an unwarranted optimism in the efficacy of the witness of individual Christian behavior. The contradiction, which was a product of Krehbiel's indomitable Progressive belief in the capacity of man to solve his problems as well as of his fundamentalist twist to the Anabaptist church-state doctrines, contributes to an understanding of why the Mennonites remained aloof from politics long after they had begun to act like Americans in so many other ways.

On one hand, Krehbiel retained and actually increased his pre-World War faith that mankind would eventually achieve peace. The war, he believed, was "the climax of man's militant criminality," but in that awful event history had turned a corner. "Need man forever remain in bondage to the sinister forces, antagonistic to those things that are right, pure, true, holy? No, the case is not hopeless. The day is approaching which the prophet foresaw . . . 'They shall beat their swords into plowshares. . . .' "[63] The coming "era of true peace and tranquility" was not consigned to the millennium but was the natural growth of certain forces already in process. "Nationalism is losing as against Internationalism. Friendship with all nations is a growing ideal."[64] Krehbiel's vision of the future warless world remained the primary inspiration for his gospel of peace. His liberal optimism remained in spite of his capitulation to fundamentalistic fears on other points.

Parallel to his persistent belief that the world was headed toward peace, Krehbiel nursed a thorough disillusionment with political reform as a means to achieving that goal. Yes, he admitted, international leagues, treaties, and pacts had made "some progress," but the problem that international diplomatic agreements and decisions "depend finally for enforcement upon the employment of armed pressure."[65] Krehbiel's pacifism did not allow him to accept military enforcement of peace. "Some other compelling force must be added. . . ." The church itself, moreover, could not contribute to a political solution, for the church was to stay out of politics. "The Church as such may not enter the field of Politics, Business, Social Reform, Labor Issues nor any other functions of activities which properly belong under the direction of the State."[66] Krehbiel believed the church should "confine itself to the spiritual and ethical realm."[67]

There was an apparent contradiction between Krehbiel's overflowing optimism for the coming world peace and his disillusionment with governments and the church as instruments of political reform. Krehbiel attempted to bridge this contradiction, but he finally failed to offer satisfactory grounds to sustain his hopes for world peace. His answer was simply that all Christians should and could begin behaving like real Christians. Somehow a great worldwide revival of Christian conviction and behavior would lead individuals to follow Jesus' way of love and reject the way of militarism. And what of politics? The ambiguities of politics miraculously dissolved in Krehbiel's vision of the coming peace. "If all the Christians the world over be thoroughly and fully instructed and grounded in all of Jesus' doctrines of love then will there be no more war between Christian nations, no violence across borders. But all international differences will be adjusted in friendly conversations."[68] Without batting an eyelash, Krehbiel leaped from the possibility of widespread individual moral rectitude to the virtual certainty of future international harmony. Political details were unimportant. Krehbiel put great stock in the growing peace movement among the churches but did not worry about how that movement could be administratively effective in world affairs. He did mention in passing that it was a "small group of diplomats and statesmen" who kept a "deadly stranglehold" on the people and led them to war, but he did not explain how the conspiracy could be converted to Christian love or how they could be dealt with in case they proved recalcitrant.[69]

Reviews of *War, Peace, Amity* in Mennonite religious papers seemed more impressed by Krehbiel's aversion to political solutions

than by his social optimism.[70] J. R. Thierstein of *The Mennonite*
read into the book a conclusion Krehbiel had not stated, "that man-
made peace will not avail."[71] Krehbiel did believe that Christian man
could achieve peace, but his book came to mark the dead end of
optimistic liberal Mennonite nonresistance. Krehbiel's optimism was
a tarnished remnant from his happy youthful years in the Progressive
era. His rejection of the church's role in politics was a curious mixture of Anabaptist church-state doctrine and fundamentalist aversion
to the social gospel. The two themes were irreconcilable. Whoever
would try to pick up the pieces of Mennonite nonresistance after the
Second World War would have to begin from a new starting point.

THE LURE OF RIGHT-WING PATRIOTISM

In 1938, Kansas fundamentalists had a chance to vote for one of
their own in an election for national office. Their man of the hour
was Gerald B. Winrod (1900-1957), candidate in the Republican
primary for United States senator. The son of a repentant Wichita
bartender whose saloon had been smashed by Carry Nation, Winrod
began a successful evangelistic career while still a teenager. By 1925
he had established sufficient reputation and authority among Kansas
fundamentalists that he was able to unite their scattered forces in a
new nondenominational organization, "The Defenders of the
Christian Faith."[72] As executive secretary, Winrod took chief responsibility for editing the organization's monthly magazine, *The
Defender,* for planning regional conferences, and for soliciting funds.
The name of the organization betrayed the mind-set of the founder.
Christianity, Winrod believed, was on the defensive. A sense of fear,
originally a generalized doctrine regarding the besieged condition of
the gospel, eventually became a personal obsession with Winrod. He
provided himself with a bodyguard and kept weapons handy for use
against enemies who were supposedly following him.[73] Winrod's personal insecurity, as well as his sense of the plight of the world, were
summed up in his biographer's paraphrase of John the Baptist, "Re-
pent, for the *Kingdom of hell* is at hand."[74]

The antidote for insecurity was self-confidence, and the pages of
The Defender resounded with the shrill certainty of embattled truth.
From 1926 to 1928 Winrod focused primarily upon religious issues—
the relation of science and religion, the godlessness of the intellectuals,
the fundamental doctrines which must be preserved at all cost.[75] The
Prohibition issue, which reached a peak in the Smith-Hoover campaign of 1928, was the bridge to a second stage (1928-1933) in

which Winrod shifted interest to political questions. Most often he conceived political issues in terms of great world movements—fascism, Communism, Nazism, revolution, war. In the interpretation of world events he could achieve desired certainty only by integrating religion and politics in an apocalyptic framework which placed current leaders and movements in roles fulfilling specific biblical prophecies for the end time of world upheaval. In January 1933, Winrod announced the discovery which completed his interpretive scheme and unlocked the mysteries of contemporary history. "Behind the scenes," he wrote, "there is *A Hidden Hand*."[76] This international conspiracy of wealthy Communist Jews, Winrod believed, planned to overthrow the present world order and establish a world dictatorship based at Palestine. From 1933 on, Winrod's anti-Semitic conspiracy theory inspired all his interpretations of political events, from the notion that Roosevelt was a Jew who was planning dictatorship for the United States to the belief that Hitler's Nazism was Europe's salvation from Communism.

The Mennonites were passive rather than active in their relationship to the Defender movement. Their influence was supportive, not formative. No Mennonites were active in the founding of the movement, nor did any exert noticeable influence upon the policies or doctrinal emphases of the organization. But the Mennonites were faithful supporters of the movement from the outset and provided Winrod with sure proof that his message was falling on fertile soil in rural Kansas. When J. W. Kliewer, former president of Bethel College, complained that Winrod was leading the Mennonites toward Nazism and draining support from Mennonite institutions, a member of Bethel's board of directors, P. H. Richert, answered, "What Winrod emphasizes is that Hitler saved Germany from bolshevism, and he gives him credit for it, as we no doubt all do. . . . I do not think that Winrod has hurt Bethel with his paper. . . ." Kliewer's criticism, which had appeared in a manuscript of his autobiography, was dropped.[77]

Winrod's fight against modernism and evolution won the support of many Mennonites. Professor A. E. Janzen of Tabor College, who later became president of that school (1935-1942), was the highest placed Mennonite in the Defender organization as chairman of the textbook committee formed in 1927. Janzen's committee was entrusted with the task of investigating and exposing public schoolbooks tainted with the theory of evolution. Janzen, who shared with

Winrod a special interest in premillennial eschatology,[78] reported in *The Defender* on the activities of his committee, but no successful purge of undesirable books from public schools was ever carried out.[79]

The Mennonite publishing houses provided the communities' closest link with the Defender movement. The Mennonite Brethren Publishing House in Hillsboro printed *The Defender* for a time during its early period, and the Herald Publishing Company of Newton won this lucrative job from 1931 to 1942. Winrod's most frequent Mennonite contact, therefore, was his association with Mennonites involved in the publishing business, such as Peter H. Berg of Hillsboro and H. P. Krehbiel, Gerhard Willms, and Menno Schrag of Newton.[80] During the financially tight depression years, the Herald Publishing Company became heavily dependent upon the business of *The Defender,* which reached a total of 100,000 copies per month in 1937.[81] By 1940 the threats to *The Defender* business represented by Winrod's domestic difficulties and growing public antipathy to his politics had taught the company a lesson. The report to the trustees of the company in that year stated, ". . . We must look for other business along with Dr. Winrod's. . . ."[82]

Most Mennonite homes subscribed to *The Defender* and many Mennonites were among those who made special gifts to the movement.[83] Winrod was a popular speaker in Mennonite churches and knew how to open Mennonite pocketbooks with appeals for funds in the midst of the depression. Mennonite newspapers carried advertisements for his meetings.[84] Mennonite names occasionally appeared as special contributors who made possible the publication of Winrod's writing in pamphlet or book form.[85]

John Jacob Kroeker, a post-World War I Mennonite immigrant from Germany, took special interest in the Defender movement as Winrod's anti-Semitism and anti-Communism led toward an embrace of the Nazi regime in Germany. Kroeker kept in close contact with Germany as a member of the German Bund, and saturated himself with Nazi propaganda. He provided Winrod with an occasional article for *The Defender* and, on at least one occasion, acted as Winrod's emissary at a far rightist meeting too suspect for Winrod to risk personal attendance. Although Kroeker counseled Mennonites to avoid religion and politics,[86] he allowed political loyalty first place in his life as he returned to Germany in time to experience the wartime disaster of the Third Reich.[87]

When Winrod declared his candidacy for the United States

Senate in 1938 the Kansas Republican party leaders, with the recent Brinkley storm to remind them of the grass roots appeal of an evangelical antipolitician, closed ranks behind the candidacy of a former governor, Clyde Reed.[88] Since both major candidates in the Republican primary (Dallas Knapp of Coffeyville and Jesse Clyde Fisher, a western Kansas clergyman, were also on the ballot) agreed on opposition to the New Deal, the campaign swirled around charges and countercharges regarding Winrod's Nazi sympathies. Winrod, in full character, saw the Jewish-Communist conspiracy behind the campaign against him, but he cautiously moderated some of the extreme positions he had earlier taken in *The Defender*.[89]

The Mennonite newspapers refrained from mixing in the campaign fight, but in issues before the election, G. H. Willms of *Der Herold* and P. H. Berg of *Vorwaerts* endorsed Winrod's candidacy. Willms and Berg mentioned no issues but rather were concerned that certain Kansas ministers had come out against Winrod. One of these ministers, wrote Willms, had had striptease artist Sally Rand speak in his church. "Is it necessary to say anything more?" he asked. Editor Berg modestly neglected to expose the depths of depravity in the anti-Winrod camp but simply expressed his belief that Winrod in the Senate "could render incalculable service to the country."[90]

Winrod lost the election and lost it badly. He ran in third place with only 21.4 percent of the vote, over 50,000 behind Reed and 10,000 behind the surprising Knapp.[91] The Mennonites came through with 60 percent for Winrod. The strongest Winrod vote was in the five Marion County Mennonite precincts which together gave him 75.4 percent. West Branch Township, home of the Reverend P. H. Richert and Tabor Church, gave Winrod a whopping 90.2 percent. In four other Mennonite townships, however (Alta, Little Valley, Mound, and Turkey Creek), Winrod failed to get plurality.

The election was a turning point toward trouble for Winrod. In 1940 his wife sued for divorce and in 1942 the federal government brought the first of three indictments for sedition against him. In the year of the first indictment, the Herald Publishing Company ceased printing *The Defender*. The Mennonites, made wealthier by wartime prosperity, saw reasons not to be identified with an accused Nazi during the Second World War. As if to symbolize Mennonite disaffection, the presiding federal judge at Winrod's sedition trial was Edward C. Eicher, a Mennonite formerly of Iowa. Mrs. M. L. Flowers of the Defenders insists that Mennonites retained their love and trust for Winrod in spite of everything. In an interview of 1966, ten years after Winrod's death, she reported that she still visited Mennonite friends and found them speaking of the great evangelist "with tears in their eyes."[92]

Winrod's success among Mennonites depended more upon his image in the community than upon his specific right-wing anti-Semitic doctrines. Mennonites knew him first of all as a preacher of the Christian gospel. Winrod took up politics only after he had established himself in the eyes of the community as a man of God. The Mennonites, long accustomed to trusting the authority of preachers, interpreted the political attacks upon Winrod (as well as Winrod's self-defense) in the light of their positive image of the man and his work. When Winrod disavowed charges of anti-Semitism (he claimed to hate only the apostate Communist Jews) or when he professed distaste for dictatorships of all types (including Mussolini, Hitler, Stalin),[93] the Mennonites were disposed to believe Winrod rather than his accusers.

The Mennonites did not share Winrod's certain knowledge of the conspiracies which were disrupting the moral order, but they did share his insecurities over current world events. Within two decades they had seen an American war against Germany, the questioning of their right to American citizenship, the depression, the repeal of Prohibition, the rise of Communism and dictatorships, the encroachments of modernism, and the tensions which accompanied the loss of German as the dominant language in the community. It was less important to decipher and evaluate Winrod's precise explanations for the world's plight than to know that here was a man who seemed to have answers while everyone else floundered. The opportunities for a demagogue to play upon the fears of the community were never greater than the decade of the 1930s.

The Mennonites could also know that Winrod reciprocated with a measure of trust in them. He sent a son to study at Hesston College; his secretary sent a daughter to Bethel College; and he endorsed the Mennonite junior college in Freeman, South Dakota, in the pages of *The Defender*. He showed interest in Mennonite leaders, such as P. H. Richert of the Tabor Church, who expressed political attitudes close to his own.[94] Despite the military metaphors which abounded in the Defender literature, Winrod attacked militarism and war as vigorously as did the Mennonites. War was not only "Hell," he believed, it was "Silly." "The Quakers and the Mennonites are right

. . . war shows ignorance and is the produce of lust."[95] Winrod was clever enough to play the proper themes when speaking to Mennonite audiences, and the community responded with willing support.

Lacking the knowledge and sophistication to evaluate properly Winrod's preposterous charges against the Jewish-Communist conspiracy, the Mennonites extended an unfortunate measure of credibility to the crusading evangelist. It was the authority of Winrod's image as preacher of the gospel and his common cause in the moral concerns of the Mennonites, however, rather than concurrence on specific political programs, which won Mennonite votes for Winrod. Winrod's dissent from the current political order was so complete that Mennonites could believe that they were voting for religion and morality and against politics. This was a well-established practice among Kansas Mennonites, as seen in the vote for the Progressive party in 1924 and for Brinkley in 1930. The confirmation of this tradition in the Republican primary of 1938 is as important to the understanding of Mennonite political acculturation as the fact that Mennonites had been duped by an evangelical anti-Semite whose fear-ridden political doctrines contradicted the core of Mennonites' peace principles.

The Kansas Mennonite attraction to Winrod is part of a broader picture of Mennonite susceptibility to right-wing political nationalism in the twentieth century. In Canada, where the Mennonites had more successfully preserved and cultivated the German culture and where thousands of Mennonite victims had fled from Communist Russia in the 1920s, many Mennonite leaders identified with the hopes and achievements of Hitler's Third Reich.[96] The Kansas Mennonites, who had been stung once on the wrong side in a war involving Germany, were less uniformly pro-German in the 1930s than they had been in 1914. Kansas Mennonites wasted no love on Communism, but their fears and frustrations were more diffuse and generalized than those of recent Mennonite exiles from Russia.

Compared to the Kansas political community which so decisively rejected Winrod in 1938, however, some Kansas Mennonites were quite distinctive in their pro-German views. Dr. J. R. Thierstein, Swiss-born professor of Bible at Bethel College since 1921, was the foremost Nazi sympathizer among Kansas Mennonites. When a Jewish-Communist revolution threatened Germany, Thierstein wrote in 1932, "An all-governing Heavenly Father did not want to allow Germany to become a second Russia. A man named Adolph Hitler

saw the danger as few others did. . . ."[97] Thierstein became editor of
The Mennonite in 1935 and gave that official General Conference
publication a pro-German, anti-Semitic bias in the years until the
Second World War.[98] That such doctrines filtered down to at least
some Mennonite farmer-laymen was evident in the writings of C. H.
Friesen of Buhler, Kansas, whose letters to Mennonite editors de-
plored the increasing influence of international Jewry, both in
Europe and America.[99]

Despite the writings of Thierstein, Friesen, and the Winrod supporters, the pro-German sentiment did not pervade the whole community as it had before the First World War. This time there were
no congregational collections of funds for the German Red Cross.
Bismark's portrait no longer appeared in Mennonite periodicals. Cultural identification with the German fatherland was less apparent.
The Kansas Mennonites produced a few voices of support for Hitler,
but the community as a whole was unwilling to complicate its problems of Americanization by flirtations with German nationalism.
Other issues, such as the renewed prospect of military conscription,
were of more immediate relevance.

CHURCHES AND CONSCRIPTION

"It is doubtful whether the next conscription act will contain an
exemption clause," wrote a Bethel College history professor in 1922,
"especially if the people themselves have a decisive voice in the
matter."[100] The Mennonite experience with popular democracy
during the First World War and the immediate postwar years raised
new questions regarding their role as a nonconforming community.
No longer could it be assumed that their privileges would be preserved simply because the American system was government by the
people. The Mennonites began to realize that they would have to
look out for their own interests, because neither the people nor the
government was necessarily on their side in a showdown. There were
two ways for the community to prepare itself. The first was to edu-
cate the church membership on the true meaning of nonresistance
and the commitments required by such a doctrine.[101] The second
was to be alert to the political situation, especially regarding the possibility of war and changes in the draft law. In both of these concerns the activities of Kansas Mennonites merged with those of Mennonites throughout the country.

The concern for peace and for favorable draft legislation drew the Mennonites, willy-nilly, into different kinds of political action. The recorded proceedings of Mennonite district and national conferences in the 1920s and 1930s tell the story of how Mennonites, including some who were quite opposed to political involvements, inadvertently found themselves expressing political attitudes and bringing the weight of their opinion to bear upon government officials. The Exemption Committee of the Western District Conference warned the churches already in 1919 that although the war was finished, the government was considering legislation for permanent military training. The committee urged the churches "to send petitions to their representatives in Washington" to defeat the proposals. Many congregations had already done so.[102] The following year the committee included in the conference minutes letters received from three United Stated senators and one congressman in response to Mennonite appeals against universal compulsory military training. All the replies (from Arthur Capper, W. A. Ayres, T. P. Gore, and Charles Curtis) agreed with the Mennonites in opposing this legislation.[103] In 1921 the Western District Conference adopted a resolution calling for President Harding and the American delegates to the Washington Disarmament Conference "to throw the whole influence of the United States into the balance for an honest disarmament and a just peace among all nations." This resolution had originated in an alliance of church councils from the Alexanderwohl, Tabor, Goessel, and Lehigh congregations.[104] The General Conference of the Mennonite Brethren Church in 1921 adopted a similar but milder resolution of "recognition and appreciation to President [Warren G.] Harding" for his "interest in the question of demobilization and abolition of war."[105] The church apparently could more easily and more safely agree to commend a Republican administration for good conduct than to criticize the government for its diplomatic or legislative failures. Even so, the Mennonite Brethren in 1924 resolved upon the church's duty to "endeavor to influence our government, especially the legislative body, to maintain peace and to abstain from war." There is little evidence that the Mennonite Brethren Church actually followed through with a political peace witness in subsequent years. They believed that their "greatest mission consists in proclaiming the Gospel of Salvation, which leads to the renewing of the inner man, for without regeneration no true and lasting peace can be attained."[106]

The KMB conference, which as recently as 1907 had admonished the brethren to avoid participation in political elections, in 1924 registered their earnest "protest against this movement of the War Department" to continue "observation of Defence Day." In a letter to President Calvin Coolidge, the gathered KMBs pointed out that this celebration was "not conductive [sic] to the promotion of world peace."[107] The triennial sessions of the General Conference of the Mennonite Church of North America did not seek to influence national public policy until war threats raised the conscription problem in the late thirties. The conference did go on record in 1926 against Reserve Officers' Training Corps, but no specific action was taken to make the resolution politically effective.[108] The 1929 session found more reason for complacency than for dismay and expressed "gratification" at the ratification of the Kellogg-Briand Pact outlawing war, and "appreciation" for President Hoover's efforts "for the reduction of naval armaments." Though unwilling to become involved in political controversy, the Mennonites were happy to pledge their "moral support" for such efforts.[109]

The Peace Problems Committee of the (Old) Mennonite Church was at least as active in political contacts with the government as was its General Conference (GC) counterpart. The (Old) Mennonite committee reported in 1927 that it had written to congressmen regarding a bill against compulsory military training in public schools and colleges. The report went on, "Other letters were forwarded at the time when the international situation as regards Nicaragua, Mexico, and China seemed acute and to encourage our President in his program of naval reduction." The committee was anxious to do more. "We owe it to the 'powers that be' to let them know our position on this question." In 1929 the (OM) General Conference session commended President Herbert Hoover for his peace efforts, and in 1931 the Peace Problems Committee reported further encouragement offered to the government in behalf of disarmament.[110] The Kansas (Old) Mennonites could know that their peace convictions were being represented before the national government, but there were some members in the (Old) Mennonite Church who felt that the committee's writing of letters to government was a misguided attempt "to run the church into the political arena."[111]

Mennonite conference statements in support of peace and disarmament were cautious and ineffective. Some members continued to grumble that Mennonites ought to stay out of politics. But when the peace question confronted the constituency as a matter of immediate self-interest, as it did on the problem of the military draft, Mennonite opposition to politics evaporated. Politics did not seem so evil when it was a matter of defending one's own rights and privileges. Mennonite desires for exemption from military service proved to be the most potent force drawing them into political activity.

The Mennonites held a set of trump cards in their political maneuvering for a draft law which would provide exemption for conscientious objectors to war. Their most persuasive weapon was their threat of civil disobedience. They politely but firmly informed the government that it was their intention, based on longstanding religious principles, to disobey any conscription law which did not provide for their exemption from military service. This threat, moreover, was credible. The historical record of conscientious objection in the First World War demonstrated that Mennonites were sincere in their convictions and that attempts to draft them into military service would produce administrative chaos and public embarrassment. No public official needed repeat Secretary of War Newton D. Baker's mistake of assuming that conscientious objectors could easily be converted into acceptance of their patriotic responsibilities.

Before 1937 the Mennonite "witness" to the national government was largely confined to occasional and ineffective official peace committee letters, conference declarations, and petitions from church congregations and other groups. During the 1920s Mennonites had often attended interdenominational peace conferences, but in 1935 H. P. Krehbiel led in the organization of a landmark conference of the "historic peace churches" in Newton, a conference which grew out of the feeling that association with humanitarian pacifists was diluting the witness of Christian nonresistance. The 1935 conference drew up preliminary plans for the event of war and established a "continuation Committee" which called later conferences, made contacts with government, and consulted on peace problems such as compulsory ROTC and naturalization of pacifists.[112] In 1937, under the advance of war clouds, a joint delegation of Mennonites, Friends, and Brethren arranged a twenty-minute audience with President Roosevelt to make a "formal presentation of convictions on war and peace." Of the three letters submitted by the denominations to the president, the Mennonite statement was most specific in declaring its purpose: the Mennonites would not respond to military conscription. A sugarcoating of patriotism helped make the harsh words palatable:

We wish to assert again our patriotism and wholehearted loyalty to our country, even now as we appear before you to state our inability, on the grounds of our conscience and religious convictions, to participate in war or military service of any type. As a matter of record now, we humbly state to our Government that, before God and our conscience, we cannot assume responsibilities or services, the purpose and end of which is the destruction of human life.[113]

The statement did not offer alternative service in the event of war, but referred to the relief work and migration assistance offered by the Mennonites during and after the First World War. The Mennonite practice of invariably referring to their benevolent enterprises in their petitions to government confirms the suggestion that Mennonite relief programs were essential to their civic identity. It was one method for them to establish their right to speak to the government and to demand special privileges.

An extended series of conferences, committee meetings, and discussions among the different Mennonite groups and the other peace churches resulted in general agreement upon a plan of action for alternative service in the case of military conscription. This plan was presented by representatives of the Mennonites, Friends, and Brethren to President Roosevelt on January 10, 1940, a full eight months before the Selective Service Act of 1940 was passed and became law. The plan had three main points: (1) A presidentially appointed civilian board should evaluate conscientious objectors and make service assignments; (2) Draft boards should route conscientious objectors to the civilian board; (3) The historic peace churches should establish and administer the alternative service projects, which might include relief to war sufferers and refugees, reclamation or forestry service, medical and health services, or farm service. The delegation pointed out the First World War precedent for a civilian board to determine conscientious objector status and President Roosevelt expressed enthusiasm for the concrete alternative service proposals. "That's getting down to a practical basis. It shows us what work the conscientious objectors can do without fighting Excellent! Excellent!"[114]

In June 1940 the Mennonites were rudely awakened to the fact that effective political action demanded more than earnest petitioning of the executive branch of government. The Burke-Wadsworth Bill, introduced to the Senate on June 20, offered no exemption from noncombatant service and had no provision for service under civilian agencies. The Mennonites and other peace groups went into an unprecedented (for Mennonites, that is) crash lobbying program to get the bill changed. The greater political experience of the Friends War Problems Committee came to the aid of politically unversed Mennonites and led the way in testimony before Senate and House hearings on the bill and in buttonholing legislators, administrative officials, and army officers. When the dust had settled, the bill in its final form had been changed to include the peace churches' demand for alternative service "of national importance under civilian direction," and it was clear that the Quaker influence had been decisive.[115] The Mennonites had found themselves reluctantly and almost inadvertently drawn into a political fight of utmost significance for their future as citizens in the United States. Hereafter, all claims of conscientious objection to political involvement would sound somewhat hollow, for Mennonites had proved their willingness to go after the political goods when the issues struck close enough home. It was nevertheless characteristically Mennonite that their own initiative was more visible in the fashioning of constructive alternatives to the draft than in the political action necessary to get the alternatives written into law.

Not until the political battle was largely won and the problems of establishing administrative machinery for alternative service became burdensome did the Mennonites appoint a full-time representative, Henry A. Fast of Newton, to represent their interests in Washington. It also became necessary to organize one central agency, the National Service Board for Religious Objectors, to avoid administrative confusion as the government negotiated with the peace churches to set up the Civilian Public Service program. One key issue was the financing of the service camps. President Roosevelt's personal objections to the use of federal funds to pay the salaries and maintenance of conscientious objectors resulted in an alternative program which was not only administered but also financed by the churches. While the Civilian Public Service program operated in the following years, nearly five thousand young Mennonite men served without pay in projects of national importance, some for longer than four years. Kansas Mennonites joined the country-wide effort which demanded unprecedented financial support of a program designed to provide Mennonites with an acceptable place in American society. While the rest of America again marched off to war, Mennonites again struggled with their problem of a dual identity by contributing to "work of national importance" on one hand through the Civilian

Public Service program, and by contributing to relief of war suffering
on the other hand through the expanded work of the Mennonite
Central Committee. It was a much more satisfactory solution than
that of the First World War, and the Mennonites had their own
political efforts to thank, at least in part, that the solution was
possible.

CONCLUSION

The interwar period was a time of readjustment for the Kansas
Mennonite community. Most acute was the problem of establishing
again a role in American society and politics out of the shambles of
their unacceptable First World War Germanism and pacifism. The
Mennonites continued to insist upon being both Mennonite and
American, but they gradually dropped their Germanism in these two
decades. Support for Hitler came occasionally from scattered Kansas
Mennonites in the 1930s, especially from those inclined to trust the
fundamentalist evangelist Gerald Winrod. But Mennonite indentifi-
cation with German national culture, so evident in their newspapers
in 1914-17, had all but disappeared. The Mennonite effort was to
be acceptably American.

The way chosen by Mennonites to fulfill the requirements of their
religious and civic loyalties was usually nonpolitical. Most successful
was the church's program of relief to victims of war during the 1920s
and the continuing benevolences of the Mennonite Central Committee. The merging of three conditions provided the impetus which
determined the character of the Mennonite relief program and made
it a success. The unsatisfied Mennonite wartime conscience provided
the initial stimulus to action. A heightened awareness of wartime
suffering and the Mennonite traditional religious emphasis upon
service and discipleship determined that the action be a form of
benevolence. And the eventual focus of the relief programs upon
Mennonite war victims lent to the project an aspect of mutual aid
among brothers and sisters in the faith. The result was the establishment of a new balance in the Mennonite self-conception as Christian
and citizen which moderated the shock of World War I, smoothed
the course of Mennonite Americanization, and prepared the community for a more creative response to the next great war.

The Mennonite relief program eventually became a permanent
feature of Mennonite institutions, but it always blossomed in wartime as Mennonites sought substitutes for the civic duties prescribed

by the warfare state. The Mennonite Central Committee relief work, the achievement of a legalized alternative to military service, and the searching for more positive applications of the biblical peace principle were forms of substitute patriotism. And because the entire process was forced into nonpolitical channels, it likewise served as a substitute for politics. The Mennonite Central Committee, standing as it did for the Mennonite positive response to the suffering world, was a kind of political surrogate for Mennonites whose distaste for politics was an ingrained tradition.

The records of Mennonite voting and officeholding in the 1920s and '30s bear out the picture of a persistently nonpolitical community. Not only did Mennonites vote in fewer numbers than did other Kansans, but they gave uncommonly large votes to candidates whose platform represented a challenge to regular party politics, such as Robert LaFollette in 1924, John R. Brinkley in 1930, and Gerald B. Winrod in 1938. To be sure, Mennonites after the First World War were not inclined to vote Socialist, except for a minority at Bethel College. Socialists never had a chance among Kansas Mennonites after the Communist Revolution and Civil War in Russia, with which Mennonites were closely acquainted through their relief work, renewed migrations from Russia to Canada, and news from Russian Mennonites about their suffering under Communism.

Aside from the LaFollette, Brinkley, and Winrod votes, the Mennonite voting percentages were not strikingly different from the Kansas norm. It was after the approach of the Second World War that the Mennonite voting pattern for the first time took on a consistently different pattern, as Mennonites settled upon the Republican party. The voting records do not indicate a peculiarly strong Mennonite negative reaction to Roosevelt and the New Deal, at least not significantly stronger than other Kansans. The year of disenchantment was 1940, when universal military conscription was adopted and war seemed increasingly imminent.

Throughout this period the Mennonites continued to be under-represented in county politics, and they produced no politicians of the capabilities of Ferdinand Funk or the young H. P. Krehbiel to represent them in the state legislature. J. A. Schowalter won political prominence through his wealth, but he was more a farmer and businessman than politician.

The course of Mennonite pacifism reflected a lack of interest or enthusiasm for politics. The influence of fundamentalism led some

Mennonite leaders (such as H. P. Krehbiel) to drain whatever political content their nonresistant doctrines once had. Even among the more liberal Mennonites, no one really attempted to define in specific political terms what the relevance of Mennonite peace doctrines might be. Mennonite pacifism remained, for the most part, a narrow doctrine of nonparticipation in war. The Kansas Institute of International Relations and other contacts with the broader American peace movement provided inspiration for a limited number of Mennonite participants, but they were heavily criticized within the fellowship and were finally abandoned.

On the draft question, however, Mennonites knew what they wanted politically and they were willing to go to the government to get it. Their efforts, together with other peace groups, to get exemption from military service, were successful. Although their threat of civil disobedience in refusing military service was a powerful political weapon which they used effectively, they did not conceive of these efforts as "political." As a special interest group attempting to influence public policy in a specific direction, however, their action was no less political than the lobbying of other special interests. By 1940 it appeared that the best school of politics for Mennonites lay in their own lobbying in government for favorable draft legislation. Whether the lessons learned here would be applied to other problems of public policy remained for the future.

"*A strong inclination toward change pervades the atmosphere in our country. The recent Mennonite immigrants have rapidly taken on the coloring of the American people in this respect. Time will tell whether the basic elements of the old original can be maintained within the manifold life-styles of the new*" (C. H. WEDEL, 1904).

CHAPTER **9**

Nonresistance, Nationalism, and Acculturation: Conclusion

THE POLITICAL ACCULTURATION OF KANSAS MENNONITES IS A chapter in the history of American nationalism. In the traditional view of immigrant history, the meaning of this story would be found in the validity of the Mennonite "contribution" to America. Although American historiography owes an immense debt to historians who wrote within such a framework, the continued evaluation of alien immigrant contributions to a composite nationality would be an injustice both to the immigrants and to America. The new task of immigrant history is to focus on the processes of social construction and disintegration of the immigrant community over longer periods of time. In the political behavior of the Kansas Mennonites, the character of this process was fundamentally shaped by the abrasive encounter of Mennonite nonresistance with American nationalism.

The statistics of Mennonite political behavior in voting, office-holding, and naturalization give only the barest hints of the drama inherent in Mennonite Americanization. The statistics show that Mennonites persistently avoided political involvement through the Second World War. But they also show that considerable numbers of Mennonites voted in elections from the beginning, and that these voters scattered their votes in a pattern not widely different from the Kansas norm. Not until 1940 and succeeding years did Mennonite voting behavior reflect a community effort to preserve group identity. Meanwhile, there was more at stake in the Mennonite civic self-conception than in Mennonite voting or officeholding habits.

The central problems of Mennonite political acculturation were all related in some way to an inescapable conflict between the ethic of modern nationalism and the ethic of traditional Mennonitism. As long as America, like all modern nations, rooted her existence in the ultimate appeal to popular military self-defense and as long as Mennonites refused military participation, a conflict between state and church was inevitable. Twentieth-century militant nationalism and Mennonitism were at odds. There were ways, however, to render this conflict less acute, less visible, less painful. The history of Mennonite Americanization was made up of attempts by the community to get around this dilemma without giving up the basic doctrine of nonresistance which accounted for it.

One way to escape was simply to ignore the problem, an alternative which was possible only in times of peace when there was no threat or possibility of military conscription. From their arrival in the 1870s until the Spanish-American War in 1898, the Mennonites were allowed an uninterrupted growth and adaptation to America. Some Mennonites became citizens and took part in elections from the very beginning. Others hesitated and harked back to the Anabaptist church-state dualism which precluded political involvements. But the empirical facts of American political life were unkind to the old dualisms. America was the land of freedom, of peace, of prosperity. The Mennonite church in America had little actual evidence of why it should be hostile to government and politics. The Mennonites began to produce a few politicians and turned in voting records which did not differ greatly from the Kansas average, even in the Populist period. They were not unified on any politically relevant ideology which could make their voting percentages consistently distinctive.

The Spanish-American War cast some brief doubts on the emerging satisfactory civic role of the Mennonite German-Americans. Stung by real or imagined charges that their patriotic contribution was less than adequate, some of them defensively affirmed their loyalty to America and obliquely mentioned the possibility of contributing to the war in some nonresistant manner. Under the pressure of the war, they began to grope for a second solution to the conflict between nationalism and nonresistance—a Mennonite substitute for military service. But the war was short and, like so many embarrassments, easily forgotten.

During the Progressive era the Mennonites continued to adapt to American society and politics. A few gadflies in the community saw problems in reconciling the Mennonite peace emphasis with American imperialism, but the community as a whole accepted Theodore Roosevelt as a national hero. Considerable numbers of Mennonites remained politically apathetic, as indicated by poor voter turnout, but several articulate Mennonite church leaders and newspaper editors enthusiastically joined the Progressive movement's optimistic demand for social reform and justice. The causes of peace and temperance were especially popular. The Mennonites seemed to be finding a comfortable home as German-Americans in the national community.

The First World War shattered the easy course of Mennonite Americanism. As pacifists and as speakers of the German language, the Mennonites were not acceptable citizens. This message was driven home as patriotic groups intimidated Mennonites into buying war bonds, camp commanders winked while nonresistant draftees were persecuted, and local editorials denounced the use of the German language. Because the Mennonites were unwilling and unable, at that point, to give up either the German language or their pacifism, they had to find substitute ways of asserting their civic dignity and of supporting their claim to American citizenship.

Two Mennonite community efforts in the post-World War I period especially dramatized the new attempts to bridge the conflict between Americanism and Mennonitism. The first was the extraordinary Mennonite voluntary benevolent program of relief to war victims and other sufferers. The second was the successful Mennonite attempt to get an alternative service program for conscientious objectors at the approach of World War II. It was not clear before 1940, however, that the Mennonites had done enough to satisfy the requirements of American citizenship and heal the ugly wounds which reinstructed them in old doctrines of the untrustworthiness and violence of the political order. It was this fact which accounted, in large measure, for continued Mennonite resistance to voting, for the continued failure of significant numbers of Mennonites to seek public office, and for the recurrent practice of voting Mennonites to get behind candidates who ran against the establishment—such as Robert LaFollette, John R. Brinkley, and Gerald B. Winrod. In that generation for whom the turning point of modern history was the First World War, the facts of life tended to support the old Anabaptist tradition which expected the state to be against the church and the Christian to be a stranger in the world.

With the Second World War the process of Mennonite political acculturation entered a new phase. Mennonite voters, reacting decisively against a Democratic administration which led the country into war, began a consistent pattern of voting about 15 percent more Republican than the Kansas average. While voting patterns became distinctive, it seemed that the tradition of nonresistance had suffered more erosion than Mennonites expected. About half of the young Mennonite draftees in the Second World War entered either combatant or noncombatant military service, even though they had the legal alternative of work in Civilian Public Service camps.[1] But Mennonite nonresistance was hardly in its death throes, for the percentage of Mennonite draftees who chose alternative service increased in the postwar decades.[2] The percentage of Mennonite voters remained low, and the numbers of office-seekers did not rise significantly. In 1956 a Bethel College-sponsored "Conference on Education and Political Responsibility" again debated the question, still unanswered after eighty years of Mennonite political acculturation, "Should Mennonites Participate in Politics?"[3]

The persistence of the Mennonite doctrine of nonresistance and its corollary aversion to political involvement is certainly the most remarkable fact of Mennonite political acculturation. Through the vicissitudes of prosperity, depression, war, peace, persecution, and toleration, the Mennonites managed to retain an identity which conflicted with the political claims of American nationalism. Not all Mennonite branches and congregations responded in the same way or at the same speed. But they all remained in some degree under the influence of the doctrine alluded to by the Mennonite leader who admonished this writer to "rightly divide the two kingdoms" in tracing the history of Mennonites in politics.[4]

No less impressive than the staying power of Mennonite apolitical attitudes and behavior is the potency of American nationalism in shaping the Kansas Mennonite experience. The tragedy of the Mennonites was not that they became Americans so slowly, but rather that they so desperately wanted to be good American citizens and could not fulfill the requirements without violating their consciences or abandoning the traditions of their forebears. Whatever was creative in the Mennonite experience arose out of this tension. The Mennonite relief programs, the development of positive alternatives to military service, and the scattered criticisms of society from a pacifist perspective were all attempts to harness the normative influence of American nationalism and bring it under the control of the Mennonite nonresistant ethic. That America had a claim to the loyalties and responsibilities of Mennonites, including a substitute for military service, was not denied. Mennonite nonconformity had been Americanized as surely as the American system had been stretched a bit to make room for these nonconformists.

The tenuous truce between church and state, which had been the hallmark of Mennonite sectarian history since the Reformation, continued its uneasy course from the arrival of the Mennonites in Kansas until the approach of their centennial. The Mennonite experience until 1940 offered little hope that simple solutions would be found. These folk were both Mennonites and Americans, which meant that until their political acculturation was complete, they were a people of two kingdoms.

Appendixes

The voting statistics in the following graphs were tabulated from data in the voting records of Marion County (West Branch, Menno, Liberty, and Risley townships), McPherson County (Lone Tree, Spring Valley, Little Valley, Superior, Turkey Creek, Mound, and Meridian townships), Harvey County (Alta and Garden townships), and Reno County (Little River Township) in Kansas. Until 1888, the first election year in which the township boundaries were established in their present form, the statistics were taken from those organized townships which most closely approximated the eventually accepted boundaries. Except in Marion County, the voting records were not carefully preserved or readily available, and considerable searching in old vaults and dusty attics was necessary. In several cases contemporary newspapers were the only source for voting records. The records before 1918 in Reno County are not available, except for the very first elections when they were recorded in the commissioners' journal. Therefore Little River Township is not included until 1918.

The single criterion governing selection of townships was density of Mennonite population. The numbers of Mennonites among voting-age residents in these townships was tabulated from the Mennonite names on the census records of 1880, 1895, and 1925. The result showed an increasing percentage of Mennonites from 50.2 percent, 65.4 percent, to 77.8 percent (see appendix F). There were considerable numbers of non-Mennonites, therefore, in areas here referred to as "Mennonite townships." The Mennonite habit of nonvoting meant that the percentage of Mennonites represented in voting statistics was somewhat smaller than the percentage of Mennonites in the population statistics.

Because religious affiliation was not recorded in census records, it was impossible to determine with precise accuracy whether or not a given resident was actually a Mennonite. There were, of course, non-Mennonites who happened to have Mennonite names, Mennonites who left the church, and some with non-Mennonite names who had joined the church. The spellings of the census taker had to be watched closely, as when, for example, a Mennonite "Janzen" was recorded as a "Johnson." Such cases were usually decided upon the basis of the census record of national origin. Despite the margin of error, the concentration of Mennonites is sufficient to justify reference to the "Mennonite vote," except, perhaps, in the earliest several elections.

On the graphs of voting percentages by party, the first bar below the center line represents a Democrat vote except for 1892 when it gives the vote for the Populist candidate. The Democrat candidates were not printed on the Kansas ballot in that year. A Democrat-Populist fusionist vote is recorded for 1896, 1898, and 1900. The third-party vote in other years was as follows: 1880, Greenback; 1882, National Labor; 1884, Greenback; 1888, National Union Labor; 1912, Progressive (Roosevelt); 1916, Socialist; 1920, Socialist; 1924, Independent (Robert LaFollette and William Allen White). Third-party votes less than 2 or 3 percent could not be recorded accurately on the graphs.

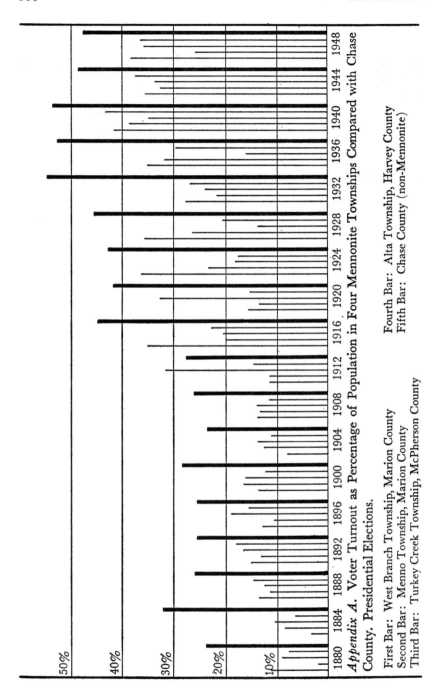

Appendix A. Voter Turnout as Percentage of Population in Four Mennonite Townships Compared with Chase County. Presidential Elections.

First Bar: West Branch Township, Marion County
Second Bar: Menno Township, Marion County
Third Bar: Turkey Creek Township, McPherson County
Fourth Bar: Alta Township, Harvey County
Fifth Bar: Chase County (non-Mennonite)

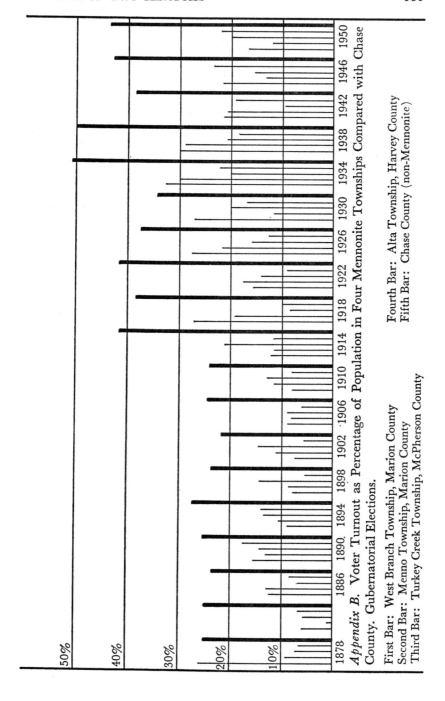

Appendix B. Voter Turnout as Percentage of Population in Four Mennonite Townships Compared with Chase County. Gubernatorial Elections.

First Bar: West Branch Township, Marion County
Second Bar: Menno Township, Marion County
Third Bar: Turkey Creek Township, McPherson County
Fourth Bar: Alta Township, Harvey County
Fifth Bar: Chase County (non-Mennonite)

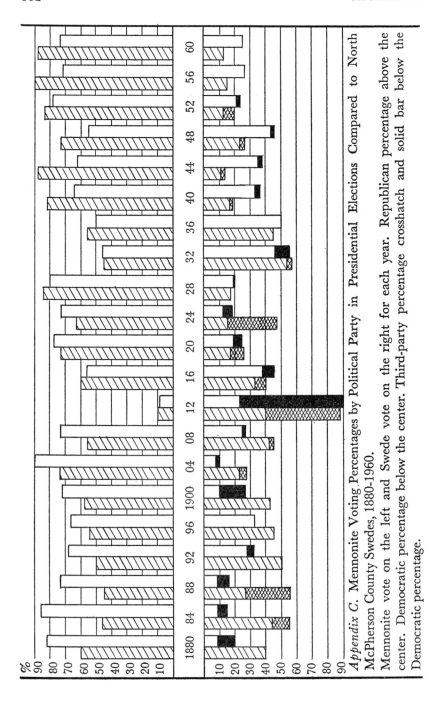

Appendix C. Mennonite Voting Percentages by Political Party in Presidential Elections Compared to North McPherson County Swedes, 1880-1960.

Mennonite vote on the left and Swede vote on the right for each year. Republican percentage above the center. Democratic percentage below the center. Third-party percentage crosshatch and solid bar below the Democratic percentage.

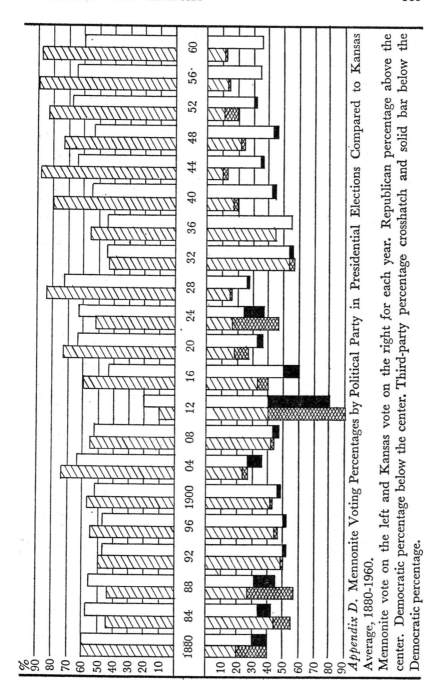

Appendix D. Mennonite Voting Percentages by Political Party in Presidential Elections Compared to Kansas Average, 1880–1960.

Mennonite vote on the left and Kansas vote on the right for each year. Republican percentage above the center. Democratic percentage below the center. Third-party percentage crosshatch and solid bar below the Democratic percentage.

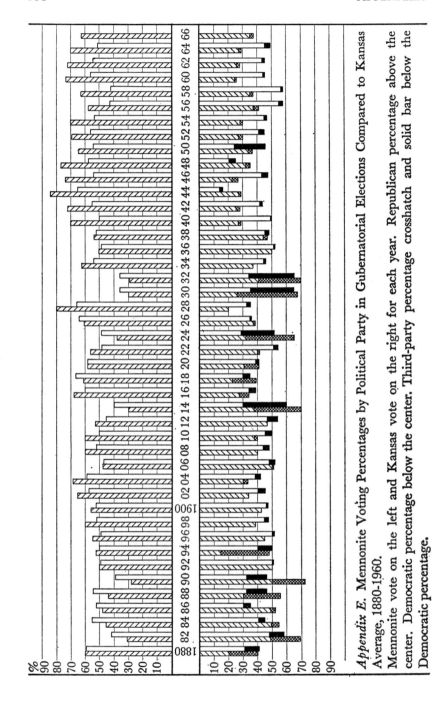

Appendix E. Mennonite Voting Percentages by Political Party in Gubernatorial Elections Compared to Kansas Average, 1880-1960.

Mennonite vote on the left and Kansas vote on the right for each year. Republican percentage above the center. Democratic percentage below the center. Third-party percentage crosshatch and solid bar below the Democratic percentage.

Appendix F

Percentage of Mennonites Among Voting-Age Residents in Selected
Central Kansas Townships

Township	1880	1895	1925
Marion Co.			
West Branch	45%*	92%	96%
Menno	62%*	91%	98%
Liberty	62%*	66%	79%
Risley	56%*	60%	78%
McPherson Co.			
Lone Tree	62%	58%	80%
Spring Valley	40%	51%	68%
Little Valley	24%	51%	68%
Superior	55%	57%	67%
Turkey Creek	57%	76%	95%
Mound	59%	60%	62%
Meridian	22%	40%	69%
Harvey Co.			
Alta	55%	78%	87%
Garden	36%	67%	73%
Reno Co.			
Little River	49%	80%	87%
Total average	50.2%	65.4%	77.8%

*Branch Township in 1880 included both present-day East Branch and West
  Branch.

*Liberty Township in 1880 included both Menno and Liberty.

*Risley Township in 1880 included present-day Lehigh Township.
  Figures for 1925 include women.

Appendix G

Votes Cast in Selected Mennonite-Populated Townships
in Presidential Elections, 1880-1964

Year	*Name*	*Party*	*Votes*	*Percentage*
1880	James A. Garfield	Republican	540	60.3%
	Winfield S. Hancock	Democrat	176	19.7
	James B. Weaver	Greenback	179	20.0
			895	
1884	James G. Blaine	Republican	493	46.8
	Grover Cleveland	Democrat	457	43.4
	Benjamin F. Butler	Greenback	3	.3
	John P. St. John	Prohibition	101	9.6
			1054	
1888	Benjamin Harrison	Republican	748	44.7
	Grover Cleveland	Democrat	453	27.1
	Clinton B. Fisk	Prohibition	21	1.3
	Andrew J. Streeter	National Union Labor	452	27.0
			1674	
1892	Benjamin Harrison	Republican	931	49.9
	James B. Weaver	Peoples	924	49.5
	John Bidwell	Prohibition	10	.5
			1865	
1896	William McKinley	Republican	982	55.0
	William Jennings Bryan	Democrat	788	44.2
	Joshua Levering	Prohibition	13	.7
			1783	
1900	William McKinley	Republican	1023	57.6
	William Jennings Bryan	Democrat	749	42.1
	John G. Woolley	Prohibition	5	.3
			1777	

1904	Theodore Roosevelt	Republican	1007	73.3%
	Alton B. Parker	Democrat	329	23.9
	Eugene V. Debs	Socialist	19	1.4
		Peoples	12	.9
	Silas G. Swallow	Prohibition	7	.5
			1374	
1908	William H. Taft	Republican	925	57.0
	William Jennings Bryan	Democrat	675	41.6
	Eugene V. Debs	Socialist	12	.7
	Eugene W. Chafin	Prohibition	12	.7
			1624	
1912	William H. Taft	Republican	177	10.7
	Woodrow Wilson	Democrat	650	39.4
	Theodore Roosevelt	Progressive	790	47.9
	Eugene V. Debs	Socialist	33	2.0
			1650	
1916	Charles E. Hughes	Republican	1462	59.3
	Woodrow Wilson	Democrat	829	33.6
	Allen L. Benson	Socialist	149	6.0
	J. Frank Hanley	Prohibition	26	1.1
			2466	
1920	Warren G. Harding	Republican	1460	73.2
	James M. Cox	Democrat	350	17.5
	Eugene V. Debs	Socialist	185	9.3
			1995	
1924	Calvin Coolidge	Republican	1365	52.4
	John W. Davis	Democrat	386	14.8
	Robert M. LaFollette	Progressive	856	32.8
			2607	
1928	Herbert Hoover	Republican	2282	83.6
	Alfred E. Smith	Democrat	437	16.0
	Norman Thomas	Socialist	12	.4
			2731	

1932	Herbert Hoover	Republican	1397	43.8%
	Franklin D. Roosevelt	Democrat	1700	53.3
	Norman Thomas	Socialist	94	2.9
			3191	
1936	Alfred M. Landon	Republican	2193	55.4
	Franklin D. Roosevelt	Democrat	1761	44.5
	Norman Thomas	Socialist	5	.1
			3959	
1940	Wendell L. Willkie	Republican	3607	81.0
	Franklin D. Roosevelt	Democrat	783	17.6
	Norman Thomas	Socialist	37	.8
	Roger W. Babson	Prohibition	26	.6
			4453	
1944	Thomas E. Dewey	Republican	3207	84.8
	Franklin D. Roosevelt	Democrat	517	14.5
	Norman Thomas	Socialist	51	1.3
	Claude A. Watson	Progressive	9	.2
			3784	
1948	Thomas E. Dewey	Republican	2982	73.3
	Harry S. Truman	Democrat	897	22.1
	Norman Thomas	Socialist	88	2.2
	Henry Wallace	Progressive	69	1.7
	Claude A. Watson	Prohibition	31	.8
			4067	
1952	Dwight D. Eisenhower	Republican	3389	79.9
	Adlai E. Stevenson	Democrat	472	11.1
	Darlington Hoopes	Socialist	15	.4
	Stuart Hamblen	Prohibition	368	8.7
			4244	
1956	Dwight D. Eisenhower	Republican	3493	85.8
	Adlai E. Stevenson	Democrat	547	13.4
	Enoch A. Holtwick	Prohibition	29	.7
			4069	

1960	Richard M. Nixon	Republican	4091	87.3%
	John F. Kennedy	Democrat	576	12.3
	Rutherford B. Decker	Prohibition	17	.4
			4684	
1964	Barry Goldwater	Republican	2042	57.7
	Lyndon B. Johnson	Democrat	1415	40.0
	E. Harold Nunn	Prohibition	84	2.4
			3541	

Appendix H

Votes Cast in Selected Mennonite-Populated Townships in Gubernatorial Elections, 1880-1948

1880	John P. St. John	Republican	533	59.8%
	Edmund G. Ross	Democrat	173	19.4
	H. P. Vrooman	Greenback-Labor	186	20.9
			892	
1882	John P. St. John	Republican	205	30.1
	George W. Glick	Democrat	318	4.0
	Charles Robinson	Greenback-Labor	139	21.0
			662	
1884	John A. Martin	Republican	495	46.8
	George W. Glick	Democrat	457	43.4
	H. L. Phillips	Greenback-Labor	39	3.7
			1058	
1886	John A. Martin	Republican	510	48.5
	Thomas Moonlight	Democrat	503	47.8
	C. H. Branscombe	Prohibition	39	3.7
			1052	
1888	Lyman U. Humphrey	Republican	729	43.2
	John Martin	Democrat	487	28.9
	Peter P. Elder	Union-Labor	451	26.7
	J. D. Botkin	Prohibition	21	1.2
			1688	

Year	Candidate	Party	Votes	%
1890	Lyman U. Humphrey	Republican	488	27.9%
	Charles Robinson	Democrat	876	50.1
	John F. Willits	Peoples-Alliance	385	22.0
	A. M. Richardson	Prohibition	1	
			1750	
1892	Abram W. Smith	Republican	933	50.1
	L. D. Lewelling	Democrat and Peoples	922	49.5
	Isaac O. Pickering	Prohibition	9	.5
			1864	
1894	E. N. Morrill	Republican	936	53.4
	David Overmyer	Stalwart Democrat	247	14.1
	L. D. Lewelling	Democrat and Peoples	560	32.0
	I. O. Pickering	Prohibition	9	.5
			1752	
1896	E. N. Morrill	Republican	980	55.6
	John W. Leedy	Democrat	782	44.4
			1762	
1898	William E. Stanley	Republican	872	60.8
	John W. Leedy	Democrat and Peoples	553	38.6
	William A. Peffer	Prohibition	9	.6
			1434	
1900	William E. Stanley	Republican	1016	57.6
	John W. Breidenthal	Democrat and Peoples	748	42.4
	Frank Holsinger	Prohibition	1	
			1765	
1902	Willis J. Bailey	Republican	783	65.1
	W. H. Craddock	Democrat	413	34.4
	F. W. Emerson	Prohibition	6	.5
			1202	

1904	Edward W. Hoch	Republican	942	68.1%
	David M. Dale	Democrat	417	30.1
	Granville Lowther	Socialist	18	1.3
	James Kerr	Prohibition	7	.5
			1384	
1906	Edward W. Hoch	Republican	514	48.9
	William A. Harris	Democrat	522	49.6
	Harry Gilham	Socialist	10	1.0
	J. B. Cook	Prohibition	6	.6
			1052	
1908	Walter R. Stubbs	Republican	970	59.8
	J. D. Botkin	Democrat	640	39.5
	George Francis Hibner	Socialist	11	.7
			1521	
1910	Walter R. Stubbs	Republican	742	59.6
	George H. Hodges	Democrat	477	38.3
	S. M. Stallard	Socialist	23	1.8
	William Cady	Prohibition	2	.2
			1244	
1912	Arthur Capper	Republican	823	53.3
	George H. Hodges	Democrat	697	45.1
	George W. Kleihege	Socialist	25	1.6
			1545	
1914	Arthur Capper	Republican	507	30.1
	George H. Hodges	Democrat	625	37.1
	Henry J. Allen	Progressive	467	27.7
	J. B. Billard	Independent	62	3.7
	Milo M. Mitchell	Socialist	22	1.3
	Silas W. Bond	Prohibition	1	.1
			1684	
1916	Arthur Capper	Republican	1535	67.0
	W. C. Lansdon	Democrat	630	27.5
	E. N. Richardson	Socialist	87	3.8
	H. R. Ross	Prohibition	40	1.7
			2292	

1918	Henry J. Allen	Republican	989	60.9%
	W. C. Lansdon	Democrat	364	22.4
	George W. Kleihege	Socialist	272	16.7
			1625	
1920	Henry J. Allen	Republican	1084	58.8
	Jonathan M. Davis	Democrat	587	31.9
	Roy Stanton	Socialist	172	9.3
			1843	
1922	W. Y. Morgan	Republican	1000	57.3
	Jonathan M. Davis	Democrat	709	40.6
	M. L. Phillips	Socialist	37	2.1
			1746	
1924	Ben S. Paulen	Republican	937	38.8
	Jonathan M. Davis	Democrat	759	31.4
	William Allen White	Independent	709	29.3
	M. L. Phillips	Socialist	11	.5
			2416	
1926	Ben S. Paulen	Republican	1127	61.2
	Jonathan M. Davis	Democrat	694	37.7
	H. Hilfrich	Socialist	20	1.1
			1841	
1928	Clyde M. Reed	Republican	1909	80.2
	Chauncy B. Little	Democrat	454	19.1
	Henry L. Peterson	Socialist	18	.6
			2381	
1930	Frank Haucke	Republican	694	30.9
	Harry Woodring	Democrat	594	26.4
	John R. Brinkley	Independent	951	42.3
	J. B. Shields	Socialist	10	.4
			2246	
1932	Alfred M. Landon	Republican	942	28.8
	Harry Woodring	Democrat	1334	40.7
	John R. Brinkley	Independent	985	30.1
	H. M. Perkins	Socialist	14	.4
			3275	

1934	Alfred M. Landon	Republican	2317	62.8%
	Omar B. Ketchum	Democrat	1352	36.6
	George M. Whiteside	Socialist	21	.6
			3690	
1936	Will G. West	Republican	2000	50.7
	Walter A. Huxman	Democrat	1935	49.1
	George M. Whiteside	Socialist	9	.2
			3944	
1938	Payne Ratner	Republican	1708	53.0
	Walter A. Huxman	Democrat	1438	43.7
	Jonathan M. Davis	Independent	54	1.7
	Ida A. Beloof	Socialist	2	.1
	C. Floyd Hester	Prohibition	19	.6
			3221	
1940	Payne Ratner	Republican	2981	70.5
	William H. Burke	Democrat	1196	28.3
	David C. White	Prohibition	39	.9
	Ida A. Beloof	Socialist	10	.2
			4226	
1942	Andrew F. Schoeppel	Republican	1500	72.3
	William H. Burke	Democrat	534	25.7
	Ida A. Beloof	Socialist	10	.5
	David C. White	Prohibition	32	1.5
			2076	
1944	Andrew F. Schoeppel	Republican	3128	84.0
	Robert Lemon	Democrat	522	14.0
	W. W. Tamplin	Socialist	20	.5
	David C. White	Prohibition	56	1.5
			3726	

1946	Frank Carlson	Republican	1777	73.6%
	Harry H. Woodring	Democrat	557	23.1
	Harry Graber	Socialist	17	.7
	David C. White	Prohibition	63	2.6
			2414	
1948	Frank Carlson	Republican	2832	75.5
	Randolph Carpenter	Democrat	773	20.6
	W. W. Tamplin	Socialist	19	.5
	N.W. Nice	Prohibition	125	3.3
			3749	

Notes and
Acknowledgments

CHAPTER 1

1. See Cornelius Krahn, "Facing the Centennial," (North Newton: xeroxed information guide, 1974); Harley J. Stucky, *A Century of Mennonite History in America* (North Newton: Mennonite Press, 1973); William E. Juhnke, ed., "A Study Guide of the Swiss Mennonites Who Came to Kansas in 1874" (Moundridge: mimeographed study guide, 1974).

2. A comparison of numbers of foreign language users in Chase County as compared with other Kansas counties can be found in J. Neale Carman, *Foreign-Language Units of Kansas,* vol. 1, *Historical Atlas and Statistics* (Lawrence: The University of Kansas Press, 1962), pp. 33, 96. On the history of Chase County see *Chase County Historical Sketches,* vol. 1 (Emporia: Chase County Historical Society, 1940). The political behavior of German-speaking Catholics who came to Kansas from Russia at the same time as the Mennonites is helpfully examined by David A. Haury, "German-Russian Immigrants and Kansas Politics: A comparison of the Catholic and Mennonite Immigration to Kansas and their Politics" (unpublished research paper, MLA, 1972).

3. A summary of Republican percentages in the Swedish precincts and in Kansas at large for these four elections is as follows:

		Swedes	*Kansas*
1880	Garfield	80.7%	60.4%
1884	Blaine	86.1%	58.2%
1888	Harrison	73.7%	55.4%
1904	Roosevelt	89.9%	64.8%

4. In one study which provides voting information from a Mennonite area, this general pattern is the same. In the Cub Creek Precinct, Jefferson County, Nebraska, a precinct which includes the Mennonite town of Jansen, the presidential election of 1940 marked a shift from the Democratic to the Republican candidate. See D. Paul Miller, "An Analysis of Community Adjustment: A Case Study of Jansen, Nebraska" (unpublished Ph.D. dissertation, University of Nebraska, 1953), p. 167, table 7.

CHAPTER 2

1. This quotation is frequently cited in Mennonite historical literature. For example, see C. Henry Smith, *The Story of the Mennonites* (3rd ed., revised

and enlarged by Cornelius Krahn; Newton: Mennonite Publication Office, 1950), p. 4. Cornelius J. Dyck, ed., *An Introduction to Mennonite History* (Scottdale: Herald Press, 1967), p. 29.

2. Contemporary Mennonite Anabaptist historiography tends to focus on the theological or biblical validity of the movement rather than upon its radical social implications in the sixteenth century context. For a stimulating dissenting view see Lowell H. Zuck, "Anabaptism: Abortive Counter-Revolt Within the Reformation," *Church History*, vol. 26 (Sept. 1957), pp. 211-226. John Howard Yoder emphasizes Zwingli's fears of the social effects of Anabaptism in "Anabaptist Origins in Switzerland," chap. 2 in *An Introduction to Mennonite History*, ed. Cornelius J. Dyck (Scottdale: Herald Press, 1967), pp. 30, 33. For a recent challenging Marxist interpretation see the historiographical essay, pp. 11-70, in Gerhard Brendler, *Das Taeuferreich zu Muenster, 1534-35* (Berlin: Veb Deutscher Verlag der Wissenschaften, 1966). Recent Mennonite Anabaptist historiography puts increasing emphasis upon the movement's radical social implications in the sixteenth century. See for example Walter Klaassen's sixth chapter, "Radical Politics: Anabaptism and Revolution," in his *Anabaptism: Neither Catholic nor Protestant* (Waterloo, Ontario: Conrad Press, 1973), pp. 48-63.

3. For a description of the Muenster uprising and evaluation of the literature see Cornelius Krahn, "Muenster Anabaptists," *Mennonite Encyclopedia*, vol. 3 (Scottdale: Mennonite Publishing House; Newton: Mennonite Publication Office; Hillsboro: Mennonite Brethren Publishing House, 1959), pp. 777-782. (*Mennonite Encyclopedia* cited hereafter as *ME*.)

4. A stimulating and perceptive essay on this topic is by Robert Friedman, "The Doctrine of the Two Worlds," *The Recovery of the Anabaptist Vision*, ed. Guy F. Hershberger (Scottdale: Herald Press, 1957), pp. 105-118. Friedman contrasts Anabaptist "kingdom theology," which is derived from the gospels and which posits a dualism of God's kingdom and Satan's kingdom, with the Reformers' "salvation theology," which is derived from the Pauline epistles and emphasizes a dualism of spirit and flesh.

5. For an appreciative summary of the Anabaptist attitude toward the state see Hans J. Hillerbrand, "The Anabaptist View of the State," *Mennonite Quarterly Review*, vol. 32 (Apr. 1958), pp. 83-110. (*Mennonite Quarterly Review* cited hereafter as *MQR*.)

6. Harold S. Bender, "Church and State in Mennonite History," *MQR*, vol. 13 (Apr. 1939), pp. 83-103.

7. For a brief survey of the Mennonites in Russia see David G. Rempel, "The Mennonite Commonwealth in Russia, a Sketch of Its Founding and Endurance," *MQR*, vol. 47 (Oct. 1973), pp. 259-308, and *MQR*, vol. 48 (Jan. 1974), pp. 5-54. See also Frank Epp, "The Mennonites in Russia," *An Introduction to Mennonite History*, ed. Cornelius J. Dyck (Scottdale: Herald Press, 1967), pp. 126-144, and Cornelius Krahn, "Russia," *ME*, vol. 3, pp. 381-393.

8. Mennonites came to Kansas in the 1870s from Prussia, Western Europe, and Mennonite settlements in America, as well as from Russia. The focus in this study is upon the Russian Mennonites who constituted the largest group.

9. Cornelius Jansen, ed., *Sammlung von Notizen ueber Amerika* (Danzig:

Paul Thieme, 1872). For a biography of Jansen and his role in the migration see Gustav E. Reimer and G. R. Gaeddert, *Exiled by the Czar* (Newton: Mennonite Publication Office, 1956). The fullest accounts of the migration as a whole include C. Henry Smith, *The Coming of the Russian Mennonites* (Berne, Ind.: Mennonite Book Concern, 1927), and Georg Leibrandt, "The Emigration of the German Mennonites from Russia to the United States and Canada in 1873-1883 and Their Settlement in Kansas" (unpublished Ph.D. dissertation, University of Minnesota, 1954). A fine short review is in the thesis by John D. Unruh, Jr., "The Burlington and Missouri River Railroad Brings the Mennonites to Nebraska, 1873-1878" (unpublished master's thesis, University of Kansas, 1959), pp. 33-56.

10. Jansen, *Sammlung*, p. 3.

11. *Ibid.*, p. 6.

12. *Ibid.*, p. 37.

13. For a brief explanation of the difference between Mennonite freedom and democratic freedom see E. K. Francis, *In Search of Utopia: The Mennonites in Manitoba* (Glencoe: Free Press, 1955), pp. 81-82.

14. Warkentin's letters to Goerz are in the MLA. A few are reprinted in "Some Letters of Bernhard Warkentin Pertaining to the Migration of 1873-1875," ed. Cornelius Krahn, *MQR*, vol. 24 (July 1950), pp. 248-262.

15. Letter from Warkentin to Goerz, no. 251, Mar. 3, 1873, *Ibid.*, p. 256.

16. Warkentin to Goerz, no. 258, Mar. 28/16, 1873. *Ibid.*, p. 260.

17. David C. Wedel, "Contributions of Pioneer David Goerz," *ML*, vol. 7 (Oct. 1952), pp. 170-175.

18. Summarized from Leonhard Sudermann, *Eine Deputationsreise von Russland nach Amerika* (Elkhart: Mennonitische Verlagshandlung, 1897), p. 10.

19. Leibrandt, "Emigration of the German Mennonites from Russia to the United States and Canada in 1873-1800," *MQR*, vol. 7 (January 1933), part 2, p. 6.

20. See the diary of delegate Tobias A. Unruh, trans. and pub. Abe J. Unruh under the title, *Great Grandfather's Diary* (Montezuma, Kan., n.p., n.d.). Entry for July 30, 1873.

21. *Ibid.*, entry for Aug. 8, 1873.

22. For the official documents relating to Grant and the Mennonites see Ernst Correll, "President Grant and the Mennonite Immigration from Russia," *MQR*, vol. 9 (July 1935), pp. 144-152.

23. C. B. Schmidt, "Reminiscences of Foreign Immigration Work for Kansas," *Transactions of the Kansas State Historical Society 1905-1906*, vol. 9, pp. 492-493.

24. Leland Harder, "The Russian Mennonites and American Democracy under Grant," *From the Steppes to the Prairies*, ed. Cornelius Krahn (Newton: Mennonite Publication Office, 1949), pp. 54-67. C. Henry Smith, *The Coming of the Russian Mennonites* (Berne, Indiana: Mennonite Book Concern, 1927), pp. 77-91.

25. The Mennonites were already leaving Russia at the time of the debates. See Leibrandt, *MQR*, vol. 7, part 2, p. 22.

26. Harold S. Bender, "Zur Heimath," *ME*, vol. 4, p. 1042.

27. *Marion County Record,* Dec. 31, 1875.

28. *Zur Heimath,* Mar. 21, 1880.

29. D.S.H., "Die Regierungschulen in Amerika," *Zur Heimath,* July 15, 1876.

30. A. J. Moser, "Regierungschulen," *Zur Heimath,* Aug. 1, 1876.

31. J. J. F., "Oeffentliche Schulen," *Zur Heimath,* Aug. 1, 1876.

32. John 15:19b, KJV.

33. D. S. H., "Zur Buergerrechts-Frage," *Zur Heimath,* Sept. 1, 1876.

34. *Zur Heimath,* June 15, 1877, and Jan. 15, 1878.

35. D. R. Hirschler, "Die Distrikt-Schulen," *Zur Heimath,* Sept. 1, 1876.

36. Ph. Schmutz, "Schule, Buergerrecht and Wehrlosigkeit," *Zur Heimath,* Mar. 15, Apr. 1, 1877.

37. Cornelius Krahn, "Ewert, Wilhelm," *ME,* vol. 2, p. 276.

38. Wilhelm Ewert, "Die Schul-und Buergerfrage," *Zur Heimath,* Apr. 1, 1877.

39. "Eine Abhandlung ueber den Krieg," *Zur Heimath,* Oct. 1, 15; Nov. 1, 15; Dec. 1, 15, 1877.

40. See, for example, A. J. Moser, "Menno Simon ueber Obrigkeit," *Zur Heimath,* June 15, 1877.

41. H. P. Krehbiel, *The History of the General Conference of Mennonites of North America* (vol. 1, St. Louis: H. P. Krehbiel, 1898), (vol. 2, Newton: H. P. Krehbiel, 1938). Samuel Floyd Pannabecker, "The Development of the General Conference of the Mennonite Church of North America in the American Environment," (unpublished Ph.D. dissertation, Yale University, 1944). For a shorter account see Cornelius J. Dyck, "The General Conference Mennonite Church," chap. 14 in *An Introduction to Mennonite History,* ed. Cornelius J. Dyck (Scottdale: Herald Press, 1967)

42. J. F. Harms, *Geschichte der Mennoniten Bruedergemeinde* (Hillsboro: Mennonite Brethren Publishing House, n.d., ca. 1924); A. H. Unruh, *Die Geschichte der Mennoniten-Bruedergemeinde* 1860-1954 (Winnipeg: The General Conference of the Mennonite Brethren Church of North America, 1955); John H. Lohrenz, *The Mennonite Brethren Church* (Hillsboro: Mennonite Brethren Publishing House, 1950); Frank C. Peters, "The Mennonite Brethren Church," chap. 15 in *An Introduction to Mennonite History,* ed., Cornelius J. Dyck (Scottdale: Herald Press, 1967), pp. 109-245.

43. Harold S. Bender, "Krimmer Mennonite Brethren," *ME,* vol. 3, pp. 242-245.

44. See Clarence Hiebert, *The Holdeman People* (South Pasadena: William Carey Library, 1973).

45. The theme of cultural interaction among Mennonite groups is central in the book published for the 1974 centennial by Harley Stucky, *A Century of Russian Mennonite History in America* (North Newton: Mennonite Press, 1973).

46. Edmund G. Kaufman, "Social Problems and Opportunities of the Western District Conference Communities of the General Conference of Mennonites of North America" (unpublished M.A. thesis, Bluffton College and Mennonite Seminary, 1917), pp. 42-57. See also Kaufman, "Non-theological Cultural Factors in the Origin and Current Relationship of

Mennonite Groups," *Proceedings of the Eleventh Conference on Mennonite Educational and Cultural Problems* (Bethel College, 1957), pp. 49-54.

47. One historian who had ambitiously planned to include all the Mennonites of Illinois in a "composite" history decided the task was impossible and wrote, "I have been disillusioned in regard to the unity of the subject." Harry F. Weber, *Centennial History of the Mennonites of Illinois, 1829-1929* (Goshen: Mennonite Historical Society, 1931), p. xi.

CHAPTER 3

1. "First Naturalization Paper" used in McPherson County.

2. Carlton J. H. Hayes, *Nationalism: A Religion* (New York: Macmillan, 1960), p. 165.

3. *Gesamtprotokolle der Kansas—und Westlichen Distrikt—Konferenzen* (n.p.: n.d.), p. 10.

4. H. P. Peters, *History and Development of Education Among the Mennonites in Kansas* (Hillsboro: n.p., 1925), p. 23.

5. Edna Nyquist, *Pioneer Life and Lore of McPherson County, Kansas* (McPherson: Democrat-Opinion Press, 1932), p. 79.

6. David V. Wiebe, *They Seek a Country* (Hillsboro: Mennonite Brethren Publishing House, 1959), p. 166.

7. *Marion County Record,* Nov. 10, 1876.

8. McPherson *Independent,* Feb. 20, 1879.

9. McPherson *Freeman,* Feb. 17, 1879.

10. Newton *Kansan,* March 6, 1879.

11. Alberta Pantle, "Settlement of the Krimmer Mennonite Brethren at Gnadenau, Marion County," *Kansas Historical Quarterly,* vol. 13 (Feb. 1945), footnote, p. 276.

12. For a summary of the vote in McPherson County, see the McPherson *Independent,* Feb. 27, 1879. C. B. Schmidt, the Santa Fe agent responsible for bringing the Mennonites to Kansas, had been soliciting railroad votes among Mennonites in the days prior to the election. See the McPherson *Independent* Feb. 20, 1879.

13. The 1892 increase in Marion County has not been fully explained, for the pileup did not occur in the days shortly before November elections. Also worth further investigation is the fact that 182 Mennonites undertook *final* naturalization proceedings in Marion County in 1892, more than three times as many as in any other year.

14. *Marion County Record,* Nov. 9, 1877.

15. Marcus Hansen, *The Immigrant in American History* (New York: Harper and Row, 1940), p. 78.

1. Alberta Pantle, *Op. Cit.,* pp. 259-285. See also David V. Wiebe, *They Seek a Country* (Hillsboro: Mennonite Brethren Publishing House, 1959), pp. 145-157.

2. Three maps which graphically illustrate the changing village settlement

CHAPTER 4

pattern of the Alexanderwohl community in Russia, in Kansas (1874), and later in Kansas (1949), were printed in *ML*, vol. 4 (Oct. 1949), pp. 21-25.

3. Quoted in Wiebe, *They Seek a Country*, p. 166.

4. D. S. H., "Die Regierrungschulen in Amerika," *zur Heimath*, July 15, 1876.

5. Menno S. Harder, "The Origin, Philosophy, and Development of Education Among the Mennonites," (unpublished Ph.D. dissertation, University of Southern California, 1949), p. 222.

6. H. P. Peters, *History and Development of Education Among Mennonites in Kansas* (Hillsboro, 1925), p. 23.

7. Harder, *Op. Cit.*, pp. 223-225.

8. Peters, *Op. Cit.*, p. 30.

9. Although the Kansas Conference is here labeled "GC," it may be kept in mind that this regional conference did not join the national General Conference as a body until 1892. See Samuel Floyd Pannabecker, "The Development of the General Conference of the Mennonite Church of North America in the American Environment," (unpublished Ph.D. dissertation, Yale, 1944), p. 402.

10. *Gesamtprotokolle der Kansas - und Westlichen Distrikt - Konferenzen,* (n.p., n.d.), vol. 3, p. 32.

11. Valentine Krehbiel, "Ist es dem wehrlosen Christen gestattet sich an politischen Wahlen zu beteiligen, und wenn so, in wie weit darf solches geschehen?" *Zur Heimath*, Mar. 21, 1880.

12. "Konferenz Beschluesse der Mennoniten Bruedergemeinde, 1878," unpublished copy by J. F. Harms, Hillsboro, 1924.

13. D. C. Eitzen, interview with the author at Hillsboro, Kansas, Nov. 23, 1966.

14. A. E. Janzen, ed., *Resolutions of the General Conference of the Mennonite Brethren Church, 1878-1963*, (Hillsboro: Board of Reference and Counsel, 1964), p. 70.

15. *Ibid.*, p. 70.

16. *Ibid.*, p. 107.

17. *Ibid.*, p. 156.

18. This explanation was suggested by A. E. Janzen, Hillsboro, interview with the author, Aug. 11, 1966.

19. *Konferenzbeschluesse der Krimmer Mennoniten Bruedergemeinde, von Nord Amerika, Zwischen den Jahren 1882-1940* (Inman: Salem Publishing House, n.d.,), p. 4.

20. *Ibid.*, p. 9.

21. *Ibid.*, pp. 15, 17.

22. *Ibid.*, pp. 25-26, 29.

23. *Ibid.*, p. 37.

24. *Conference Record Containing the Proceedings of the Kansas-Nebraska Mennonite Conference, 1876-1914*, ed. L. O. King, et. al., n.d.; n.p., p. 10.

25. *Ibid.*, p. 10.

26. *Ibid.*, p. 16. These concerns were expressed at the Kansas-Nebraska conference in the Pennsylvania Church, Harvey County, April 6-7, 1888.

27. *Ibid.*, p. 29.

28. *Ibid.,* p. 39.

29. *Ibid.,* p. 87.

30. From June G. Cabe and Charles A. Sullivant, *Kansas Votes, National Elections, 1859-1956* (Lawrence: Governmental Research Center, University of Kansas, 1957).

31. Herman Loewen, interview with the author in Newton, Kansas, May 9, 1967.

32. *Marion County Record,* Nov. 10, 1876.

33. McPherson *Republican,* Oct. 5, 1882.

34. The quotations are used here in referring to the "Mennonite" vote because there is no way of determining what percentage of votes recorded in a single township was actually cast by Mennonites. In 1880 the heaviest concentration of Mennonites in any single township was 62% and the average in a group of selected Mennonite townships was only 50.2%. The percentage of Mennonites in these townships increased gradually to 65.4% in 1895 and 77.8% in 1925. But it was only in Menno and West Branch townships, with over 90% Mennonites among potential voters, that one was able to speak with certainty about the Mennonite vote. See Appendix F, Percentage of Mennonites Among Voting-Age Residents in Selected Central Kansas Townships.

It should also be kept in mind that a smaller percentage of Mennonites turned out to vote on election day. In the 1880 presidential election, for example, 67% of the potential voters cast ballots in King City Township, McPherson County, where almost no Mennonite families had settled. In adjacent Lone Tree Township, with 62% of potential voters Mennonites, only 42.5% voted. And in Liberty Township in Marion County (which included the area of present Menno Township), also with 62% of potential voters Mennonites, only 10.6% went to the polls. The high number of Mennonite nonvoters meant that even in a township of 70% Mennonites, only half of the voters in any given election may have actually been cast by Mennonites.

35. For a general article on Mennonites and temperance see Harold S. Bender, "Alcohol," *ME,* vol. 1, pp. 36-40.

36. The sale of alcohol was forbidden in the KMB village of Gnadenau. See Pantle, "Settlement," p. 273.

37. "Ein arger Feind," *Zur Heimath,* July 15, 1878; "Murphy Clubs oder Christi Gemeine?" *Zur Heimath,* Aug. 1, Oct. 1, 1878.

38. Quoted in J. W. Kliewer, *Memoirs* (North Newton: Bethel College Press, 1943), p. 61.

39. Wilhelm Ewert, "Unsre ersten Schritten zur Befolgung des Milizgesetzes in Kansas," *Zur Heimath,* Feb. 15, 1877. David Goerz, "Die Gefahren einer Revolution beseitigt," *Ibid.*

40. J. H. Loewen, "Harms, John F.," *ME,* vol. 2, 665. Cornelius Krahn, conversation with the author, May 8, 1967.

41. *Newton Anzeiger,* June 22, 1888.

42. *Marion County Anzeiger,* June 1, 1888.

43. *Marion County Anzeiger,* July 27, 1888.

44. *Marion County Anzeiger,* Sept. 14, 28, 1888.

45. *McPherson Anzeiger,* Nov. 2, 1888.

46. *Newton Anzeiger,* Aug. 10, 1888.

47. *McPherson Anzeiger,* Aug. 17, 1888.

48. *Newton Daily Republican,* Aug. 15, 1888.

49. *Newton Anzeiger,* Aug. 17, 24, 1888.

50. Freely translated: Dear Fatherland, you can rest at ease, the people stand staunchly behind Cleveland.

51. *Hillsboro Herald,* Nov. 1, 8, 1888.

52. *Marion County Anzeiger,* Oct. 5, 1888.

53. For background on the history and practice of Mennonite mutual aid see J. Winfield Fretz, "Mutual Aid Among the Mennonites," *MQR,* vol. 13 (1939), pp. 28-58, 187-209.

54. *McPherson Anzeiger,* Feb. 17, 1888.

55. *Hillsboro Anzeiger,* Supplement, July 31, 1896.

56. P. M. Friesen, *Die Alt-Evangelische Mennonitische Bruderschaft in Russland,* 1889-1910 (Halbstadt: Verlagsgesellschaft Raduga, 1911), pp. 498-499. *Marion County Anzeiger,* Oct. 23, 1887. *McPherson Anzeiger,* June 1, 1888.

57. Herman Loewen, Newton, Kansas, interview with the author, May 8, 1967.

58. John E. Goering, son of Joseph C. Goering, interview with the author at Moundridge, Kansas, May 7, 1967. See also Walter T. K. Nugent, *The Tolerant Populists* (Chicago: University of Chicago Press, 1963), p. 140.

59. *Hillsboro Anzeiger,* April 18, 1890.

60. *Hillsboro Anzeiger,* Nov. 7, 1890.

61. *Hillsboro Anzeiger,* Oct. 9, 1891. Quoted in Michael J. Brodhead, "The Early Career of E. W. Hoch," (unpublished M.A. thesis, University of Kansas, 1962), p. 65.

62. *Hillsboro Anzeiger,* Sept. 29, 1893.

63. *Hillsboro Anzeiger,* June 26, 1896.

64. Brodhead, "The Early Career," p. 63.

65. Marion County Record of Votes Cast, 1897.

66. *Newton Post und Volksblatt,* Oct. 27, 1904. Gerhard Zerger, retired farmer and McPherson County commissioner, interview with the author, Moundridge, Dec. 6, 1966.

67. The first issue of the *Marion County Anzeiger,* July 15, 1887, addressed the question in broader terms which included German immigrants in general rather than Mennonites in particular.

68. Ernest E. Leisy, "On a Kansas Farm," *ML,* vol. 1 (Jan. 1946), p. 18.

69. W. J. Groat, "The Russo-German Colonies of Kansas," *Brown's Industrial Gazetteer and Handbook* (n.p.: n.d. [1881]), p. 200.

70. McPherson *Republican,* April 24, 1884.

71. Newton *Kansan,* Aug. 24, 1882. See also the praise for the Mennonites in the McPherson *Republican,* May 25, 1882.

72. Jacob Stucky, "Auswanderungslied," *Zur Heimath,* June 1875.

73. *Marion County Anzeiger,* June 1, 1888.

CHAPTER 5

1. Samuel S. Haury, *Die Wehrlosigkeit in der Sonntagsschule* (Dayton: United Brethren Publishing House, 1894).

2. *Der Herold,* Apr. 5, 1917.

3. See the announcement of the special session and the questions to be discussed in *Christlicher Bundesbote,* May 12, 1898.

4. *Gesamtprotokolle der Kansas - und Westlichen Distrikt - Konferenzen,* p. 264.

5. Charles M. Skinner, "The Mennonites of Kansas," St. Louis *Globe-Democrat,* Sept. 30, 1900.

6. *Kansas Volksblatt und Anzeiger,* Mar. 10, 1898.

7. For other examples of Mennonite trust in McKinley as a peacemaker see John P. Thiessen, "Wie stehen unsere Mennoniten in Amerika zur Wehrpflicht," Hillsboro *Post,* June 3, 1898, and the editorial by H. P. Krehbiel in *The Review,* Oct. 1900.

8. See, for example, "Spaniens barbarische Kreigsfuehrung," *Kansas Volksblatt und Anzeiger,* June 23, 1898.

9. *Volksblatt und Anzeiger,* Aug. 18, 1898.

10. *Ibid.,* Sept. 8, 1898.

11. H. O. Kruse, "The Coming World Conflict," *The Review,* May 1899.

12. Krehbiel began *The Review* as an English-language paper in Canton, Ohio, in April 1899, but moved it to Newton, Kansas, in December 1899. He continued the paper through 1904 and then switched to German-language publication.

13. An Inquiring Observer, "How About That Doctrine of Non-Resistance?" *The Review,* Sept. 1900.

14. J. J. Funk, letter to the editor, *The Review,* Oct. 1900.

15. *The Review,* Oct. 1900.

16. P. H. Richert, "Neither a Republican Nor a Democratic Principle," *The Review,* Nov. 1900.

17. *The Review,* Dec. 1900, Jan. 1901.

18. C. Frey, "Etliche Gedanken bezueglich der gegenwaertigen Kampagne," Hillsboro *Post,* Sept. 23, 1900.

19. Ferdinand J. Funk, "Die Philippinen-Frage," Hillsboro *Post,* Aug. 24, 1900.

20. Ferdinand J. Funk, "Ein Brief von Herrn Roosevelt," Hillsboro *Post,* Oct. 26, 1900.

21. Only the General Conference Mennonites officially stated their approval of noncombatant war work. The more conservative and isolated groups, such as the (Old) Mennonites and Church of God in Christ (Holdeman) Mennonites, were less affected by wartime patriotism.

CHAPTER 6

1. Unpublished M.A. Thesis, Bluffton College and Mennonite Seminary, 1917.

2. *Ibid.,* pp. 70-71, 73, 87, 95-97, 99, passim.

3. *Ibid.,* pp. 86-87.

4. *Ibid.,* pp. 165-173, 174. It should be kept in mind that Kaufman wrote primarily of General Conference Mennonites, though he wrote in his last chapter with regard to his final summary that "in a large measure most of these things apply to American Mennonites in general" (p. 165).

5. *Ibid.,* pp. 149-163.

6. Walter A. Huxman, governor of Kansas 1937-39, interview with the author, Oct. 7, 1966. Huxman's father was a Mennonite who joined the Swedenborgian Church near Pretty Prairie.

7. Kansas Mennonites never had a single leader who embodied the politics of the entire community. In this respect they may be contrasted with the Swedes of North McPherson County who came under the dominant Republican influence of Dr. Carl A. Swensson (1857-1904). Emory K. Lindquist, chancellor of Wichita State University, interview with the author, Oct. 3, 1966. For a biographical sketch of Swensson, see Lindquist's *Smoky Valley People* (Lindsborg: Bethany College, 1953), pp. 126-146.

8. Marcus Hansen, *The Problem of the Third Generation Immigrant* (Rock Island, Ill.: Augustana Historical Society, 1938), pp. 6-7.

9. *Vorwaerts,* July 14, 1911.

10. *Vorwaerts,* July 8, 1910.

11. Edward Bartel, North Newton, interview with the author, Sept. 2, 1966.

12. Hillsboro *Journal,* Dec. 4, 1908.

13. J. G. Ewert, *Der Gute Kampf* (Elkhart, Ind.: Mennonite Publishing Co., 1900).

14. J. G. Ewert, *Christentum und Sozialismus* (Hillsboro: Journal Press [1909]). An enlarged second edition was printed in 1914. Ewert occasionally spelled his name with a "v," especially when writing in English.

15. *Ibid.,* p. 10.

16. H. P. Krehbiel, "Sozialist Debs ueber Religion und der Hillsboro Schriftleiter als Verteidiger," *Der Herold,* June 2, 1910.

17. *Vorwaerts,* June 3, 1910. *Der Herold,* June 9, 1910.

18. Renatta Schultz Friesen (Mrs. J. V.), Hillsboro, interview with the author, May 2, 1967.

19. J. G. Ewert, *Die Bibel und die Enthaltsamkeit,* 2nd ed. (Berne: Christlichen Maessigkeits Verein, n.d.), pp. 30-31.

20. J. G. Ewert, *Christentum und Prohibition* (n.p.: n.d.), p. 7-8.

21. J. G. Ewert, 1874-1923," *Vorwaerts-Kalender* (Hillsboro: Mennonite Brethren Publishing House, 1925), p. 48.

22. See the bitter exchange between Ewert and Ferdinand Funk in the Hillsboro *Journal,* Oct. 30, Nov. 20, Dec. 4 and 11, 1908.

23. *Die Christliche Lehre von der Wehrlosigkeit,* trans. J. G. Ewert (Hillsboro: n.p., 1899).

24. Ewert, *Christianity and Socialism,* p. 5.

25. J. G. Ewert, "Ist Bryan unzuverlaessig?" *Der Deutsche Westen,* Oct. 22, 1908.

26. J. G. Ewert, "Warum ich nicht fuer Roosevelt waehlen wuerde," *Vorwaerts,* Oct. 25, 1912.

27. Christian Krehbiel, *Prairie Pioneer* (Newton: Faith and Life Press, 1961). Olin A. Krehbiel, "Krehbiel, Christian," *ME,* vol. 3, p. 236.

28. *The Review,* Aug. 1899.

29. *The Review,* Nov. 15, 1904.

30. C. H. Wedel, "Die Friedensidee auf sozial-politischem Gebiet," *Monatsblaetter aus Bethel College,* VIII (June 1903), pp. 63-64.

31 H. P. Krehbiel, "Progress of Peace," *The Review* (Oct. 15, 1904).

32. H. P. Krehbiel, *War, Peace, Amity* (Newton: H. P. Krehbiel, 1937).
33. *The Review,* Oct. 1900.
34. Elva Krehbiel Leisy, "Henry Peter Krehbiel (1862-1946)," *ML,* vol. 9 (Oct. 1954), p. 162.
35. *Post und Volksblatt,* July 3, 1902. See also *Ibid.,* Oct. 30, 1902, and May 4, 1905, for Mennonite reaction to labor-management disputes.
36. *Post und Volksblatt,* Nov. 2, 1905.
37. *Post und Volksblatt,* June 22, 1905.
38. *Post und Volksblatt,* May 22, 1902.
39. *Post und Volksblatt,* Oct. 11, 1906.
40. *Post und Volksblatt,* Aug. 16, 1906; July 16, 1908.
41. *Post und Volksblatt,* Oct. 29, 1908.
42. C. D. Amstutz, "Roosevelt and Nonresistance," *The Review,* Nov. 1900.
43. Hillsboro *Journal,* Oct. 30, 1908. *Vorwaerts,* Oct. 25, 1912.
44. *The Review,* Nov. 15, 1904.
45. Cornelius Krahn, Bethel College, interview with the author, June 12, 1967.
46. Romans 13:1.
47. D. C. Wedel, letter to the author, Nov. 19, 1966.
48. *Topeka Daily Capital,* Mar. 7, 1909.
49. The records for Krehbiel's term in the legislature are meager. The list of committees and proposed legislation are to be found in the *House Journal, State of Kansas, 1909* (Topeka: State Printing Office, 1909). There are also a few items in the H. P. Krehbiel Collection, folder 51.
50. H. P. Krehbiel to Christian Krehbiel, Mar. 2, 1909. H. P. Krehbiel Collection, folder 50. H. P. Krehbiel to H. E. Suderman, Jan. 23, 1909. H. P. Krehbiel Collection, folder 49.
51. Schellenberg also served a second term in this office from 1922 to 1929. See T. R. Schellenberg, "Editor Abraham L. Schellenberg," *ML,* vol. 9 (Jan. 1954), pp. 19-28.
52. Quoted in *Ibid.,* p. 23.
53. From 1907 to 1913 the Mennonite Brethren Publishing Company headquarters had been in McPherson where Schellenberg, for a time, edited *Der Deutsche Westen.* Personal differences between the editors and publisher reduced the effectiveness of the newspaper. See Schellenberg's summary of the history of the paper in the final issue, *Der Deutsche Westen,* Dec. 29, 1910.
54. *Vorwaerts,* Feb. 13, 1914.
55. *Vorwaerts,* Feb. 20, 1914.
56. *Vorwaerts,* Feb. 27, 1914.
57. *Vorwaerts,* Oct. 30, 1914.
58. T. R. Schellenberg, "Editor Abraham L. Schellenberg," op. cit., p. 25.
59. Hillsboro *Journal,* Oct. 30, 1908.
60. *Vorwaerts,* May 1 and Sept. 11, 1914.
61. *Vorwaerts,* Oct. 30, 1914.
62. See, for example, Schellenberg's biting reference to "food dictator" Herbert Hoover with the implicit suggestions that Hoover's appeals contradict the "yet higher word" of the Bible. *Zionsbote,* June 20, 1917.

63. Schellenberg returned to his job in Hillsboro from 1922 to 1929, after which he again took up farming and preaching in Texas. He died in 1941. See T. R. Schellenberg, "Editor Abraham L. Schellenberg," op. cit., pp. 26-28.

64. See for example, *Post und Volksblatt,* June 12 and Oct. 9, 1902, and *Der Deutsche Westen,* Nov. 3, 1910.

65. Kruse's paper was reprinted in *Der Herold,* Mar. 31, 1910.

66. *Ibid.*

67. Richard Hofstadter, *The Age of Reform* (New York: Vintage, 1955), pp. 131-173; Christopher Lasch, *The New Radicalism in America 1889-1963* (New York: Vintage, 1965), pp. 36-37, 101.

68. *Vorwaerts,* Oct. 2, 1914.

69. Ewert, *Christentum und Sozialismus,* p. 6.

CHAPTER 7

1. A. L. Schellenberg, "1914," *Vorwaerts,* Jan. 2, 1914.

2. T. R. Schellenberg, "Editor Abraham L. Schellenberg," *ML,* vol. 9 (Jan. 1954), pp. 19-28. J. H. Lohrenz, "Schellenberg, Abraham L.," *ME,* vol. 4, p. 448. "Krehbiel, Christian E.," and "Krehbiel, Henry Peter," *Who's Who Among the Mennonites,* A. Warkentin, ed. (n.p., 1937), pp. 86-87. Olin A. Krehbiel, "Krehbiel, Christian Emmanuel," *ME,* vol. 3, pp. 237-238. Elva Krehbiel Leisy, "Krehbiel, Henry Peter," *ME,* vol. 3, pp. 237-238. The most important official Mennonite periodicals were (GC) *Christlicher Bundesbote,* Berne, Ind., C. van der Smissen, ed.; *The Mennonite,* Berne, Ind., S. M. Grubb, ed.; (MB) *Zionsbote,* Hillsboro, Kan., Abraham L. Schellenberg, ed.; (KMB) *Der Wahrheitsfreund* (begun in 1915), Chicago, M. B. Fast, ed.; (OM) *The Gospel Herald,* Scottdale, Pa., Daniel Kaufman and John F. Funk, eds.

3. *Der Herold,* Aug. 6, 1914.

4. *Vorwaerts,* Aug. 7, 1914.

5. *Vorwaerts,* Sept. 11 and 18, 1914.

6. *Der Herold,* Aug. 13, 1914.

7. Quoted in *Der Herold,* Oct. 8, 1914. Freely translated: Dear Fatherland, you can rest at ease; strong and faithful stands the watch on the Rhine.

8. *Der Herold,* Nov. 12, 1914. Letter from Franziska Muller dated Steglitz, Sept. 15, 1914.

9. *Der Herold,* Dec. 10, 1914. Letter from Ernst Meyer dated Koenigsburg, Oct. 22, 1914.

10. *Der Herold,* Nov. 5, 1914.

11. Friedrich Adam Julius Von Bernhardi, *Germany and the Next War,* trans., Allen H. Powles (London: Edward Arnold, 1912). This book was given to the Bethel College library in 1928 by E. B. Krehbiel as part of the Christian Krehbiel collection.

12. *Vorwaerts,* Oct. 30, 1914.

13. *Der Herold,* Oct. 29, 1914.

14. *Vorwaerts,* Nov. 6, 1914.

15. See Appendix D.

16. Clifton J. Child, *The German-Americans in Politics, 1914-1917* (Madison: University of Wisconsin, 1939), pp. 22-28.

17. Mennonite history is full of instances in which members stood ready to do something regarded as useful to warring nations. J. W. Nickel, "An Analytical Approach to Mennonite Ethics" (unpublished Ph.D. dissertation, Iliff School of Theology, 1959) p. 65, writes that such service "was rendered to the armies marching for William of Orange, Frederick the Great, Catherine the Great and Nicholaus II, for Karl XII of Sweden as well as for the armies of the United States of America, Canada, Brazil, Paraguay, and also for those of Hitler and Stalin.

18. *Vorwaerts,* Nov. 27, 1914.

19. *Vorwaerts,* Dec. 18, 1914.

20. C. C. Wedel, "Wo ist dein Bruder Abel?" *Der Herold,* April 8, 1915. See 2 Kings 5:20-27.

21. G. B. Ruth, "Hans und Peter," *Der Herold, Aug. 26, 1915.* Ruth was a Mennonite who had received no Mennonite support in his bid for the office of Harvey County superintendent of public instruction on the Socialist ticket in 1906 and for county commissioner in 1912.

22. *Der Herold,* Aug. 26, 1915.

23. *Vorwaerts,* Mar. 19, 1915.

24. *Vorwaerts,* April 9 and 16, 1915.

25. *Vorwaerts,* May 28, 1915.

26. *Vorwaerts,* May 21, 1915.

27. *Der Herold,* May 13, 1915.

28. J. G. Ewert, "Die ersten Praesidentschaftskandidaten fuer 1916," *Vorwaerts,* Mar. 17, 1916.

29. See Vorwaerts, July 20, 1915; May 19, 1916; Aug. 18, 1916. For an analysis of the German-American press, especially in Ohio, see Carl Wittke, *German-Americans and the World War* (Columbus: Ohio State Archaeological and Historical Society, 1936).

30. *Vorwaerts,* Sept. 22, 1916.

31. *Der Herold,* Oct. 21, 1915.

32. *Der Herold,* July 15, 1915.

33. J. D. Fast, "Allerlei," *Vorwaerts,* May 26, 1916.

34. *Vorwaerts,* Mar. 17, June 23, July 7, and Sept. 22, 1916. *Der Herold,* July 13 and Oct. 12, 1916.

35. J. G. Ewert, "Fragen, die Hughes nicht beantwortet," *Vorwaerts,* Sept. 22, 1916.

36. *Vorwaerts,* Oct. 27, 1916. On the wartime role of J. G. Ewert, A. L. Schellenberg, and the Hillsboro newspaper, *Vorwaerts,* see Gregory J. Stucky, "Fighting Against War: The Mennonite *Vorwaerts* from 1914 to 1919," *Kansas Historical Quarterly,* vol. 38 (Summer 1972), pp. 169-186.

37. *Vorwaerts,* Nov. 3, 1916.

38. *Der Herold,* Nov. 9, 1916.

39. *Christlicher Bundesbote,* Nov. 16, 1916, p. 4.

40. Interview with Gerhard Zerger, Moundridge, Dec. 6, 1966.

41. Letter from D. C. Wedel, Nov. 19, 1966.

42. Gerhard Dalke, *A Defense of the Mennonites Against Recent Attacks Made Upon Them* (n.d.; n.p. [1917]), p. 9.

43. *Der Herold,* Apr. 19, 1917. Only Western District (GC) Mennonites had the right to vote in this meeting.

44. Committee members were P. H. Richert, Gerhard Penner, J. C. Goering, P. H. Unruh, H. P. Krehbiel, and W. J. Ewert.

45. "Bericht der Spezialsitzung der Westlichen Distrikt-Konferenz, (17) Mai 1898," *Gesamtprotokolle der Kansas - und Westlichen Distrikt - Konferenzen,* p. 264.

46. *Der Herold,* Apr. 19, 1917.

47. *Ibid.*

48. Newton *Evening Kansan Republican,* Apr. 12, 1917. The press release was written by H. P. Krehbiel.

49. Newton *Evening Kansan-Republican,* Apr. 26, 1917.

50. William Frank Zornow, *Kansas* (Norman: University of Oklahoma, 1957), p. 229.

51. H. C. Peterson and Gilbert C. Fite, *Opponents of War 1917-1918* (Madison: University of Wisconsin Press, 1957), pp. 10-11.

52. H. P. Krehbiel, "Militaerdienst in der Ver. Staaten," *Der Herold,* Mar. 16, 1916.

53. Public Law No. 85, 64th Cong., 1st Session.

54. H. P. Krehbiel, "Ein neues Militaergesetz," *Der Herold,* Mar. 15, 1917.

55. *Der Herold,* Apr. 26 and May 10, 1917.

56. *Der Herold,* May 24, 1917. Public Law No. 12, 65th Cong., 1st Session. Selective Service Act of May 18, 1917.

57. The KMBs later adopted a conference resolution advising their men not to report to the camps. See *Konferenzbeschluesse der Krimmer Mennoniten Bruedergemeinde, von Nord Amerika, zwischen den Jahren 1882-1940* (Inman: Salem Publishing House, n.d.), p. 37. However, there is no record that the KMB young men abided by this resolution.

58. Minute Book of the Committee on Exemptions of the Western District Conference 1917-1922, p. 19.

59. *Ibid.* Letter to Newton D. Baker, June 28, 1917, Metropolitan Hotel, Washington, D.C. The letter was signed by J. W. Kliewer, P. H. Unruh, and H. P. Krehbiel for the GCs; M. M. Just and H. W. Lorenz for the MBs; and D. E. Harder for the KMBs. The letter also claimed to represent a group of Hutterite Mennonite churches of South Dakota, pp. 23-25.

60. *Ibid.,* p. 26.

61. *Ibid.,* p. 27. Copy of letter from the committee to General E. H. Crowder, Provost Marshal General, July 2, 1917.

62. *Ibid.,* p. 27.

63. *Ibid.,* p. 33.

64. T. M. Erb, Hesston, June 18, 1917, letter to P. H. Unruh, Goessel, P. H. Unruh Collection, General Correspondence 1906-1917, MLA folder 1.

65. Aaron Loucks, Scottdale, Pa., July 24, 1917, letter to H. P. Krehbiel, Newton, H. P. Krehbiel Collection, Petitions and Reports, MLA microfilm 78. There were no Conservative Amish congregations in Kansas at this time.

66. "A Statement of Our Position on Military Service as Adopted by The Mennonite General Conference, August 29, 1917," *Gospel Herald,* X (Sept. 6, 1917), pp. 420-421.

67. See *The Mennonite,* vol. 30 (Sept. 13, 1917), p. 1, for a view of how Mennonites understood Baker and what they expected.

68. Quoted in Frederick Palmer, *Newton D. Baker, America at War* (New York: Dodd, Mead & Co., 1931), vol. 1, p. 342. For a newer critical but balanced evaluation of Baker's attitude toward the conscientious objector see Daniel R. Beaver, *Newton D. Baker and the American War Effort, 1917-1919* (Lincoln: University of Nebraska, 1966), pp. 231-233.

69. Order from the Adjutant General of the Army to the commanding generals of all National Army and National Guard division camps. Printed in James S. Easby-Smith, *Statement Concerning the Treatment of Conscientious Objectors in the Army* (Washington: Government Printing Office, 1919), p. 37.

70. H. P. Krehbiel, Newton, Aug. 22, 1917, telegram to Provost Marshal General E. H. Crowder, Washington, D.C. Crowder to Krehbiel Aug. 23, 1917, Records of Selective Service System 1917-1919, RG 163. MLA microfilm 208.

71. J. S. Hartzler, *Mennonites in the World War* (Scottdale: Mennonite Publishing House, 1921, p. 68.

72. Gustav Baergen, interview with the author at Hutchinson, Kansas, Jan. 22, 1967.

73. Interviews with D. C. Pauls, Henry Cooprider, Gustav Gaeddert, Cornelius Voth, Gustav Baergen. See also Noah Leatherman, *Diary Kept by Noah L. Leatherman While in Camp During World War I* (Linden, Alberta: Aaron L. Toews, 1951), and the unpublished diaries of Gustav Gaeddert and Menno Claassen. J. S. Hartzler reviews the experiences of the boys in camp and in the disciplinary barracks throughout the country in *Mennonites in the World War,* pp. 122-149.

74. Henry Cooprider, interview with the author in McPherson County, Kansas, Oct. 23, 1966. A taped interview and typescript copy of Mr. Cooprider's reminiscences on World War I experiences are included in the Schowalter Oral History Collection in the Mennonite Library and Archives at Bethel College. There is a published index to the 273 interviews in the collection. Keith L. Sprunger, James C. Juhnke, and John D. Waltner, eds., *Voices Against War* (North Newton: Bethel College, 1973).

75. H. P. Krehbiel, "Ein Besuch in Camp Funston," *Vorwaerts,* Oct. 12, 1917.

76. H. W. Lohrenz, President of Tabor College, Hillsboro, Oct. 19, 1917, letter to P. H. Unruh, member of Western District Exemption Committee. P. H. Unruh Collection, MLA folder 1, general correspondence 1906-1917.

77. *Vorwaerts,* Oct. 26, 1917.

78. *Minutes of the 26th Western District Conference,* Oct. 24-25, 1917 (Newton: Herald Press, n.d.), p. 725.

79. Gustav Gaeddert, interview with the author, North Newton, Kansas, Jan. 18, 1967.

80. Gustav Gaeddert diary. Entries for Jan. 1, 1918, and Feb. 5, 1918. MLA microfilm no. 79.

81. H. P. Krehbiel, Newton, Dec. 3, 1917, letter to F. M. Regier, Freeman, South Dakota, H. P. Krehbiel Collection, MLA folder 144, Exemption Committee Correspondence, Nov. 1917—Mar. 1918. See also the report by Aaron Loucks (OM). "To Our Drafted Brethren," *Gospel Herald,* vol. 10 (Mar. 21, 1918), p. 938.

82. E. H. Crowder, *Second Report of the Provost Marshal General to the Secretary of War* (Washington: Government Printing Office, 1919), pp. 58-59.

83. See Arlyn John Parish, *Kansas Mennonite During World War I* (Fort Hays: Kansas State College, 1968), p. 45.

84. Guy F. Hershberger in *War, Peace, and Nonresistance* (Scottdale: Herald Press, 1953), p. 111, gives a brief summary of the records of Mennonite drafted men.

85. *Vorwaerts,* June 28, 1918.

86. For examples of the experiences of Mennonite draftees in military camp, see J. S. Hartzler, *Mennonites in the World War* (Scottdale: Mennonite Publishing House, 1921), pp. 86-149.

87. Guy F. Hershberger, *War, Peace and Nonresistance* (Scottdale: Herald Press, 1953), p. 111.

88. Edwin S. Wertz, Cleveland, Aug. 20, 1918, telegram to Attorney General, Washington, D.C., General Records of the Department of Justice, Record Group 60, Straight Numerical File 194642, MLA microfilm no. 208.

89. Edwin S. Wertz, Cleveland, Sept. 12, 1918, letter to U.S. Attorney General, Washington, D.C.

90. Alfred Bettman, Washington, D.C., Aug. 30, 1918, memorandum to John Lord O'Brian, MLA microfilm no. 208.

91. John Lord O'Brian, Washington, D.C., Sept. 19, 1918, letter to Edwin S. Wertz, Cleveland, Ohio, MLA microfilm no. 208.

92. Edwin S. Wertz, Cleveland, Aug. 9, 1921, letter to the U.S. Attorney General, MLA microfilm no. 208.

93. H. P. Krehbiel, "Die Stellung der Gemeinde Jesu Christi zum Modernen Staat," *Herold,* April 25, 1918.

94. *Conference Reports, 1896-1956, Church of God in Christ, Mennonite* (Lahoma, Oklahoma: Church of God in Christ Mennonite, 1956), p. 20. For an account of Holdeman Mennonite World War I experiences see Hiebert, *Holdeman People,* pp. 249-258.

95. P. P. Wedel, Church Chronicle of the First Mennonite Church of Christian, Kansas, located at Moundridge, Kansas (n.p.; n.p., 1957), p. 30.

96. James A. Ray, "An Explanation by James A. Ray," *Vorwaerts,* Sept. 21, 1917, p. 4. See also J. G. Ewert, "Ein Angriff auf die deutschen Schulen in Marion County," in the same issue and "Ray's Answer" in *Vorwaerts,* Sept. 28, 1917, p. 5.

97. Peter J. Wedel, *The Story of Bethel College* (North Newton: Bethel College, 1954), p. 237.

98. For details on Mennonite community wartime experiences, see the Schowalter Oral History Collection at MLA and J. S. Hartzler, *Mennonites in the World War* (Scottdale: Mennonite Publishing House), 1921, pp. 150-166.

99. Burrton *Graphic,* Nov. 14, 1918.

100. *Ibid.* Hutchinson *News,* Nov. 16, 1918. The report in the *News* was probably written by a Burrton citizen.

101. Newton *Evening Kansan-Republican,* Dec. 24, 1918. See also the Wichita *Eagle,* Dec. 27, 1918.

102. Newton *Evening Kansan-Republican,* Dec. 24, 1918.

103. Allan Teichroew, "World War I and the Mennonite Migration to Canada to Avoid the Draft," MQR, vol. 45 (July 1971), 219-249.

104. For an example of a war-crusading Mennonite, see the roport on Rudolph Goerz in the Newton *Evening Kansan-Republican,* Apr. 26, 1917.

105. *Der Herold,* Aug. 26, 1915.

106. *Der Herold,* April 19, 1917.

107. The most recent book on Mennonite history, Cornelius J. Dyck, ed., *An Introduction to Mennonite History* (Scottdale: Herald Press, 1967) says that Mennonites rejected the purchase of war bonds in the war (p. 296). This generalization needs to be checked against evidence in local areas. Many Mennonites in Kansas did buy war bonds, especially those of the most numerous GC congregations. See "Mennonites Get into Line on Bond Drive," clipping from unnamed newspaper in H. R. Voth Collection, MLA folder 88; and the suggestion in *Der Herold* of May 23, 1918, that Mennonites make gifts of the bonds to Mennonite institutions such as hospitals, orphans' homes, and colleges. The gifts of liberty bonds enabled the Western District Conference successfully to complete a $100,000 endowment fund drive for Bethel College. See Peter J. Wedel, *The Story of Bethel College,* p. 250.

108. *Der Herold,* July 4, 1918.

109. W. P. Rempel, Pasadena, Calif., Sept. 9, 1918, letter to H. P. Krehbiel, Newton, H. P. Krehbiel Collection, MLA folder 146. H. P. Krehbiel, Newton, October 28, 1918, letter to F. P. Keppel, Washington, D.C., H. P. Krehbiel Collection, MLA folder 147.

110. *The Mennonite,* Jan. 31, 1918.

111. Gerhard Dalke, *A Defense of the Mennonites Against Recent Attacks Made Upon Them* (n.d.; n.p., 1917).

112. *Ibid.,* p. 15.

113. J. G. Ewert, "A Correction and a Declaration," *Vorwaerts,* May 17, 1918.

114. John A. Hawgood, *The Tragedy of German-America* (New York: Putnam 1940), pp. xvii-xviii, p. 295.

CHAPTER 8

1. P. P. Hilty, *Gifts Received by the Emergency Relief Commission of the General Conference of Mennonites of North America since Aug. 28, 1917, to Aug. 12, 1920* (n.p.; n.d.).

2. Levi Mumaw, "Facts and Figures of the Secretary Treasurer," in *Feeding the Hungry,* ed. P. C. Hiebert and Orie O. Miller (Scottdale: Mennonite Central Committee, 1929), pp. 323-330.

3. The history of the Mennonite Central Committee (MCC) from 1920 to 1951 was written by John D. Unruh, *In the Name of Christ* (Scottdale: Herald Press, 1952). The MCC-directed Civilian Public Service program for conscientious objectors in World War II was described by Melvin Gingerich, *Service for Peace* (Akron, Pa.: Mennonite Central Committee, 1949).

4. *Ibid.,* Unruh, p. 9.

5. Cornelius Krahn, J. Winfield Fretz, and Robert Kreider, "Altruism in Mennonite Life," *Forms and Techniques of Altruistic and Spiritual Growth,* ed. Pitirim Sorokin (Boston: Beacon Press, 1954), pp. 309-328.

6. Leland Harder, "The Quest for Equilibrium in an Established Sect: A Study of Social Change in the General Conference Mennonite Church" (unpublished Ph.D. dissertation, Northwestern University, 1962), p. 208.

7. For a brief discussion of the salutary effects of war upon community anxieties, see Sebastian de Grazia, *The Political Community* (Chicago: University of Chicago Press, Phoenix edition, 1963), pp. 156-161.

8. Hiebert, *Feeding the Hungry,* p. 29.

9. Payson Miller, "Mennonites and Relief Work," *Report of the Fourth All-Mennonite Convention* (Goshen: n.p., 1922), pp. 23-24.

10. A corollary to the argument of the foregoing section is that the Mennonite relief program would not have arisen had there been no contact with American culture and no desire to be good Americans. A comparison of Mennonites with the Amish, who remained isolated and uninterested in relief programs, would be instructive in this regard, especially since acculturation has eventually led to relief and missionary work in recent years among the more progressive of the Amish. See John A. Hostetler, *Amish Society* (Baltimore: John Hopkins Press, 1963), p. 324. The link between American nationalism and Mennonite discipleship was again revealed in 1972 and 1973 when the number of Mennonites volunteering for church-related service leveled off and declined, partly in response to the end of the military draft. See Edgar Stoesz, "More Dollars, but Fewer Volunteers," *The Mennonite,* vol. 88 (Oct. 9, 1973), p. 584.

11. Hiebert, *Feeding the Hungry,* pp. 287-292.

12. J. Neale Carman, *Foreign-Language Units of Kansas* (Lawrence: University of Kansas Press, 1962), pp. 2, 164-165, 188-189, 192-193. The 1935 date applies to descendants of Mennonite immigrants from Europe and Russia in the 1870s. The shift was made about ten or fifteen years earlier among (Old) Mennonites of Pennsylvania German origin.

13. Cornelius Voth, interview with the author, Feb. 13, 1967.

14. *Vorwaerts,* Oct. 31, 1924.

15. *Der Herold,* Oct. 23, 1924.

16. H. P. Krehbiel, "Nass oder Trocken!" *Der Herold,* Oct. 4, 1928. Ferdinand J. Wiens, "The World Is Watching!" *Mennonite Weekly Review,* Oct. 24, 1928.

17. See Raymond L. Flory, "McPherson—The Community That Missed the Depression," in *McPherson at Fifty* (McPherson: McPherson College, 1970), pp. 147-159.

18. Quoted in Gerald Carson, *The Roguish World of Doctor Brinkley* (New York: Rinehart and Co., 1960), p. 115.

19. William G. Clugston, *Rascals in Democracy* (N.Y.: Richard R. Smith, 1941) p. 160.

20. *Vorwaerts,* Nov. 14, 1930.

21. There is abundant literature on Brinkley, but reliable analysis of his political success is lacking. The authorized biography is Clement Wood, *The Life of a Man* (Kansas City: Goshorn Publishing Co., 1934). See also Clugston, *Rascals in Democracy;* Thomas W. Bonner, *The Kansas Doctor* (Lawrence: University of Kansas Press, 1959), pp. 207-220; Carson, *The Roguish World of Doctor Brinkley;* Don B. Slechta, "Dr. John R. Brinkley: A Kansas Phenomenon" (unpublished M.A. thesis, Fort Hays Kansas State College, 1952);

Francis W. Schruben, "Dr. John R. Brinkley, Candidate for Governor" (unpublished M.A. thesis, University of Wichita, 1953).

22. George Mack, Jr. (ed.), *The 1933 Kansas Legislature Blue Book* (Lawrence: The World Co., [1933]), p. 56. The meager Jacob A. Showalter papers are in the Mennonite Library and Archives. For a brief review of Showalter's life see Robert Schrag, "The Story of a Mennonite Millionaire, Jacob A. Showalter, 1879-1953," *ML*, vol. 12 (Apr. 1957), pp. 64-69.

23. *House Journal, State of Kansas*, 1933, 1935, and 1937.

24. Undated chapel speech, "The Purpose of an Education," Jacob A. Showalter Collection, MLA folder 8. Undated notes, Jacob A. Showalter Collection, MLA folder 8.

25. Clarence J. Hein and Charles A. Sullivant, *Kansas Votes. Gubernatorial Elections, 1859-1956* (Lawrence: University of Kansas Governmental Research Center, 1958), p. 71.

26. McPherson County Record of Votes. The totals in nine Swedish precincts were: against repeal, 1635 (70.4%); for repeal, 687 (29.6%).

27. Krehbiel, "Welches! Trunkenheit oder Nuechternheit?" *Der Herold*, Oct. 6, 1932; Krehbiel, "Depression," *Der Herold*, Oct. 13, 1932.

28. *Vorwaerts*, Nov. 4, 1932.

29. *Mennonite Weekly Review*, Oct. 30, 1940.

30. J. W. Kliewer, "A Sermon on Christian After War Questions," *Der Herold*, Mar. 20, 1919. Kliewer's sermon was also printed and distributed in pamphlet form (Newton: Herald Press, [1918]).

31. J. W. Kliewer, "A Memorial Day Message of Peace," *The Review*, July 15, 1903.

32. *Der Herold*, Feb. 20, 1919.

33. *Der Herold*, July 8, 1920.

34. J. G. Ewert, "Wie hat Harding sich bewiesen?" *Vorwaerts*, Oct. 22, 1920.

35. "Ein Mahnruf an die Amerikaner deutscher Abstammung," *Vorwaerts*, Oct. 29, 1920.

36. *Der Herold*, Oct. 14, 1920. Article X of the League Covenant provided for collective military action against aggressors in international relations.

37. Newton *Evening Kansan-Republican*, Nov. 8, 1921. The Bethel student newspaper, "Collegian," appeared as a regular feature in the *Kansan-Republican* during these years.

38. Philip A. Wedel, "Why Internationalism?" *Bethel College Monthly*, vol. 28 (June 1923), pp. 8-10.

39. Albert J. Penner, "The Old and the New," *Bethel College Monthly*, vol. 31 (May 1925), p. 3.

40. *Bethel College Monthly*, vol. 31 (Nov. 1925), p. 5.

41. Newton *Evening Kansan-Republican*, Oct. 30, 1923, Bethel *Collegian* section.

42. Newton *Evening Kansan-Republican*, Oct. 26, 1921, Bethel *Collegian* section.

43. See, for example, D. H. Richert, "A Movement To Abolish War," *Bethel College Monthly*, vol. 28 (June 1923), pp. 8, 10.

44. Newton *Evening Kansan-Republican*, Nov. 6, 1928.

45. Esko Loewen, interview with the author, North Newton, Kansas, May 25, 1967.

46. E. L. Harshbarger, "Why Should Mennonite C.E. Societies Support the Kansas Institute of International Relations," *The Mennonite,* vol. 54 (May 16. 1939), p. 9. Records relating to the institute are in the Mennonite Library and Archives, here called the "Institute Collection." See also Theodore W. Loewen, "Mennonite Pacifism: The Kansas Institute of International Relations," (unpublished research paper, MLA, 1971).

47. Newton *Evening Kansan-Republican,* June 3, 1936.

48. Letter from Harshbarger to Capper, June 23 [1937].

49. Evaluation sheet on 1937 institute by W. F. Unruh, missionary to India, Institute Collection, MLA.

50. Letter from P. H. Richert to E. G. Kaufman, May 14, 1936. P. H. Richert Collection, MLA folder 61.

51. Letter from M. Horsch to E. L. Harshbarger, June 25, 1936. Institute Collection, MLA.

52. Evaluation sheet on 1936 institute by J. R. Thierstein, Institute Collection, MLA.

53. Minutes of a "Special Mennonite Committee" on institute affairs, June 17, 1940. Institute Collection, MLA.

54. Duplicated letter from E. L. Harshbarger, Dean of the Institute, to "Fellow Christian Worker," n.d. [1939]. William E. Juhnke personal collection.

55. P. J. Wedel, *The Story of Bethel College* (North Newton: Bethel College, 1954), p. 509.

56. P. H. Richert to D. H. Richert, Apr. 13, 1918. P. H. Richert collection, MLA folder 139.

57. See angry faculty letters to the Bethel College Board of Directors by Helene Riesen, Apr. 3, 1919; J. H. Doell, Apr. 4, 1919; Frieda van der Smissen, Apr. 4, 1919; Helena L. Isaac, Apr. 5, 1919; D. H. Richert, Apr. 12, 1919; and A. B. Schmidt, Apr. 2, 1919. P. H. Richert Collection, MLA folder 139. See also Wedel, *Bethel College,* pp. 241-246.

58. Jacob F. Balzer, Bethel College professor of Greek and Bible, 1913-1918. Interview with the author, May 27, 1967. On the fundamentalist controversy at Bethel College see Mark Stucky, "Bethel Meets the Modernist Challenge," (unpublished research paper, MLA, 1969), and Delores Reimer, "Jacob Frank Balzer and the Experience at Bethel College 1913-1918," (unpublished research paper, MLA, 1974).

59. See C. Norman Kraus, "American Mennonites and the Bible, 1750-1950," MQR, vol. 41 (Oct. 1967), pp. 309--329.

60. P. H. Richert to P. A. Kliewer, June 3, 1940. P. H. Richert collection, MLA folder 67.

61. See, for example, Samuel S. Haury, *Wehrlosigkeit in der Sonntagsschule* (n.p.: [1894]).

62. Richert's numerous manuscripts on this problem are in MLA folder 142 of his collection. One draft was eventually published during the Second World War as *A Brief Catechism on Difficult Scripture Passages and Involved Questions on the Use of the Sword* (Newton: n.p., 1942).

63. Krehbiel, *War, Peace, Amity,* pp. 30-31.

64. *Ibid.*, pp. 327, 334.

65. *Ibid.*, pp. 110, 112.

66. *Ibid.*, p. 269.

67. *Ibid.*, p. 287.

68. *Ibid.*, p. 327.

69. *Ibid.*, pp. 59-60.

70. Christian Doctrine (A Quarterly Supplement to the *Gospel Herald*), (Apr. 21, 1938), pp. 79-80.

71. *The Mennonite*, vol. 52 (July 27, 1937), p. 14.

72. G. H. Montgomery, *Gerald Burton Winrod* (Wichita: Mertmont, 1965), pp. 13-15. Written by Winrod's successor at the head of the Defender organization, this is the official biography to which the researcher is referred when denied access to the closed Winrod papers. Winrod's politics until 1938 have been competently treated by Ann Mari Buitrago, "A Study of the Political Ideas and Activities of Gerald B. Winrod, 1926-1938" (unpublished M.A. thesis, Kansas University, 1955). James Schrag briefly touched on Winrod's relationship to the Mennonites in a 1966 Bethel College undergraduate social science seminar paper, "Gerald Burton Winrod: The Defender."

73. Schrag, "Winrod," pp. 4-5.

74. Montgomery, *Winrod*, p. 24.

75. This interpretation of Winrod's intellectual development follows Buitrago, "Political Ideas," p. 25.

76. G. B. Winrod, "Ten Deadly Enemies," *The Defender*, vol. 7 (Jan. 1933), p. 1, quoted in Schrag, "Winrod," p. 14.

77. P. H. Richert to E. G. Kaufman, Jan. 8, 1937. P. H. Richert collection, MLA folder 62. J. W. Kliewer, *Memoirs of J. W. Kliewer* (North Newton: Bethel College, 1943), p. 107. Copies of Kliewer's original manuscript are in the MLA.

78. A. E. Janzen, *The Two Kingdoms and Closely Related Events* (Hillsboro: Mennonite Brethren Publishing House, 1927).

79. Buitrago, "Political Ideas," pp. 29-30.

80. Winrod's secretary, Mrs. Myrtle Ludwig Flowers, who was business manager of the Defenders in 1967, mentioned these four men when asked for names of Mennonite friends of the Defenders in the 1920s and 1930s. Interview with the author, Kansas City, Kansas, Oct. 6, 1966.

81. Schrag, "Gerald Burton Winrod," p. 11.

82. "Report to the Trustees of the Herald Publishing Company, Oct. 7, 1940," P. H. Richert Collection, MLA folder 131.

83. These generalizations are supported by random questioning of Mennonite community residents, although official figures are not available.

84. See, for example, *Der Herold*, Oct. 4, 1934 and Feb. 17, 1938.

85. Winrod credited Mrs. J. F. Franz, among others, for publication of his book, *Christ Within* (Wichita: Winrod Publication Center, 1925).

86. John J. Kroeker, "International Relations and Our Denomination," *Mennonite Weekly Review*, June 16, 1937.

87. The information on Kroeker is taken from Schrag, "Gerald Burton Winrod," pp. 28.30.

88. William F. Zornow, *Kansas: A History of the Jayhawk State* (Norman: University of Oklahoma Press, 1957), p. 259.

89. Buitrago, "Political Ideas," pp. 118-124.

90. *Der Herold*, July 28, 1938. *Vorwaerts*, July 29, 1938.

91. *Thirty-first Biennial Report of the Secretary of State, State of Kansas, 1937-1938*. (Topeka: Kansas State Printing Plant, 1938). The totals were: Reed, 104, 918 (42.3%); Knapp, 64,068 (25.8%); Winrod, 53,149 (21.4%); Fisher, 26,034 (10.5%).

92. Interview with the author, Kansas City, Kansas, Oct. 6, 1966.

93. Gerald B. Winrod, *Terse Talks* (n.p.: [1938]), pp. 8-9.

94. Schrag, "Gerald Burton Winrod," p. 40.

95. Buitrago, "Political Ideas," p. 77. This is an indirect quotation from *The Defender*, Dec. 1932, p. 2.

96. Frank Epp, "An Analysis of National Socialism in the Mennonite Press in the 1930s" (unpublished Ph.D. dissertation, University of Minnesota, 1965).

97. J. R. Thierstein, "Adolf Hitler von deutscher Seite betrachtet," *Bethel College Monthly*, XXXIX (Apr. 1934), p. 14.

98. William E. Juhnke, Jr., "A World Gone Mad: Mennonites View the Coming of the War, 1938-1939," (unpublished undergraduate research paper, MLA, 1966). Juhnke suggests that Thierstein did not shift to a tone of criticism of Germany until October 1939, pp. 17-18.

99. See Friesen's letters in *Vorwaerts*, Dec. 2, 1938; Jan. 20, May 5, and June 30, 1939. For a brief biography of Friesen and a list of some of his writings see Ronald M. Friesen, "The Writings of C. H. Friesen, A Partial Bibliography," (unpublished undergraduate research paper, MLA, 1962).

100. C. Henry Smith, "Mennonites and War," *Report of the Fourth All-Mennonite Convention* (Goshen: n.p., 1922), p. 83.

101. For a review of Mennonite peace education efforts between the wars see Melvin Gingerich, *Service for Peace: A History of Mennonite Civilian Public Service* (Akron: Mennonite Central Committee, 1949), pp. 18-23.

102. *Protokoll der achtundzwanzigsten Westlichen Distrikt-Konferenz* (n.p.: 1919), p. 819.

103. *Protokoll der neunundzwanzigsten Westlichen District-Konferenz* (n.p.: 1920), pp. 856-858.

104. *Protokoll der dreissigsten Westlichen Distrikt-Konferenz*, p. 929.

105. A. E. Janzen, compiler, "Resolutions of the General Conference of the Mennonite Brethren Church, 1878-1963," duplicated by The Board of Reference and Counsel, 1964, p. 121.

106. *Ibid.*, pp. 121-122.

107. *Konferenzbeschluesse der Krimmer Mennoniten Bruedergemeinde, von Nord Amerika, Zwischen der Jahren 1882-1940* (Inman, Kansas: Salem Publishing House, n.d.), p. 48.

108. *Official Minutes and Reports of the Twenty-Fourth Session of the General Conference of the Mennonite Church of North America* (n.p.: 1926), p. 17.

109. *Official Minutes and Reports of the Twenty-Fifth Session of the General Conference of the Mennonite Church of North America* (n.p.: 1929), p. 42.

110. Guy F. Hershberger, *The Mennonite Church in the Second World War* (Scottdale: Mennonite Publishing House, 1951), p. 5.

111. Quoted and answered in *Ibid.*, p. 248.

112. Gingerich, *Service for Peace*, p. 28. Rufus D. Bowman, *The Church of the Brethren and War* (Elgin, Ill.: Brethren Publishing House, 1944), pp. 271, 272.

113. A. J. Neuenschwander, "Representatives from Historic Peace Churches Present Position to Government," *The Mennonite*, vol. 52 (Mar. 9, 1937), pp. 4-5. The letter and accompanying statement on the Mennonite attitude toward war are also reproduced in Gingerich, *Service for Peace*, pp. 430-431.

114. Quoted in *Ibid.*, p. 44, and in Rufus D. Bowman, *The Church of the Brethren and War* (Elgin, Ill.: Brethren Publishing House, 1944), p. 279.

115. Gingerich, *Service for Peace*. p. 20.

CHAPTER 9

1. Guy F. Hershberger, *The Mennonite Church in the Second World War* (Scottdale: Mennonite Publishing House, 1951), p. 39. Howard Charles, "A Presentation and Evaluation of MCC Draft Status Census," Proceedings of the Fourth Annual Conference on Mennonite Cultural Problems (North Newton: n.p., 1945), pp. 82-106. Comparisons with the First World War are difficult to assess because the definition and status of the different kinds of service (regular, noncombatant, and alternative service) were not parallel for both wars. According to a tabulation by C. C. Janzen, "A Social Study," pp. 66-67, most Kansas Mennonite draftees in the First World War accepted noncombatant service under military administration. This would suggest that the change in Mennonite draft preferences from the First to the Second World War was perhaps not very large.

2. Harder, "The Quest for Equilibrium," table 34, p. 324.

3. See the following articles in *Mennonite Life,* vol. 11 (July 1956): J. Winfield Fretz, "Should Mennonites Participate in Politics?" pp. 139-140; Esko Loewen, "Church and State," pp. 141-142; Elmer Ediger, "A Christian's Political Responsibility," pp. 143-144.

4. John Jost, interview with the author, Jan. 15, 1967.

Bibliography

BOOKS

Beaver, Daniel R. *Newton D. Baker and the American War Effort, 1917-1919.* Lincoln: University of Nebraska Press, 1966.

Bernhardi, Friedrich Adam Julius Von. *Germany and the Next War.* Translated by Allen H. Powles. London: Edward Arnold, 1912.

Biennial Reports of the Kansas State Board of Agriculture. Topeka: Kansas State Board of Agriculture, 1931, 1937.

Bonner, Thomas Neville. *The Kansas Doctor.* Lawrence: University of Kansas Press, 1959.

Bowman, Rufus D. *The Church of the Brethren and War.* Elgin, Illinois: Brethren Publishing House, 1944.

Brendler, Gerhard. *Das Taeufferreich Zu Muenster, 1534-35.* Berlin: Veb Deutscher Verlag der Wissenschaften, 1966.

Brunk, Harry Anthony. *History of the Mennonites in Virginia, 1727-1900.* Harrisonburg: Privately printed, 1959.

Burkholder, L. J. *A Brief History of the Mennonites in Ontario.* Markham, Ontario: Mennonite Conference of Ontario, 1937.

Butcher, Walter. *Presidential Election Returns for Kansas, 1864-1952.* Emporia: The Emporia State Research Studies, 1956.

Cabe, June G., and Sullivant, Charles A. *Kansas Votes. National Elections, 1859-1956.* Lawrence: University of Kansas Governmental Research Center, 1957.

Carman, J. Neale. *Foreign-Language Units of Kansas,* vol. 1, *Historical Atlas and Statistics.* Lawrence: University of Kansas Press, 1962.

Carson, Gerald. *The Roguish World of Doctor Brinkley.* New York: Rinehart and Co., 1960.

Chase County Historical Sketches. n.p.: Chase County Historical Society, vol. 1, 1940, vol. 2, 1948.

Clugston, William George. *Rascals in Democracy.* New York: Richard R. Smith, 1940.

Conference Record Containing the Proceedings of the Kansas-Nebraska Mennonite Conference, 1876-1914. Compiled by L. O. King, T. M. Erb, and D. H. Bender. n.p.: Kansas Nebraska Mennonite Conference. [1914].

Conference Reports, 1896-1956, Church of God in Christ, Mennonite. La Roma. Oklahoma: Church of God in Christ, Mennonite, 1956.

Connelley, William E., ed. *A Standard History of Kansas and Kansans.* Chicago: Lewis Publishing Co., 1918.

Connelley, William E., ed. *History of Kansas Newspapers.* Topeka: Kansas State Printing Plant, 1916.

Dalke, Gerhard. *A Defense of the Mennonites Against Recent Attacks Made upon Them.* n.p.: [1917].

Dalke, Gerhard. *Das Verlorene und Wiedergefundene Paradis.* Hillsboro: Mennonite Brethren Publishing House, n.d.

Dalke, Gerhard. *Jubilaeums-Gedanken zum fuenfzigsten Jubilaeumsfests der Einwanderung der Mennoniten in Amerika.* n.p.: n.d.

Dalke, Gerhard. *Wo Wuenschest du deine Ewegkeit zu Verleben?* n.p.: n.d.

Die Deutschen Ansiedlungen in Sued West Kansas auf den Laendereien der Atchison, Topeka und Santa Fe Eisenbahngesellschaft. Halstead: Westlichen Publikations Gesselchaft, 1878.

Die Entstehung der Kansaskonferenz der Mennoniten-Gemeinden, 1877-1892. n.p.: n.d.

Dyck, Cornelius J., ed. *An Introduction to Mennonite History.* Scottdale, Pennsylvania: Herald Press, 1967.

Ehrt, Adolf. *Das Mennonitentum in Russland von seiner Einwanderung bis zur Gegenwart.* Langensalza: Julius Beltz, 1931.

Ewert, Jacob Gerhard, *Die Bibel und die Enthaltsamkeit.* 2nd ed. Berne, Indiana: Christlichen Maessigkeitsverein, n.d.

Ewert, Jacob Gerhard. *Christentum und den Socialismus.* Hillsboro: J. G. Ewert, n.d.

Ewert, Jacob Gerhard. *Christentum und Prohibition.* Hillsboro: J. G. Ewert, n.d.

Ewert, Jacob Gerhard. *Die Christliche Lehre von der Wehrlosigkeit.* Hillsboro: J. G. Ewert, 1899.

Ewert, Jacob Gerhard. *Der Gute Kampf: Eine Allegorie.* Elkhart: Mennonite Publishing Co., 1900.

Faust, Albert Bernhardt. *The German Element in the United States with Special Reference to its Political, Moral, Social, and Educational Influence.* New York: The Steuben Society of America, 1927. 2 vols.

Francis, E. K. *In Search of Utopia: The Mennonites in Manitoba.* Glencoe: Free Press, 1955.

Friesen, P. M. *Die Altevangelischen Mennoniten Bruderschaft.* Halbstadt, Russia, 1911.

Gallaher, Art Jr. *Plainville Fifteen Years Later.* New York: Columbia University Press, 1961.

Gesamtprotokolle der Kansas—und Westlichen Distrikt-Konferenzen. n.p.: n.d.

Gingerich, Melvin. *The Mennonites in Iowa.* Iowa City: The State Historical Society of Iowa, 1939.

Gingerich, Melvin. *Service for Peace: A History of Mennonite Civilian Public Service.* Akron, Pennsylvania: Mennonite Central Committee, 1949.

Goerz, David. *Die Mennoniten-Niederlassung auf den Laendereien der Atchison, Topeka und Santa Fe Eisenbahn Gesellschaft.* St. Joseph: 1874.

Grazia, Sebastian de. *The Political Community.* Chicago: University of Chicago Press, 1963.

Hansen, Marcus. *The Immigrant in American History.* New York: Harper and Row, 1940.

Hansen, Marcus. *The Problem of the Third Generation Immigrant.* Rock Island, Illinois: Augustana Historical Society, 1938.

Harms, John Foth. *Geschichte der Mennoniten-Bruedergemeinde.* Hillsboro: Mennonite Brethren Publishing House, 1927.

Hartzler, John Ellsworth. *Education Among the Mennonites of North America.* Danvers, Illinois: Central Mennonite Publishing Board, 1925.

Hartzler, J. S. *Mennonites in the World War,* Scottdale: Mennonite Publishing House, 1921.

Hartzler, J. S. *Mennonites in the World War.* 2nd ed. Scottdale: Mennonite Publishing House, 1922.

Haury, Samuel S. *Die Wehrlosigkeit in der Sonntagsschule.* Dayton, Ohio: United Brethren Publishing House, 1894.

Hawgood, John A. *The Tragedy of German-America.* New York: G. P. Putnam's Sons, 1940.

Hayes, Carlton J. H. *Nationalism: A Religion.* New York: Macmillan, 1960.

Hein, Clarence J., and Sullivant, Charles A. *Kansas Votes. Gubernatorial Elections, 1859-1956.* Lawrence: University of Kansas Governmental Research Center, 1958.

Hershberger, Guy F. *The Mennonite Church in the Second World War.* Scottdale: Mennonite Publishing House, 1951.

Hershberger, Guy F., ed. *The Recovery of the Anabaptist Vision.* Scottdale: Herald Press, 1957.

Hershberger, Guy F. *War, Peace, and Nonresistance.* Scottdale: Herald Press, 1953.

Hiebert, Clarence. *Holdeman People.* South Pasadena: William Carey Library, 1973.

Hiebert, P. C., and Miller, Orie O., eds. *Feeding the Hungry: Russia Famine, 1919-1925.* Scottdale: Mennonite Central Committee, 1929.

Hilty, P. P. *Gifts Received by the Emergency Relief Commission of the General Conference of Mennonites of North America since Aug. 28, 1917, to Aug. 12,1920.* n.p.: n.d.

Hofstadter, Richard. *The Age of Reform.* New York: Vintage, 1955.

Hostetler, John A. *Amish Society.* Baltimore: Johns Hopkins Press, 1963.

Hostetler, John A. *The Sociology of Mennonite Evangelism.* Scottdale: Herald Press, 1954.

House Journal, State of Kansas, 1909. Topeka: State Printing Office, 1909.

Jansen, Cornelius, ed. *Sammlung von Notizen ueber Amerika.* Danzig: Paul Thieme, 1872.

Janzen, A. E. *The Two Kingdoms and Closely Related Events.* Hillsboro: Mennonite Publishing House, 1927.

Janzen, A. E., compiler. *Resolutions of the General Conference of the Mennonite Brethren Church, 1878-1963.* [Hillsboro]: The Board of Reference and Counsel, 1964.

Kaufman, P. R. *Unser Volk und seine Geschichte.* Basil, Kansas: S. Mouttet, 1931.

King, L. O., et. al., eds. *Conference Record Containing the Proceedings of the Kansas-Nebraska Mennonite Conference, 1876-1914.* n.p.: n.d.

Kliewer, J. W. *Memoirs of J. W. Kliewer.* North Newton: Bethel College, 1943.

Kliewer, J. W. *A Sermon on Christian After War Questions*. Newton: Herald Press, [1918].

Konferenzberichte der Mennoniten Bruedergemeinde von Nord Amerika 1885-1919 nebst Konstitution der Mennoniten Bruedergemeinde von Nord Amerika. Hillsboro: Mennonite Brethren Publishing House, 1920.

Konferenzbeschluesse der Krimmer Mennoniten Bruedergemeinde, von Nord Amerika, zwischen den Jahren 1882-1940. Inman: Salem Publishing House, n.d.

Krahn, Cornelius, ed. *From the Steppes to the Prairies*. Newton: Mennonite Publication Office, 1949.

Krehbiel, Christian. *Prairie Pioneer. The Christian Krehbiel Story*. Newton: Faith and Life Press, 1961.

Krehbiel, Henry Peter. *The History of the General Conference of Mennonites of North America*. vol. 1, St. Louis: H. P. Krehbiel, 1898. vol. 2, Newton: H. P. Krehbiel, 1938.

Krehbiel, Henry Peter. *War, Peace, Amity*. Newton: H. P. Krehbiel, 1937.

Lasch, Cristopher. *The New Radicalism in America 1889-1963*. New York: Vintage, 1965.

Lindquist, Emory K. *Smoky Valley People, A History of Lindsborg, Kansas*. Lindsborg: Bethany College, 1953.

Lohrenz, John H. *The Mennonite Brethren Church*. Hillsboro: Mennonite Brethren Publishing House, 1950.

Lujan, Herman D. *Kansas Votes, National and Statewide General Elections 1958-1964*. Lawrence: University of Kansas Governmental Research Center, 1965.

Lynd, Robert S., and Lynd, Helen M. *Middletown*. New York: Harcourt, Brace, 1929.

Mack, George Jr., ed. *The 1933 Kansas Legislative Blue Book*. Lawrence: The World Co., [1933].

Malin, James C. *Winter Wheat in the Golden Belt of Kansas*. Lawrence: University of Kansas Press, 1944.

Mennonite Encyclopedia. Scottdale: Mennonite Publishing House, 4 vols. 1955-1959.

Miller, Mary. *A Pillar of Cloud: The Story of Hesston College 1909-1959*. North Newton: Mennonite Press, 1959.

Montgomery, G. H. *Gerald Burton Winrod*. Wichita: Mertmont, 1965.

Nyquist, Edna. *Pioneer Life and Lore of McPherson County, Kansas*. McPherson: The Democrat-Opinion Press, 1932.

Parish, Arlyn John, *Kansas Mennonites During World War I*. Fort Hays: Kansas State College, 1968.

Peters, H. P. *History and Development of Education among the Mennonites in Kansas*. Hillsboro: 1925.

Redfield, Robert. *The Little Community*. Chicago: University of Chicago Press, 1955.

Regier, C. C. *Pioneer Experiences of Father, Mother, and Grandfather*. n.p.: C. C. Regier, 1963.

Reimer, Gustav E., and Gaeddert, G. R. *Exiled by the Czar: Cornelius Jansen and the Great Mennonite Migration, 1874*. Newton: Mennonite Publication Office, 1956.

Richert, Peter H. *A Brief Catechism on Difficult Scripture Passages and Involved Questions on the Use of the Sword.* Newton: 1942.

Sibley, Mulford Q., and Jacob, Philip E. *Conscription and Conscience: The American State and the Conscientious Objector, 1940-1947.* Ithaca: Cornell University Press, 1952.

Smith, C. Henry. *The Coming of the Russian Mennonites.* Berne, Indiana: Mennonite Book Concern, 1927.

Smith, C. Henry. *The Story of the Mennonites.* 3rd. ed. rev. and enl. by Cornelius Krahn. Newton: Mennonite Publication Office, 1950.

Sprunger, Keith L.; Juhnke, James C.; and Waltner, John D., *Voices Against War.* North Newton: Bethel College, 1973.

Sudermann, Leonhard. *Eine Deputationsreise von Russland nach Amerika.* Elkhart: Mennonitisches Verlagshandlung, 1897.

Thirty-first Biennial Report of the Secretary of State, State of Kansas, 1937-8. Topeka: Kansas State Printing Plant, 1938.

Toennies, Ferdinand. *Community and Society, Gemeinschaft und Gesellschaft.* Trans. and ed. by Charles P. Loomis. East Lansing: Michigan State University Press, 1957.

Troeltsch, Ernst. *The Social Teaching of the Christian Churches.* Trans. by Olive Wyon. London: Geo Allen & Unwin, 1931.

Unruh, A. H. *Die Geschichte der Mennoniten-Bruedergemeinde,* 1860-1954. Winnipeg: The Christian Press, 1955.

Unruh, Abe J., ed. Great Grandfather's Diary. Montezuma, Kansas: n.d.

Unruh, John D. *In the Name of Christ: A History of the Mennonite Central Committee and Its Service 1920-1951.* Scottdale: Herald Press, 1952.

Warkentin, Abraham, ed. *Who's Who Among the Mennonites.* Newton: Bethel College, 1937. New edition, 1943.

Weber, Harry F. *Centennial History of the Mennonites of Illinois, 1829-1929.* Goshen: Mennonite Historical Society, 1931.

Wedel, Peter J. *The Story of Bethel College.* ed. Edmund G. Kaufman. North Newton: Bethel College, 1954.

Wedel, P. P., *Kurze Geschichte der aus Wolhynien, Russland, nach Kansas ausgewanderten Schweizer-Mennoniten.* n.p.: 1929.

Wenger, John C. *History of the Mennonites of the Franconia Conference.* Telford: Franconia Mennonite Historical Society, 1937.

Wenger, John C. *The Mennonites in Indiana and Michigan.* Scottdale: Herald Press, 1961.

Wiebe, David V. *They Seek a Country: A Survey of Mennonite Migrations with Special Reference to Kansas and Gnadenau.* Hillsboro: Mennonite Brethren Publishing House, 1959.

Winrod, Gerald B. *Christ Within.* Wichita: Winrod Publication Center, 1925.

Winrod, Gerald B. *Terse Talks.* Wichita: Gerald B. Winrod, 1938.

Wittke, Carl Frederick. *German-Americans and the World War with Special Emphasis on Ohio's German Language Press.* Columbus: Ohio State Archaeological and Historical Society, 1936.

Wood, Clement. *The Life of a Man.* Kansas City: Goshorn Publishing Co., 1934.

Zornow, William F. Kansas: *A History of the Jayhawk State.* Norman: University of Oklahoma Press, 1957.

ARTICLES

Baehr, Karl. "The Secularization Process among Mennonites." In *Conference on Mennonite Cultural Problems,* pp. 35-40. Newton: Bethel College Press, 1942.

Bender, Harold S. "Alcohol." *ME* 1:36-40.

Bender, Harold S. "Church and State in Mennonite History." *MQR* 13 (April 1939):83-103.

Bender, Harold S. "Krimmer Mennonite Brethren." *ME* 3:242-245.

Bender, Harold S. "Zur Heimath." *ME* 4:1042.

Charles, Howard. "A Presentation and Evaluation of MCC Draft Status Census." In *Proceedings of the Fourth Annual Conference on Mennonite Cultural Problems,* pp. 83-106. North Newton, 1945.

Correll, Ernst. "President Grant and the Mennonite Immigration from Russia." *MQR* 9 (July 1935): 144-152.

Correll, Ernst, ed. "Sources on the Mennonite Immigration from Russia in the 1870s." *MQR* 24 (October 1950):327-352.

Correll, Ernst. "The Congressional Debate on the Mennonite Immigration from Russia, 1873-74." *MQR* 20 (February 1946):174-188.

Correll, Ernst. "President Grant and the Mennonite Immigration from Russia." *MQR* 9 (July 1935):144-152.

Ediger, Elmer. "A Christian's Political Responsibility." *ML* 11 (July 1956): 143-144.

Entz, J. E. "First Mennonite Church—Newton (1878-1953)." *ML* 8 (October 1953):152-158.

Flory, Raymond L. "McPherson—The Community that Missed the Depression." In *McPherson at Fifty,* pp. 147-159. McPherson College, 1970.

Fretz, J. Winfield. "Mutual Aid Among the Mennonites." *MQR* 13 (January, July 1939): 28-58, 187-209.

Fretz, J. Winfield. "Should Mennonites Participate in Politics?" *ML* 11 (July 1956): 139-140.

Gingerich, Melvin. "The Reactions of the Russian Mennonite Immigrants of the 1870s to the American Frontier." *MQR* 34 (April 1960): 137-146.

Gingerich, Melvin. "Russian Mennonites React to Their New Environment." *ML* 15 (October 1960):175-180.

Groat, W. J. "The Russo-German Colonies of Kansas." In *Brown's Industrial Gazetteer and Handbook,* pp. 198-201. n.p., n.d.

Handlin, Oscar. "Immigration in American Life: A Reappraisal." In *Immigration in American History: Essays in Honor of Theodore C. Blegen,* edited by Henry Steele Commager. Minneapolis: University of Minnesota Press, 1961.

Harder, Leland. "The Russian Mennonites and American Democracy under Grant." In *From the Steppes to the Prairies,* edited by Cornelius Krahn, pp. 54-67. Newton: Mennonite Publication Office, 1949.

Hillerbrand, Hans. "The Anabaptist View of the State." *MQR* 32 (April 1958): 83-110.

Hofer, J. M. "The Diary of Paul Tschetter, 1873." *MQR* 5 (April 1931): 112-128 and *MQR* 5 (July 1931): 198-220.

Kaufman, Edmund G. "Nontheological Cultural Factors in the Origin and Current Relationship of Mennonite Groups." In *Proceedings of the Eleventh Conference on Mennonite Educational and Cultural Problems,* pp. 49-54. n.p., 1957.

Krahn, Cornelius; Fretz, J. Winfield; and Kreider, Robert. "Altruism in Mennonite Life." In *Forms and Techniques of Altruistic and Spiritual Growth,* edited by Pitirim Sorokin, pp. 309-328. Boston: Beacon Press, 1954.

Krahn, Cornelius. "Ewert, Wilhelm." *ME* 2:276.

Krahn, Cornelius. "Muenster Anabaptists." *ME* 3:777-782.

Krahn, Cornelius. "Russia." *ME* 4:381-393.

Krahn, Cornelius. "Some Letters of Bernhard Warkentin Pertaining to the Migration of 1873-1875." *MQR* 24 (July 1950):248-263.

Kraus, C. Norman. "American Mennonites and the Bible, 1750-1950." *MQR* 41 (October 1967): 309-329.

Krehbiel, Olin A. "Krehbiel, Christian." *ME* 3:236.

Kreider, Robert. "The Anabaptist Conception of the Church in the Russian Mennonite Environment, 1789-1870." *MQR* 25 (January 1951):17-33.

Leibrandt, Georg. "The Emigration of the German Mennonites from Russia to the United States and Canada in 1873-1880." *MQR* 6 (October 1932): 205-226 and *MQR* 7 (January 1933):5-41.

Leisy, Elva Krehbiel. "Henry Peter Krehbiel (1862-1946)." *ML* 9 (October 1954):162-166.

Leisy, Ernest E. "On a Kansas Farm." *ML* 1 (January 1946):18-21.

Loewen, Esko. "Church and State." *ML* 11 (July 1956):141-142.

Loewen, J. H. "Harms, John F." *ME* 2:665.

Miller, Payson. "Mennonites and Relief Work." In *Report of the Fourth All-Mennonite Convention Held in Eighth Street Mennonite Church,* pp. 13-25. Goshen, Indiana, 1922.

Pantle, Alberta. "Settlement of the Krimmer Mennonite Brethren at Gnadenau, Marion County." *Kansas Historical Quarterly* 13 (February 1945): 259-285.

Penner, Albert J. "The Old and the New." *Bethel College Monthly* 31 (May 1925):1-3.

Redekop, Calvin. "Patterns of Cultural Assimilation Among Mennonites." In *Proceedings of the Eleventh Conference on Mennonite Educational and Cultural Problems,* pp. 99-112. n.p., 1957.

Regier, C. C. "An Immigrant Family of 1876." *Social Science* 7 (July 1932): 250-266.

Richert, D. H. "A Movement To Abolish War." *Bethel College Monthly* 28 (June 1923):8-10.

Schellenberg, T. R. "Editor Abraham L. Schellenberg." *ML* 9 (January 1954):19-28.

Schmidt, C. B. "Reminiscences of Foreign Immigration Work for Kansas." In *Transactions of the Kansas State Historical Society 1905-1906,* vol. 9 (1905-1906):485-497.

Schrag, Robert. "The Story of a Mennonite Millionaire, Jacob A. Showalter, 1879-1953." *ML* 12 (April 1957):64-69.

Skinner, Charles M. "The Mennonites of Kansas." *St. Louis Globe-Democrat*, Sept. 30, 1900.

Smith, C. Henry. "Mennonites and War." In *Report of the Fourth All-Mennonite Convention Held in Eighth Street Mennonite Church*, pp. 77-85. Goshen, Indiana, 1922.

Stucky, Gregory J. "Fighting Against War: The Mennonite *Vorwaerts* from 1914 to 1919." *Kansas Historical Quarterly* 38 (Summer 1972):169-186.

Stucky, Harley J. "The German Element in Kansas." In *Kansas: The First Century*, edited by John D. Bright, pp. 329-354. New York: Lewis Historical Publishing Co., 1956.

Stucky, Harley J. "Should Mennonites Participate in Government?" *ML* 14 (January 1959):34-38.

Teichroew, Allan. "World War I and the Mennonite to Canada To Avoid the Draft." *MQR* 45 (July 1971):219-249.

Thierstein, J. R. "Adolf Hitler von deutscher Seite betrachtet." *Bethel College Monthly* 39 (April 1934):14.

[Warkentin, Abraham]. "Second in National Contest." *Bethel College Monthly* 31 (November 1925):5.

Wedel, C. H. "Die Friedensidee auf sozial-politischem Gebiet." *Monatsblaetter aus Bethel College* 8 (June 1903):63-64.

Wedel, D. C. "Contributions of Pioneer David Goerz." *ML* 7 (October 1952):170-175.

Wedel, Philip A. "Why Internationalism?" *Bethel College Monthly* 28 (June 1923):8-10.

Zuck, Lowell H. "Anabaptism: Abortive Counter-Revolt Within the Reformation." *Church History* 26 (September 1957):211-226.

Ph.D. DISSERTATIONS AND M.A. THESES

Albrecht, Abraham. "Mennonite Settlement in Kansas." Master's thesis, Kansas University, 1924.

Brodhead, Michael J. "The Early Career of E. W. Hoch." Master's thesis, University of Kansas, 1962.

Buitrago, Ann Mari. "A Study of the Political Ideas and Activities of Gerald B. Winrod, 1926-1938." Master's thesis, Kansas University, 1955.

Epp, Frank. "An Analysis of National Socialism in the Mennonite Press in the 1930's." Ph.D. dissertation, University of Minnesota, 1965.

Harder, Leland D. "The Quest for Identification in an Established Sect: A Study of Social Change in the General Conference Mennonite Church." Ph.D. dissertation, Northwestern University, 1962. Published by the author in multilith form.

Harder, Menno S. "The Origin, Philosophy, and Development of Education Among the Mennonites." Ph.D. dissertation, University of Southern California, 1949.

Harshbarger, Eva G. "The Status of Mennonite Women in Kansas in their Church and Home Relationships." Master's thesis, Kansas State University, 1945.

Janzen, Cornelius. "Americanization of the Russian Mennonites in Central Kansas." Master's thesis, Kansas University, 1914.

Janzen, Cornelius Cicero. "A Social Study of the Mennonite Settlement in the Counties of Marion, McPherson, Harvey, Reno, and Butler, Kansas." Ph.D. dissertation, University of Chicago, 1926.

Kaufman, Edmund G. "Social Problems and Opportunities of the Western District Conference Communities of the General Conference of Mennonites of North America." Master's thesis, Bluffton College and Mennonite Seminary, 1917.

Miller, D. Paul. "An Analysis of Community Adjustment: A Case Study of Jansen, Nebraska." Ph.D. dissertation, University of Nebraska, 1953.

Nickel, Jacob Winrod. "An Analytical Approach to Mennonite Ethics." Ph.D. dissertation, Iliff School of Theology, 1959.

Pannabecker, Samuel F. "The Development of the General Conference in the American Environment." Ph.D. dissertation, Yale University, 1944.

Peters, H. P. "History and Development of Education Among the Mennonites in Kansas." Master's thesis, Bluffton College, 1925.

Redekop, Calvin W. "The Sectarian Black and White World." Ph.D. dissertation, University of Chicago, 1959.

Rempel, David G. "The Mennonite Colonies in New Russia: A Study of their Settlement and Economic Development from 1789 to 1914." Ph.D. dissertation, Stanford University, 1933.

Shipley, Helen B. "The Migration of Mennonites from Russia 1873-1883 and their Settlement in Kansas." Master's thesis, University of Minnesota, 1954.

Slechta, Don B. "Dr. John R. Brinkley." Master's thesis, Fort Hays Kansas State College, 1952.

Stucky, Harley J. "Cultural Interaction Among the Mennonites Since 1870." Master's thesis, Northwestern University, 1947.

Stucky, Milo O. "The Mennonites of McPherson County, Kansas." Master's thesis, University of Washington, 1940.

Unruh, John D., Jr. "The Burlington and Missouri River Railroad Brings the Mennonites to Nebraska, 1873-1878." Master's thesis, University of Kansas, 1959.

Unruh, Otto D. "Schisms of the Russian Mennonites of Harvey, McPherson, and Reno Counties, Kansas." Master's thesis, Kansas University, 1940.

Waltner, Erland. "An Analysis of the Mennonite Views on the Christian's Relation to the State in the Light of the New Testament." Th.D. dissertation, Eastern Baptist Theological Seminary, 1948.

Yoder, Gideon. "The Oldest Living American Mennonite Congregations of Central Kansas." Master's thesis, Phillips University, 1948.

UNDERGRADUATE RESEARCH PAPERS

Friesen, Ronald M. "The Writings of C. H. Friesen: A Partial Bibliography." Research paper, MLA, 1962.

Haury, David A. "German-Russian Immigrants and Kansas Politics: A Comparison of the Catholic and Mennonite Immigration to Kansas and Their Politics." Research paper, MLA, 1972.

Juhnke, William E., Jr. "A World Gone Mad: Mennonites View the Coming of the War, 1938-1939." Research paper, MLA, 1966.

Kaufman, Letha. "Excerpts Pertaining to Mennonites Printed in the *McPherson Republican* in the Years 1880 to 1884 Inclusive." Research paper, MLA, 1945.

Loewen, Theodore W. "Mennonite Pacifism: The Kansas Institute of International Relations." Research paper, MLA, 1971.

Reimer, Deloris. "Jacob Frank Balzer and the Experience at Bethel College 1913-1918." Research paper, MLA, 1974.

Schrag, James. "Gerald Burton Winrod: The Defender." Research paper, MLA, 1966.

Stucky, Harley J. "A Survey of Mennonite Progress in McPherson, Marion, Harvey, and Reno Counties." Research paper, MLA, 1941.

Stucky, Mark. "Bethel Meets the Modernist Challenge." Research paper, MLA, 1969.

Voth, Cornelius, Jr. "Reverend P. H. Richert as a Peace Leader." Research paper, MLA, n.d.

Wedel, Garman H. "Miscellaneous News Items Concerning the Mennonites as Found in the *Newton Kansan* During the Years of 1874 to 1900." Research paper, MLA, 1945.

Yoder, Robert L. "Mennonite Participation in Politics from 1860-1918." Research paper, Goshen College, 1962.

NEWSPAPERS AND RELIGIOUS PERIODICALS

Note: For more detailed information regarding editors, changes of name, and place of publication of these newspapers, see the following bibliographical sources:

Arndt, Karl J. R., and Olson, May E., *German-American Newspapers and Periodicals, 1732-1955.* Heidelberg: Quelle and Meyer, 1916.

Bender, Harold S. *Two Centuries of American Mennonite Literature.* Goshen: Mennonite Historical Society, 1929.

Connelley, William E. *History of Kansas Newspapers.* Topeka: Kansas State Historical Society and Department of Archives, 1916.

Anzeiger (Hillsboro) 1887-1897
Anzeiger (McPherson) 1887-1890
Anzeiger (Newton) 1887-1892
Bethel College Monthly 1912-1934
Christlicher Bundesbote 1882-1956 (Merged with *Der Bote* in 1947)
Deutsche Westen (McPherson) 1907-1910
Freundschafts-Kreis (Hillsboro) 1885-1886
Gospel Herald (Scottdale, Pennsylvania) 1908-
Herold (Newton) 1897-1941
Hillsboro Journal 1902-
Kansan-Republican (Newton) 1876-
Monatsblaetter aus Bethel College 1896-1912
Marion Record 1875-
McPherson Republican 1879-
Mennonite 1885-
Mennonite Weekly Review 1922
Post (Hillsboro) 1898-1902

Review 1898-1904
Vorwaerts (Hillsboro) 1909-1940
Wahrheitsfreund 1915-1947
Zionsbote 1884-1964
Zur Heimath (Halstead) 1875-1881

PRIMARY MATERIALS AND COLLECTIONS

Note: The following holdings of the Mennonite Library and Archives at Bethel College constitute a small portion of the valuable resources of that library. The H. P. Krehbiel Collection and the P. H. Richert Collection, for example, together contain more than 375 file folders and several drawers of diaries, sermons, and other material.

Gaeddert, Gustav. Diary of Experiences as a Draftee in the First World War. MLA microfilm 79.
Janzen, Cornelius. Collection.
Kansas Institution of International Relations, 1936-1940. Uncatalogued Collection.
Krehbiel, Christian. Collection.
Krehbiel, H. P. Collection.
Minute Book of the Committee on Exemptions of the Western District Conference, 1917-1922.
Richert, P. H. Collection.
Schowalter, Jacob A. Collection.
Selected Items from the Miscellaneous Correspondence File. Records of the Selective Service System, 1917-1919. National Archives and Records Service, General Services Administration. MLA microfilm 208.
Unruh, P. H. Collection.
Voth, H. R. Collection.

INTERVIEWS

Baergen, George. First World War draftee. Hutchinson, Kansas, January 22, 1967.
Balzer, Jacob F. Bethel College professor of Greek and Bible, 1913-1918. North Newton, Kansas, May 27, 1967.
Bartel, Edward. Retired Mennonite farmer. North Newton, Kansas, September 2, 1966.
Cooprider, Henry. Retired Mennonite minister and farmer. Rural Inman, Kansas, October 23, 1966.
Eitzen, D. C. Retired Mennonite farmer and amateur historian. Hillsboro, Kansas, September 15, 1966.
Flowers, Myrtle Ludwig, Business manager of *The Defenders*. Kansas City, Kansas, October 6, 1966.
Friesen, Renatta Schultz (Mrs. J. V.). Wife of Mennonite politician. Hillsboro, Kansas, May 2, 1967.
Funk, Mrs. Jacob. Daughter of Mennonite politician. Hillsboro, Kansas, November 23, 1966.

Goering, John E. Son of Mennonite Populist. Moundridge, Kansas, May 7, 1967.

Goering, Joseph D. C. Retired Mennonite farmer. McPherson, Kansas, July 31, 1966.

Gordon, Charles. First World War American patriot. Hutchinson, Kansas, April 23, 1967.

Huxman, Walter, Governor of Kansas, 1935-1937. Topeka, Kansas, October 7, 1966.

Jost, John. Mennonite farmer and minister, Bethel College, January 15, 1967.

Lindquist, Emory K. Chancellor of Wichita State University. Wichita, Kansas, October 3, 1966.

Loewen, Esko. Bethel College Dean of Students, North Newton, Kansas, May 25, 1967.

Loewen, Herman. Son of Mennonite Populist. Newton, Kansas, May 8, 1967.

Pauls, D. C. Retired Mennonite farmer and minister, Inman, Kansas, September 18, 1966.

Ruppenthal, Lloyd. Attorney, McPherson, Kansas, December 10, 1966.

Zerger, Gerhard. Retired farmer, businessman, and politician. Moundridge, Kansas, December 6, 1967.

Index